DECOLONIZING 1968

DECOLONIZING 1968

TRANSNATIONAL STUDENT ACTIVISM IN TUNIS, PARIS, AND DAKAR

BURLEIGH HENDRICKSON

CORNELL UNIVERSITY PRESS
Ithaca and London

Copyright © 2022 by Cornell University

First published 2022 by Cornell University Press

Library of Congress Cataloging-in-Publication Data

Names: Hendrickson, Burleigh J. (Burleigh Joe), author.
Title: Decolonizing 1968 : transnational student activism in Tunis, Paris, and Dakar / Burleigh Hendrickson.
Description: Ithaca, New York : Cornell University Press, 2022. | Includes bibliographical references and index.
Identifiers: LCCN 2022001268 (print) | LCCN 2022001269 (ebook) | ISBN 9781501766220 (hardcover) | ISBN 9781501767715 (paperback) | ISBN 9781501766237 (epub) | ISBN 9781501766244 (pdf)
Subjects: LCSH: Students—Political activity—Tunisia—Tunis—History—20th century. | Students—Political activity—France—Paris—History—20th century. | Students—Political activity—Senegal—Dakar—History—20th century. | Student movements—Tunisia—Tunis—History—20th century. | Student movements—France—Paris—History—20th century. | Student movements—Senegal—Dakar—History—20th century. | Decolonization—Tunisia—History—20th century. | Decolonization—Senegal—History—20th century. | Youth protest movements—Tunisia—Tunis—History—20th century. | Youth protest movements—France—Paris—History—20th century. | Youth protest movements—Senegal—Dakar—History—20th century. | Student movements—International cooperation—History—20th century. | Youth protest movements—International cooperation—History—20th century. | Tunisia—Politics and government—1956–1987. | France—Politics and government—1958–1969. | Senegal—Politics and government—1960–2000.
Classification: LCC DT264.46 .H46 2022 (print) | LCC DT264.46 (ebook) | DDC 371.8/109611—dc23/eng/20220422
LC record available at https://lccn.loc.gov/2022001268
LC ebook record available at https://lccn.loc.gov/2022001269

For Addie and my teachers at Sheldon Elementary School

Contents

ACKNOWLEDGMENTS

This book would not have been possible without the input, guidance, and hospitality of several individuals. My editors, Emily Andrew and Bethany Wasik, at Cornell took a chance on this book, and their consistent and clear communication greatly facilitated the revising process. All of the anonymous reviewers improved the manuscript tremendously.

Laura Frader of Northeastern University has been a wonderful mentor. She expertly struck a delicate balance between high standards of excellence and nurturing encouragement. Laura's expertise, generosity, and tireless work ethic have provided me with a scholarly role model I can only strive to emulate. In addition to quenching my thirst for 1960s culture and radical politics, Tim Brown helped me to write more clearly and to locate the heart of the matter. His support early in my career gave me the courage to pursue lofty goals. Kate Luongo shared her deep knowledge of postcolonial theory and piqued my interest in African history and anthropology. Her creative approaches to material are matched only by her amazing red sauce.

Bob Hall, in my eyes a pillar of integrity in a world where that can seem scarce, was extremely generous with his time in guiding me in the early stages of my research. I owe so much to my graduate colleagues at Northeastern University, in particular those who welcomed me into the department or joined me in our writing group: James Bradford, Stephanie Boyle, Rachel Gillett, Samantha Christiansen, Zach Scarlett, Stacy Fahrenthold, Malcolm Purinton, Andrew Jarboe, Seneca Joyner, Yan Li, Colin Sargeant, Ross Newton, Ethan Hawkley, Olivier Schouteden and many others. James gave wonderful advice about academic presses and strengthened my writing with keen insights. Special thanks to Chris Gilmartin for bringing kindness and humanity into scholarly endeavors. We miss you, Chris.

Thanks to a postdoctoral fellowship at Boston College, I was able to carry out the bulk of revisions. I benefited in particular from intellectual exchanges with colleagues Robin Fleming, Julian Bourg, Ginny Reinburg, Thomas Dodman, Priya Lal, and Hannah Farber. Extra special thanks to Elise Franklin, who read multiple drafts of my introduction and conclusion and helped reorganize and clarify my arguments. Carrie O'Connor, Liz Stein, Alexandra Steinlight, and Ram Natarajan offered their friendship in Boston and talked me through writing challenges, often over drinks at Christopher's. We miss you, Carrie.

At Dickinson College, the French and Francophone studies department, as well as David Commons and the history writing group, offered me opportunities and engaged with my work. Bénédicte Monicat and Willa Silverman graced the French and Francophone studies department at Penn State University with leadership in trying times. Colleague Jennifer Boittin provided important professional guidance and friendship. The department gave me employment and generous research funds to carry the manuscript to the finish line. Thanks to Cyanne Loyle, Magalí Armillas-Tiseyra, and my faculty writing group at Penn State. This community provided emotional support and accountability through the final stages. Scholars and colleagues Daniel Gordon, Julia Clancy-Smith, Sara Pursley, Sarah Curtis, Stephen Harp, Megan Brown, Liz Fink, Jess Pearson, and Herrick Chapman generously gave their time and knowledge and sharpened related material along the way. Liz Foster and Michaël Béchir Ayari shared invaluable resources from their own research on Dominican priests in Senegal and interviews with *coopérants* in Tunisia, respectively.

Tom Luckett and John Ott were great professors at Portland State. The moniker "Tommy Guns," which a few of us grad students loved to throw around in the safe confines of local pubs, does not just appear out of nowhere. It is earned through rigorous teaching and scholarship, and quirky anecdotes about imagination and money. I do hope the deck is holding up well. Marc Harris taught me the finer points of Hegel and Marx, and Michael Grutchfield reminded me that the role of the historian is not to apply Sartrean existentialism to every historical inquiry. Lloyd Kramer at UNC has been a great role model and resource to navigate academia. And Dana Tessin of Sheldon Elementary School in Vermont taught me how cool social studies can be.

Some material from chapters 2 and 4 appeared in the *International Journal of Middle East Studies* and in *The Global 1960s: Convention, Contest, and Counterculture*, respectively. I acknowledge and thank them for permission to reproduce the material. I wish to acknowledge the generous support of the US Department of Education's Fulbright-Hays program, the Social Science Research Council, the Council for European Studies, the Andrew W. Mellon Foundation, the Society for French Historical Studies, and the Boston College Clough Center for the Study of Constitutional Democracy. These funds allowed me to travel, conduct research, learn new cultures and histories, think, write, and meet a number of amazing people along the way.

In Tunisia I would not have survived the revolution without the gracious hospitality of the Menchaoui family in La Marsa. They provided me with shelter, sound cultural advice, and delicious home-cooked meals. Tom DeGeorges, Laryssa Chomiak, and Riadh Saadaoui of CEMAT oriented me to local research resources and connected me with other scholars. I will never forget conversations over rosé with Tom and Kyle Liston at La Plaza—but maybe even more I will miss the long taxi rides into the archives with Kyle when Western and postcolonial worlds collided as we battled over questions of lingua franca, (neo-)imperialism, and cultural power. Mabrouk Jebahi at the Tunisian National Archives, a true gentleman, exposed me to the nooks and crannies of the Kasbah in Tunis. The Clark family offered me a welcoming home abroad. Clement Henry Moore, Habib Kazdaghli, and, of course, Simone Lellouche Othmani provided me with useful contacts in Tunisia. Kazdaghli stood strong in the face of bullying in the academy during the uncertain times of regime change and demonstrated how to speak truth to power. Simone is quite simply one of the most amazing people I have ever encountered, working tirelessly for human rights and penal reform in Tunisia and elsewhere for her entire life.

In France I received guidance from Françoise Blum, Boris Gobille, Pascale Barthélemy, Michelle Zancarini-Fournel, and Franck Veyron of the BDIC (now la Contemporaine). Françoise was incredibly generous with me and other junior scholars, sharing sources on 1960s activism in Senegal and creating inclusive spaces. Emmanuelle Santelli and Makram Abbès in Lyon were a great help on the finer points of French academic writing, and, in addition to our many long exchanges about the Maghreb, Emmanuelle pointed me to the utility of the grille d'entretien. I am saddened by the news that the Association Génériques has dissolved owing to lack of funding. Former employees Pierre Pavy, Tatiana Sagatni, Tiffen Harmonic, and Louisa Zanoun all went out of their way to grant me special access to the Othmani Papers and worked with me to promote the memory of France's immigrant communities. I would like to thank the French taxpayers who funded the shuttle bus from Porte d'Orléans to the archives at Fontainebleau, though I wished they would have shelled out a bit more for heating in that frigid building. Thanks to Raymond Beltran, who picked me up at the train station in Carcassone, fed me delectable cassoulet and Madiran, and recounted his souvenirs of Alain Geismar, Ambassador Sauvagnargues, and 1960s Tunis.

In Senegal the Cissé family showed my wife and me Senegalese hospitality, opening their home to us, sharing tips on cab fares and fabric markets, and giving us an unforgettable cultural experience by inviting us to join their celebration of Tabaski. The West African Research Center in Fann was a wonderful home base from which to write. Mariane Yade's warm morning greetings were surpassed only by the WARC cooks' unparalleled thiboudienne, which always gathered a packed house. Ousmane Sène, Ibrahima Thioub, and Penda

Mbow pointed me toward textual and living sources. Colleagues Aleysia Whitmore and Erin Pettigrew shared laughter and travel stories and offered perspective on music and life in West Africa. Thanks to the Boulangerie Jaune for existing and acting as our North Star to orient in a foreign land. I must thank Muhammad, a friendly young bus driver who walked with me for what seemed like several miles to deliver me to the doorstep of an interview subject. On that note, thank you, thank you, to all my interviewees!

To my parents, Patsy and Victor, who brought me into this world and gave me excellent examples of how to approach life, however unconventional. They never questioned my decisions or pressured me in any way and gave me the freedom to follow my dreams. When I got out of line, my mother's disapproving raised brow was enough to put me back on track. They instilled in me a very grounding set of values and the old-school virtues of hard work and persistence. Carrying concrete forms and swinging a hammer are honorable ways to make a living, and if you are not interested in such work, you had better hit the books. Thanks to my grandfather for supporting my higher education. My amazing in-laws kept me grounded and always made an effort to travel and see my wife and me while I was conducting research abroad. Jim Soldin remains—to my knowledge—the only person other than my wife and my advisors at Portland State to have read my earlier academic work on venality in France. My brother Vic made me want to achieve excellence in the classroom and on the basketball court. Trying to compete on his level was an uphill battle, even though he did not always realize he was in a competition. Those were some great footsteps to try to follow, and now that our career trajectories have diverged, he has been a steady shoulder to lean on. Thanks also to my original furry friends Puckett and Gracie, and my new ones Pogba and Cléopâtre, who were welcomed distractions when they intervened on my lap and protected me from my computer screen. John Coltrane, Seepeoples, and Karen Dalton provided the soundtrack for my last push at writing.

Finally, I would like to acknowledge my wife, Adeline Soldin. Her sense of adventure, intellectual capacity, and merits provided encouragement and support while creating opportunities for me to grow as a person and as a scholar. Her individual successes opened doors that took us to Boston, France, and Carlisle, Pennsylvania. I admire her moral compass and endeavor to match her high standards of academic and human character.

Abbreviations

AEMNA(F)	Association des Étudiants Musulmans Nord-Africains (en France)
	Association of Muslim North African Students (in France)
AESF	Association des Étudiants Sénégalais en France
	Association of Senegalese Students in France
AOF	Afrique-Occidentale Française
	French West Africa
CAL-UGET	Comités d'Action et de Lutte-Union Générale des Étudiants de Tunisie
	Committees of Action and Struggle-General Union of Tunisian Students
CFDT	Confédération Française Démocratique du Travail
	French Democratic Confederation of Labor
CGT	Confédération Générale du Travail
	General Confederation of Labor
CISDHT	Comité International pour le Sauvegarde des Droits de l'Homme en Tunisie
	International Committee for the Protection of Human Rights in Tunisia
CP	Comités Palestine
	Palestine Committees
CRS	Compagnies Républicaines de Sécurité
	Republican Security Companies
CTIDVR	Comité Tunisien d'Information et de Défense des Victimes de la Répression
	Tunisian Committee of Information and Defense of the Victims of Repression
CVN	Comité Vietnam National
	National Vietnam Committee
FEANF	Fédération des Étudiants de l'Afrique Noire en France
	Federation of Students of Black Africa in France

FEN   French Federation of National Education
           Fédération de l'Éducation Nationale
FF-FLN   Fédération de France du Front de Libération Nationale
           Federation of France of the National Liberation Front
FIDH   Fédération Internationale des Droits de l'Homme
           International Federation of the League of Human Rights
FLN   Front de Libération Nationale
           National Liberation Front
GEAST   Groupe d'Études et d'Action Socialiste Tunisien
           Group of Study and Tunisian Socialist Action
GILT   Groupe d'Information pour les Luttes en Tunisie
           Information Group for Struggles in Tunisia
JCR   Jeunesse Communiste Révolutionaire
           Revolutionary Communist Youth
MDS   Mouvement des Démocrates Socialistes
           Democratic Socialist Movement
MEOCAM   Mouvement des Etudiants de l'Organisation Commune Afric-
           aine et Malgache
           Student Movement of the African and Malagasy Common
           Organization
MJUPS   Mouvement des Jeunes UPS (Union Progressiste Sénégalaise)
           UPS (Senegalese Progressive Union) Youth Movement
MTA   Mouvement des Travailleurs Arabes
           Arab Workers' Movement
MUP   Mouvement d'Unité Populaire
           Popular Unity Movement
OAS   Organisation de l'Armée Secrète
           Secret Army Organization
PAI   Parti Africain de l'Indépendance
           African Independence Party
PCF   Parti Communiste Français
           French Communist Party
PCT   Parti Communiste Tunisien
           Tunisian Communist Party
PDS   Parti Démocratique Sénégalais
           Senegalese Democratic Party
PSD   Parti Socialiste Destourien
           Socialist Destourian Party
SNESup   National Union of Higher Education
           Syndicat National de l'Enseignement Supérieure

Sonacotra	National Company of Housing Construction for Workers Société Nationale de Construction de Logements pour les Travailleurs
UDES	Union Démocratique des Étudiants Sénégalais Senegalese Democratic Student Union
UED	Union des Étudiants de Dakar Dakar Student Union
UGEAO	Union Générale des Étudiants de l'Afrique Occidentale General Union of West African Students
UGET	Union Générale des Étudiants de Tunisie General Union of Tunisian Students
UGTT	Union Générale Tunisienne du Travail Tunisian General Labor Union
UIE	Union Internationale des Étudiants International Union of Students
UJC(ml)	Union des Jeunesses Communistes marxistes-léninistes Union of Marxist-Leninist Communist Youth
UNEF	Union Nationale des Étudiants de France National Union of French Students
UNTS	Union Nationale des Travailleurs Sénégalais National Union of Senegalese Workers
UPS	Union Progressiste Sénégalaise Senegalese Progressive Union

DECOLONIZING 1968

Prologue
An (In)Tense Reflection

I arrived in Tunisia to conduct research for this book on 1968 activism in late February 2011, just weeks after the fall of dictator Zine al Abidine Ben Ali (1987–2011). With great courage, the people of Tunisia, led by an invigorated youth, accomplished a major step that the protesters of 1968 before them had only envisioned: removing a corrupt power and launching an international democratic movement. *Decolonizing 1968* attempts to retrace early expressions of postcolonial nationalism on university campuses—in which students in decolonizing nations demanded expedited democratization and political rights—that have recently resurfaced.

Time and space affected this book in meaningful ways. Temporally, my reading of Tunisia's '68 was, and is, assuredly marked by the context of the Arab Spring, in which I carried out this research. Not only did the streets of Tunis appear filled with boundless possibility, but a new political awakening was also taking place before my eyes. Prior to the Tunisian Revolution, researchers with local expertise had warned me about the potential futility, or even the danger, of trying to mine archives and carry out interviews on politically sensitive topics under a dictatorship. But Ben Ali's timely departure removed tedious bureaucratic procedures to access archives and, more importantly, opened up exciting conversations with former and current activists that would not have been possible before the moment of political euphoria generated by the Arab Spring. Time and again Tunisians spoke to me about the process of learning how to have honest, productive, and civil dialogue about their nation's political future. This was something they had never been able to do safely, or at least publicly, having passed from thirty years of "the Supreme Combatant" under Tunisia's first president, Habib Bourguiba (1956–1987), to twenty-six years of "Ben à Vie" ("president for life," or 1987–2011, having been cut short by a revolution). Surely the conversations we had, and my research outcomes, would have been far different had I undertaken this project in the prerevolutionary era.

I found that postcolonial spaces continued to act as sites of solidarity and places of collective remembrance and historical-present reflection. When I returned to France from Tunisia for quick follow-up research in the spring of 2011, I happened upon a sizable local community meeting of mostly Tunisians and a handful of French sympathizers who had gathered in Paris to discuss the impact of the Arab Spring. The event was intergenerational, bringing together men and women, including both former 68ers and college-age youth. A historian spoke about what she had witnessed in Tunis as events unfolded in December 2010 and January 2011, while another 68er paid homage to the Tunisian youth who catalyzed the movement and achieved what his group had been unable to accomplish in 1968. After an impassioned speech about the important role played by women in the Tunisian Revolution, the female members of the crowd spontaneously broke out into a high-pitched, howling ululation. They expressed a new kind of transnational solidarity reminiscent of one that I had uncovered from the past, and one not necessarily founded in new practices of social media with which Western journalists seem so enamored.

After decimating the adversarial Tunisian Left in the 1960s and 1970s, the Bourguiba administration created space for a new bastion of regime critique on the religious right. Politico-religious organizations like the Islamic Tendency Movement—al-Nahda (Renaissance Party) under its current iteration—endured similarly repressive measures under Ben Ali. After its reintegration as a legal political party in 2011, al-Nahda has emerged as a political force in post–Ben Ali Tunisia. The Tunisian Workers' Party has also been legalized under the new government, headed by activists formerly oppressed under both regimes. After twenty years of injunction, al-Nahda dominated Tunisia's 2011 elections, the first free elections since 1956. Unlike the one-party states of Bourguiba or Ben Ali, al-Nahda opted to maintain a semblance of political openness and national unity. After winning a plurality of elections in October 2011, the party voluntarily relinquished power in the executive after two opposition leaders were murdered by fanatics. In 2021, Tunisians are still torn between accusations of political corruption within al-Nahda and President Kaïs Saïed's unconstitutional dissolution of Parliament. Though a work in progress, the Tunisian political transition has thus far largely been a beacon of light for the region, in contrast to

Egyptian elections that were followed first by retribution against the judiciary and then by the usurpation of power from the Muslim Brotherhood by General Abdel Fattah el-Sisi's military coup in 2014. As contemporary Tunisia grapples with corruption and obstructionism while also integrating formerly repressed political currents, human rights—a key feature of 1968 Tunisia—remain at the forefront of Tunisia's future political landscape.

Having spent several months in both Tunis and Paris, I expected my final research destination, Dakar, to provide a calmer backdrop following some of the unsettling scenes of looting and occasional clashes with authorities that I witnessed during the political transition in Tunis. While this was generally the case, there were exceptions, like when I politely asked my taxi driver to turn around before the entrance of the Cheikh Anta Diop University library because the car was nearly hit by a tear gas canister. Police launched the tear gas at protesting university students, who then hurled them back in our direction. Following President Léopold Sédar Senghor's initial heavy investments in Senegalese higher education in the 1960s, which complemented French subsidies, the International Monetary Fund gradually replaced France as the primary resource for questions of development, including higher education. Structural adjustment handed down by the IMF diverted funds away from education and instituted massive cuts to the public sector, designed to gradually decrease the role of the state in economic affairs.

The 1968 protests led to the Africanization of teaching corps once dominated by French educators. The next wave of major reforms in the 1980s has led to massive overcrowding in Senegalese universities, where underresourced professors and students face a learning environment in crisis. Designed to handle twenty-five thousand students, the Cheikh Anta Diop University in Dakar is bursting at the seams with enrollments of over one hundred thousand, where law students arrive three to four hours before the start of a class in hopes of obtaining a seat.[1] After students were served rotten fish in the university cafeteria in 2011, it is not shocking that they raised Cain at the footsteps of the library I was trying to access. Fifty years after 1968, universities across the nation mobilized to declare solidarity following the tragic death of Mohamed Fallou Sène at Gaston Berger University during clashes with police while protesting the university's failure to distribute scholarship funds. Like what their Tunisian counterparts found in Mohamed Bu'azizi, whose self-immolation sparked nationwide outrage with a morally bankrupt state, Senegalese students have identified their own martyr with slogans like "Stop killing us" and "We are all Mamadou Fallou Sène."[2] These slogans also closely mirror French students' earlier chants of "We are all undesirables" after student leader Daniel Cohn-Bendit was denied reentry into France by authorities, and speak to the continued echoes of 1968. Anticorruption protests denouncing President Macky Sall's repression of opposition leaders persisted even through a global pandemic, along with renewed calls in 2021 to sever ties with French business interests.

Though Tunisia and Senegal shed the French colonial yoke in 1956 and 1960, respectively, many are still frustrated with old forms of oppression that have taken on new faces. Even after the departures of Abdoulaye Wade (2012) and Ben Ali (2011), both of whom had been accused of neocolonialism, pillaging of local resources, and a lack of democratic representation in government, watchful citizens still deploy the language of anticolonialism to assess the quality of life available in their nations. From Tunisian revolutionaries' use of French to call for Ben Ali and his corrupt ruling party, the Democratic Constitutional Rally, to *dégage* (get out) to the Senegalese *y'en a marre* (enough is enough) and #FreeSenegal movements, at the heart of both sets of demands, from the Maghreb to sub-Saharan Africa, is a notion that the goals of national independence have not been fully realized. The concept of unfulfilled independence reared its head after the initial elation of independence in the turbulent 1960s. As Tunisia's contemporary history of both secularism and government repression lies in the balance, leadership must approach its challengers with caution or face the wrath of protest.

Democratic freedoms, along with economic opportunity, are at the core of protesters' demands in the Arab world and sub-Saharan Africa today. We should all be watching with great curiosity as the Tunisian government reintegrates long-suppressed political parties and as Senegal's leaders face ongoing pressure to cut neo-imperial ties with French corporations. Likewise in France, the place of May '68 in the history of antiracism continues to challenge anti-immigrant politics emanating from groups like Marine Le Pen's right-wing National Rally (formerly Front National), and students across France continue to rail against Emmanuel Macron's proposed reforms to centralize university administration and limit access to higher education.[3] And new transnational antiracist solidarities have emerged, linking activists seeking justice for victims of police brutality across the Atlantic. Former French president Nicolas Sarkozy was unsuccessful in his attempts to "liquidate May '68" from France's history.[4] His comments do, however, underscore the importance of revisiting divisive events in national pasts so that politically interested parties do not act as sole judges or arbiters of history.

The revolutionary fervor of the Arab Spring indeed captured the attention of the world and propelled French 68er and prominent philosopher Alain Badiou toward an optimism for the future. Badiou remarked that the oligarchic "democracies" of the West were not providing much in the way of models for nations in the process of shedding dictatorships. Instead, the West has much to learn from its Arab and African counterparts that are causing a "rebirth of history," where new ideas for a free future society are being generated at sites of "movement communism," such as Tahrir Square in Cairo or the Kasbah Square in Tunis. Yet this time, for Badiou they are absent the weight of outmoded Cold War party structures.[5] If we continue the work of "decolonizing 1968," we can see not only that the sub-Saharan and Maghrebi world has a longer history of contestation than Badiou would suggest, but that for decades it has had much to offer the West in modeling transnational activism. In the wake of the Arab Spring and the rumblings on Senegalese and French university campuses and city streets, I propose yet another kind of "rebirth of history." If the pages of this book have any bearing, perhaps 68ers like Badiou in the future will no longer merely reference May '68 in France when drawing comparisons to contemporary movements. When reflecting on the Tunis of today, philosophers and onlookers should bear in mind that Tunis had its own '68, '72, and '78. And may "1968" henceforth come to englobe action beyond the dominant French case. Indeed, may 1968 be reborn to hold a broader place in Tunisian, French, Senegalese, and Francophone world history broadly, as the shot across the bow that finally achieved one of its targets in 2011.

Introduction

1968 in Postcolonial Time and Space

> *In each action we must look beyond the action at our past,*
> *present, and future state, and at others whom it affects, and*
> *see the relations of all those things.*
>
> —Blaise Pascal, *Pensées*

In March 1968 at the University of Tunis, stu-
dents seeking the liberation of incarcerated militant Mohamed Ben Jennet occupied university buildings. Participation was so widespread that administrators
announced an early spring break that year to rid the campus of troublemakers.
Less than two months later, massive university strikes started in Paris and spread
throughout the country. Clashes with police elicited nationwide sympathy for
the student movement and brought the French Republic to its knees. Just weeks
after events erupted in France, students in Senegal occupied the University of
Dakar in protest of financial cuts to student stipends. Material claims transformed into political ones and, as in France, workers supported student demonstrations while making their own demands for higher wages. How is it, then,
that disparate campuses across the Francophone world spawned strikingly similar acts of revolt within a span of three months? This book proceeds from the
premise that the movements of 1968 were intrinsically linked to the processes of
decolonization across the globe. Likewise, the activist revolts examined specifically in Tunis, Paris, and Dakar cannot be disentangled from the web of connections forged during the French colonial period, many of which persisted in its
aftermath. In other words, beyond all the transnational exchanges that characterized it, 1968 must also be understood as a *postcolonial* moment.

The upsurge of radical politics in the 1960s and 1970s shook the globe. Youth
activism encompassed the capitalist West and the communist East.[1] Equally

important, it broke out throughout many of the regions now referred to as the global South. Despite wide variance in local conditions, nearly every 1968 movement was a decolonizing one occurring in postcolonial states of all sorts. Though scholars often view 1960 as the banner year for decolonization, especially in Africa, the transition from colonized state to independent nation does not happen immediately with the pen stroke of a treaty or the election of a new president. It is an ongoing process steeped in imperial residue: economic and military accords, enduring educational institutions, and various forms of violence often orchestrated by either new national authoritarians or old colonial ones (or both). Examples exist in every geopolitical sphere of 1968. The intergenerational activists of the Prague Spring contested Soviet imperialism and authoritarian encroachment on Czechoslovakia's national sovereignty. The Black Panthers in the United States denounced American involvement in Vietnam and the practice of forced conscription. Meanwhile, their neighbors in Mexico channeled Cuban anticolonialists to decry their own nation's authoritarian, neo-imperial, and clientelist practices.[2] More broadly, movements frequently drew intellectual inspiration from anticolonial and Third World thinkers, in the process decolonizing Western minds and reshaping worldviews as revolutionary ideas traveled the globe.[3]

Yet while all of these movements were linked to various aspects of decolonization, I focus particular attention on the former French empire, exploring very specific sets of postcolonial interconnectivity. In addition to well-documented cases of student protests like France's May '68, activists from former French colonial territories of the Third World likewise occupied university campuses seeking radical political change. The Third World was not simply a fantasy location for Western radicals enchanted by Mao and Che but a site of activism in its own right.[4] Decolonization thus played a multifaceted and paradoxical role in the movements of 1968. On the one hand, the messy and complex process of decolonization was impossible to achieve in its entirety owing to ongoing postcolonial relationships and influences; on the other hand, these exchanges facilitated important transnational activist networks of students, intellectuals, and labor organizers, effectively globalizing local movements and causes. In the literal sense, decolonization itself was what people were protesting, by seeking either to accelerate it or to sever neocolonial ties. In the figurative, the idea of decolonization bonded distant and disparate groups and formed global activist sensibilities and communities. Whether Tunisian and Senegalese students and workers lamented authoritarian behavior in their newly minted governments, or French intellectuals appropriated Maoist slogans to mobilize immigrant workers, decolonization permeated their actions. Anticolonial affinities and practices similarly governed relations between Western and Third World radicals, as evidenced in the mobilizing power of transnational opposition to the Vietnam War. At the same time, the historical memory of colonialism continued to shape postcolonial France and its former colonies as they emerged from the ruins of a crumbling empire.[5]

This book raises three key questions: How might we study the transnational elements of the global 1960s in manageable and concrete ways without essentializing moments like 1968 in universal terms? Under what circumstances did movements travel beyond university campuses and even across national borders, and which forces of civil society propelled their momentum? Finally, how does our understanding of the political geography of the global 1960s shift if we reconsider the imperial remains of the postcolonial world?[6] I explore these questions by investigating the global 1960s in a way that is at once transnational—to determine the intensity of global connections—and comparative, taking into account local contexts with varying student demographics, levels of state repression, and states of postcolonial existence. Examining the colonial histories linking political action in Tunis, Paris, and Dakar, *Decolonizing 1968* charts the transformation of activist networks from their colonial-era origins through the 1970s.

What did 1968 look like in this triangle of postcolonial relations in the era of decolonization? As former axes of imperial France, Tunis, Paris, and Dakar shared the colonial imprints of French language, culture, and authority. Both newly independent nations, Tunisia and Senegal faced similar challenges with rapidly expanding government bureaucracies, national programs, and development projects. After independence in 1956, Tunisian president Habib Bourguiba's pro-Western economic policies fractured a Tunisian population that was reconstructing a national identity in the wake of French colonialism. In Senegal, President Léopold Sédar Senghor's efforts at "African Socialism" presented postcolonial challenges related to overdependence on single-crop agriculture, originally established to serve colonial France, and the continued presence of French and Levantine foreigners in economic and educational sectors that nationalists grew to resent. These efforts by Bourguiba and Senghor to forge postindependence states sparked tensions that flamed into full-on protest movements. In each case, leaders' reluctance to tolerate dissent and the ensuing resistance to authoritarianism were the result of both colonial legacies and the incomplete state of national autonomy. In other words, decolonization was at the forefront of state-society confrontations.

Like Tunisia and Senegal, France was also a postcolonial state, as colonies and metropoles alike navigated the decolonizing process.[7] The recent memory of the Algerian War and the live updates of conflict in Vietnam and Palestine inflected 1968 protests in all three sites. France also felt the effects of postcolonial social change as an industrial center that was, by the 1960s, heavily dependent on the labor of immigrants recruited from its former colonies. This influx altered France's demographics, producing an updated "immigrant question" around which French activists on the left and right staked new political identities. Across the Mediterranean, by 1968, the hangover following celebrations of liberation from France had set in, as empowered youth and a growing intellectual base called into question the new governments formed out of imperial fragmentation. As Tunisia and Senegal turned nationalist independence movements into autocratic one-party states, Paris became a center from which oppositional organizations were launched. Immigrant intellectuals and foreign students often returned to home institutions in the former colonies to participate in political activism and, in some cases, teamed up with national labor unions to demand change. Like the colonial officials and subjects before them, 1960s state leaders and activists continued to complicate and strategically deploy traditional notions of what Antoinette Burton has termed "nation-home" and "empire-away" in an era of transnational activism for anticolonial causes.[8]

Institutions rooted in imperial projects, especially the French university system, shaped postcolonial protest and linked activists across Europe, Africa, and the Middle East. Universities created opportunities for contact and exchange. On the one hand, these institutions represented lasting imperial ties through French-influenced education; on the other hand, they also functioned as sites of anticolonial resistance by clustering large numbers of informed and disenchanted youth. Likewise, the networks, language, and collective memory of post-1945 anticolonialism provided the base on which new forms of 1960s contestation were built. Past and present melted together in 1968 as colonial legacies shaped the nature of protests in postcolonial states. After 1968, colonial-era activist networks transformed into important immigrant, human rights, and democratic initiatives, as agents for change unfurled anti-imperialist agendas against both French policymakers and authoritarian acts in emerging African nations. State leaders and student activists alike deployed colonial history—accusing each other of imitating French colonial behavior—to make claims on the present and future of postcolonial states well after empire. Furthermore, Third World actors articulated clear positions on global issues, and Third World action could take place in the First World.

The global 1960s should be evaluated, then, not just on some (im)measurable level of "global impact" or reach but on the form of revolutionary practice, on the ideological identification of movements, and on the actual mechanisms of circulation for ideas and the physical bodies that transported them across postcolonial frontiers. To that end, this book situates the most well-known

"1968"—France's May '68—as part of a broader complex of events and connections encompassing France's former colonial possessions. I begin this global history in Tunis in March 1968, during which Paris acted as a central node connecting activists that were not the sole possession of one particular political or historiographic unit. This transnational activism did not come after an original, or French, May '68; rather, Tunis, Paris, and Dakar were part and parcel of a global and postcolonial moment of contestation.

Nineteen sixty-eight was not, then, a uniquely Western phenomenon, nor should it be considered as an event sovereign to the history of France. It occurred in a postcolonial paradox where colonial pasts created the objects of protest, while enduring relationships between metropole and postcolony enabled transnational networks of social mobilization. *Decolonizing 1968* is in part a political reclamation project that—through comparative, transnational, and postcolonial perspectives—seeks to liberate 1968 from the narratives that have constrained it to France's national history.[9] At the same time, it endeavors to release and to decolonize historical actors originating in the Third World from analyses that have left them "'spatially incarcerated' in that 'other place.'"[10] A postcolonial framework provides the necessary tools of excavation to bring to the surface previously peripheral histories of France's ex-colonies, thereby challenging the universal character of the Western experience of 1968.[11]

Decolonizing and Globalizing the 1960s in the Former French Empire

If historians have reached a fragile consensus that 1968 was somehow global, we still lack a framework to properly study the material and imagined bonds between political activists across north/south geographic, economic, and ethnic divides.[12] Given the significant importance of decolonization in the global 1968, surprisingly few scholars of postcolonial and empire studies have focused on this crucial year of contestation. Even fewer historians have incorporated the tools of postcolonial or decolonial studies to understand the global 1960s.[13] This book draws on the rich body of postcolonial theory as well as its emerging counterpart in decolonial studies to "decolonize" the study of 1968.[14] To decolonize 1968, as suggested in the book's title, is to engage in a particular type of theoretical and historical work. Its most notable impact here resides in rethinking our spatial and temporal understandings of 1968 and its aftermath. While there are other possible (and viable) spatial structures around which one could organize a global study of this period—for example, Cold War alliances, transatlantic cultural and political appropriations, or discrete

Third World centrism—the spaces under scrutiny in this book are decidedly postcolonial in nature. The former empire provided the canvas on which *Decolonizing 1968* paints a postcolonial picture of transnational activism in and around 1968. It maintains the goal of liberating 1968 from place-bound analyses by both unraveling the legacies of colonialism that inspired movements for change and weaving together a patchwork of postcolonial activism.

And yet, the imagery of a tripartite geospatial oeuvre detailing border-crossing activists participating in—and imagining themselves as part of—a global community does not fully capture the range of possibilities for doing decolonial work. We must also consider the temporal. The gerund *decolonizing* in the book's title suggests that this historical work is unfinished, not meant to ever reach foreclosure. Temporally, the book incorporates the colonial past; the 1968 events themselves, which occurred in a postcolonial present for the historical actors living them in real time; and the shifting historical place that 1968 will hold as politicians and historians continue to remake it in the future. Since the late 1990s, new formulations of "the long 1960s," or "the '68 years," have helped free 1968 studies from the events of that year alone. But there is also another temporal dimension at issue. That is to say, new versions of 1968 will surely arise as historians, armed with the theoretical tools accumulated as we navigate historiographic turns (in the present, the global, the imperial, and postcolonial/decolonial; and surely in the near future, the digital), continue to revisit this series of events. Even in the absence of immediate political regime change in any of the three cases investigated here, the legacies of 1968 continue to wield a major influence on the present-day political landscapes that they have altered.

Whereas postcolonial theory provides a window into the many legacies of colonialism that produced the 1968 moment, decolonial studies explains protesters' desire for a future devoid of neocolonial exploitation. This approach acknowledges the coupling of colonialism and modernity by Latin Americanists while uncovering what those in decolonial studies have termed "resistance to the colonial matrix of power" and "positionalities that displace Western rationality."[15] Yet while many scholars in this nascent field argue for a concept that is "always already decolonial, delinking from the good, the bad, and the ugly of modernity and postmodernity," the case of 1968 in the former French empire does not present such a purely clean break from colonial constructs.[16]

For example, imperial institutions shaped the modernization projects of North and West African officials after independence, from modeling African universities after French ones to infrastructure investments in the tourism industry designed to attract Europeans to African shores. And while African students sought to displace European influence, they did so through the modern channels available to them. I prefer to think of decolonial action here along the same lines as radical network theorist Ilham Khuri-Makdisi, where "different groups of actors in the non-Western world felt confident they could assemble their own visions of social and world order, borrowing, adapting, synthesizing, perhaps plundering ideas from 'the West and the rest' and melding them with local practices and ideas."[17]

Rather than completely severing (delinking) from modernity and postmodernity, the 1968 activists of this book more often instrumentalized networks and institutions rooted in the colonial project to engage in anticolonial resistance. *Decolonizing 1968* is thus about the discovery of the power of postcolonial activists and the global dimensions of protest in interrelated Francophone spaces.

Taken together, postcolonial and decolonial readings of 1968 reorient our thinking about both space (the interconnected former French empire and the spatial imaginary of the global 1960s) and time (the deployment of the colonial past in postcolonial presents and imagined decolonial futures).[18] Spatially, this book looks beyond purely national contexts, calling into question the degree of rupture after empire. Ideas and events taking place in both the metropole and the colonies often created "colonial situations" that were mutually constitutive, and we should thus consider Western nations and their overseas colonies as single entities across transnational spaces.[19] After the end of formal empire, France, West Africa, and North Africa likewise produced one particular "*postcolonial situation*"—1968—through their shared colonial pasts and the transnational activist networks of the time. These formulations allow for what Gary Wilder has termed a deterritorialization of political activism "in which supposedly European categories . . . belong as much to [African] actors who coproduced them as to their continental counterparts."[20] The protests in Tunis, Paris, and Dakar thrust into relief the tensions between the provincial and global elements of 1968. While some 68ers used international platforms to make claims about the autochthonous nature of their movements—often to counter accusations of imitating students in the West—others acted locally in solidarity with causes in distant lands. In making sense of these countervailing forces, the global in this case is not a stand-in for universal experiences; rather, the work of "decolonizing 1968" reveals a constellation of local, interconnected, and overlapping networks of border-crossing agents acting on postcolonial symbols of identification across Francophone spaces.

Though the book is geographically centered on three important sites of decolonization, I also open up discussion on the university as a fixed place where students imagined new landscapes of ideological and discursive space. African and Maghrebi students in Paris collaborated with activist groups at home institutions in Tunis and Dakar to organize multisited strikes. While Paris connected 1968 activists from across the globe, it also reflected its own specific set of understudied postcolonial formations. French students at the University of Nanterre, built in 1964, were brought to action in 1968 in part because of their proximity to immigrant communities on the outskirts of Paris. The physical location of the university next to worker shantytowns (bidonvilles) placed France's social inequalities in plain sight and opened the spatial imagination of activists to envision new ideals for the French university and French nation.[21] Many French leftists—frustrated with reformist stances of the French Communist Party (which did not support revolution in Algeria)—turned to immigrant causes as sources of revolutionary inspiration. The relationship between French left-wing activists and non-Western students and workers thus produced a domestic (France-based) ideology of a more globalized and meaningful struggle. Yet 1968 also produced a form of nationalism in postcolonial France on the far right. Evidence of increased racist attacks by French whites against immigrants in and immediately after 1968 reveals a shifting demographic landscape in the workplace, the university, and the streets of France's industrial cities. These developments threatened notions of a universalist (i.e., white) French culture, otherwise known as white nationalism.[22]

Walter Benjamin commented that the bourgeois urban space of the nineteenth-century Arcades in Paris was where one experienced the "intoxication of possibility and desire."[23] In the 1960s, the Parisian suburb of Nanterre functioned similarly in that it reflected newly imagined possibilities for students who inhabited that particular space. However, rather than producing a desire for bourgeois consumption, Nanterre generated a yearning to revolutionize society. It forced students to confront the failures of France's postwar welfare state where cultural, social, and economic differences between students and immigrant workers were ever present in daily life. As Henri Lefebvre commented, "Right now [Nanterre] contains misery, shantytowns, excavations for an express subway line, low-income housing projects for workers, industrial enterprises. This is a desolate and strange landscape . . . [that] might be described as a place of damnation."[24] Improvements in public education, combined with a postwar demographic boom, led to much more socially diverse campuses in France than in past generations. Yet even students from working-class backgrounds who populated university dormitories still held a position of relative privilege over immigrant laborers dwelling next door. Beyond Nanterre, while activists themselves physically crossed borders to engage in radical politics on either side of the Mediterranean, demonstrating against the Vietnam War at home was also a way to imagine themselves as members of a global activist community that was both abstract and real.

Decolonizing 1968 retraces the French colonial influences on African universities that made possible the transnational networks of migrant intellectuals established before national independence. I consider the "postcolonial" not in its chronological sense as the history of the former colonies "after" independence; rather, the "postcolonial" operates as an ongoing state of being in the world and a set of experiences that are "produced by" colonialism.[25] Particular institutions of the French empire, such as universities, shaped life in the decolonizing societies of 1968. Shining a light on their enduring legacies is an effort to concretely link colonial pasts and postcolonial presents by actually tracking the movement of people, ideas, and political culture both across time and in the unfolding of global protest.

After and Beyond Empire

Moving beyond event-centered histories of the year 1968 to understand its colonial heritage and the transforming of the political currents of the 1970s, this book falls in line with what French scholars like Michelle Zancarini-Fournel have termed *les années 68* (the 1968 years), or "the long 1960s," that look beyond the year itself.[26] Colonial pasts set the stage for the events themselves, whose characterizations were rewritten, erased, or reconfigured by activists, state actors, and counterrevolutionaries.[27] While campuses in Tunis, Paris, and Dakar erupted in 1968, each movement had its own specific chronologies, trajectories, and reference points that, in instances that this book explores, became imbricated with each other. And while nationalist historiographies have subverted cross-cultural analyses, postcolonial state leaders like Léopold Sédar Senghor and Habib Bourguiba erroneously depicted student activism on their national university campuses as an imitation of French students. Beyond merely rebalancing the historical scales, this book is about the myriad ways that colonialism and decolonization were key determinants in the activism of 1968.

Colonial education in service of the French empire transformed into postcolonial universities in Tunisia and Senegal. Though designed to train the next generations of Tunisians and Senegalese to usher in a new era of African prosperity, these institutions emulated French models of higher education. Just as French universities became sites from which anti-imperialist articulations emanated before independence, postcolonial campuses were also sites of conflict in the 1960s between activist youth and the state over the future of the nation. African universities were both state-building institutions and institutions of the state that took on extremely important roles as new governments implemented ambitious modernization schemes across all sectors of society. The university was at once a product and a producer of modernity. It was a national symbol of progress and a source of pride for developing nations. It would train its doctors, engineers, teachers, and politicians. Thus, both the state and the youth of the nation had a great stake in the university and its implications for determining the future.

University campuses provided the building blocks for newly independent societies. They also became postcolonial battlegrounds where states and educated youth expressed and debated conflicting notions of modernity, national identity, and democracy. Moreover, students leveraged increased political power as part of the process of decolonization. By 1960, those under twenty-five in both Tunisia and Senegal made up approximately 60 percent of the total population, compared with approximately 30 percent for France.[28] Concerned about shifting demographics, governments in Tunisia and Senegal carried out large-scale education projects to accommodate rising numbers of youth, increasing literacy rates and elevating social status for young people lucky enough to have access to higher education. Societal transformations in education coincided with the consolidation of state power into single nationalist parties and student and labor unions in Tunisia and Senegal. Extralegal student organizations with links to banned political parties found refuge on campuses. As the Senegalese historian Mamadou Fall has pointed out, "Each time the opposition is muzzled and forced underground, the university becomes the natural site of expression for political currents."[29] The former colonizer/colonized antagonisms from the days of struggle for independence were replaced by stark divisions between disillusioned youth and heavy-handed postcolonial state leaders.

Using campus lecterns, students articulated alternative nationalisms that resisted neoimperial projects and rejected authoritarian state leadership. Bourguiba frequently referenced the importance of national solidarity when arguing for a united one-party state that delivered independence in 1956 and that would best carry out future nation-building. Senghor likewise condemned and banned the African Independence Party in 1960 to secure unchallenged power within his Senegalese Progressive Union. Though France experienced a comparatively greater degree of political pluralism in the postwar period, Charles de Gaulle had just concentrated executive power with the constitution of the Fifth Republic in 1958 under the guise of resolving the Algerian War.

In short, the university was in many ways a microcosm of the tensions between nationalism and independence, on the one hand, and persistent colonial and neoimperial ties, on the other. By 1968, the revolutionary moment and climax of most studies of the global 1960s, the university had become the mouthpiece for many societal claims against state power in the three overlapping case studies presented here. The French university, developed in the metropole and exported to colonial centers of power like Tunis and Dakar to meet the needs of the empire, became an important and enduring remnant of the colonial system after independence. If Tunisian and Senegalese universities were inspired by the French model, so too were student and activist organizations. Created in Paris during the colonial era, African student organizations came home to roost after the collapse of the empire. Senegalese students who called for the replacement of French faculty and curricula with African alternatives were actively seeking to decolonize these remains of French imperial education. When regimes in Tunisia and Senegal repressed political dissent, Paris continued to act as a nexus in international networks of information dissemination and antigovernment protests. In addition to calling for education reforms, student activists used the university as a platform to resist the state and to articulate their own versions of what I term "postcolonial nationalism." A new postcolonial nationalism emerged in which Tunisian and Senegalese activists defined and deployed anti-imperialist claims that had once been designated for the French state, converting and redirecting them toward their own new university and state leaders.

While the major clashes between students and the state often ignited on campuses, and their catalytic nature is undeniable, students frequently engaged with other important stakeholders. Beyond student activism, 1968 witnessed a resurgence in the grassroots activism of teachers and industrial workers, as well as immigrant intellectuals and laborers. In Paris and Dakar, worker activism arguably eclipsed what students had set in motion. In Tunisia, worker participation in 1968 was less prevalent owing to close ties between worker unions and the state, yet workers challenged the state more effectively than did students in the late 1970s. Though campuses were of fundamental importance as launching sites for protest, these often spilled into popular urban quarters or to factories whose spaces striking workers reclaimed.

The notion of "beyond" thus operates on two levels, as the book traces activism beyond the campus and beyond the moment its student protagonists were enrolled. For example, Tunisian activist Ahmed Ben Othmani was radicalized as a college student in the 1960s, incarcerated for protesting in 1968, and continued to advocate for human and political rights issues well after terminating university studies. Likewise, the unfolding of 1968 in France inspired the creation of the French group Cahiers de mai, whose primary function was to engage with and advocate for France's immigrant workers in the 1970s, and who ultimately led their own autonomous, post-1968 antiracist movement.

The activists of 1968 and beyond who highlight the pages of this book drew on the colonial past to imagine new and alternative futures for their decolonizing societies. These were often based on racial and religious tolerance, participatory democracy, increased wages and protections for workers, and human rights, if not tolerance of the political Right or the soft middle. Though it is unsurprising that many of the institutions of colonialism persisted after independence, the very education systems that the French hoped would make colonial subjects useful to the state ultimately functioned as the crucible of postcolonial revolt. Rather than terminating the colonial era, to decolonize 1968 is to interrogate the multiple ways that decolonization determined and connected the protests in three important postcolonial states and beyond the borders of France.

CHAPTER 1

Colonialism, Intellectual Migration, and the New African University

> *Postcolonial studies considers the manner in which traces of a colonial past become, in the present moment, the object of symbolic and pragmatic work, as well as the conditions under which these practices give rise to unprecedented hybrid or cosmopolitan forms of life, politics, culture, and modernities.*
>
> —Achille Mbembe, "Provincializing France?" *Public Culture*

Though French presence in Senegal dates to at least the seventeenth century, when Gorée Island acted as an important hub in the French slave trade, it was not until 1895 that the French established the Government General of French West Africa (Afrique-Occidentale Française [AOF]). From 1895 to 1956, the Government General oversaw an area nine times the size of France, consisting of present-day Mauritania, Senegal, Ivory Coast, Guinea, Burkina Faso, Mali, Niger, and Benin.[1] Saint-Louis was named the seat of the colonial government in the AOF until 1902, when the outpost was transferred to Dakar. Senegal had long held a special place in the French colonial hierarchy, where designated coastal regions were the only places in AOF in which French citizenship was possible, at least nominally, as early as 1848.[2] Native residents were considered colonial subjects in all other regions of the AOF. Yet in Senegal, *originaires* from one of four communes (Saint-Louis, Dakar, Rufisque, Gorée) were able to elect their own deputies in the French National Assembly, paving the way for the first Black African deputy from Senegal, Blaise Diagne, in 1914. Diagne obtained recognition of citizenship for *originaires* and their descendants with 1916 legislation and led massive efforts to successfully recruit some sixty thousand *tirailleurs sénégalais* into the colonial army to fight in World War I.[3] This privileged status for Senegalese was measured, however. Nominal citizenship was not without its complexities, as legal categories differentiated citizenship based on ethno-racial lines and even divided single African social groups from the same families or ethnic origins.[4]

Additional rights were extended to subjects from France's African colonies during the "imperial civil war" between de Gaulle's Free French and Maréchal Pétain's Vichy.[5] To help defeat the Nazis and regain France's territories, de Gaulle curried favor with leading African politicians by offering representation in France's Constituent Assembly at the Brazzaville conference in 1944.[6] In a parallel effort to quell rising anticolonialism in the aftermath of World War II, French administrators later hung their hopes on the 1946 French Union, which granted a new form of imperial citizenship to colonial subjects in Africa. Two years into the Algerian War (1954–1962), France renewed legislative efforts to avoid the spread of conflict beyond Algeria's borders with the passing of the 1956 loi-cadre in French West Africa. Demands for local autonomy in the AOF increased with Indigenous leaders empowered to exercise administrative authority while colonial subjects gained voting rights. By 1958, as the French military was entrenched in a costly and bloody war in Algeria, it became clear to observers and colonial administrators alike that France did not have the resources to maintain control over its African colonies. When Charles de Gaulle returned to power in 1958 in a sweeping referendum to solve the "Algerian Question," he brought with him the new Constitution of the Fifth Republic, which increased executive power and established the French Community, a federation of African member states.

Only in 1958 after the creation of the French Community did France acknowledge eventual independence in "Black Africa." This new apparatus extended citizenship to all subjects of its African member states and laid out favorable trade agreements and aid packages with individual states known as coopération.[7] These close ties to France were first termed France-Afrique and, later, Françafrique ("Africa of France" or "Moneyed France") to criticize the dependence they created for sub-Saharan African nations with currencies tied to the French franc. Beyond the attacks on the sovereignty of currencies, Françafrique also enabled the French military to intervene and prop up authoritarian rulers, and established collaboration between French and African authorities to surveil and often deport politically active Africans living in France.[8] Under the leadership of Sékou Touré, French Guinea was the only former AOF colony to refuse membership to the French Community, forgoing development aid in favor of immediate independence. The aid to the remainder of the community's members proved insufficient to satisfy the growing desire for complete national independence. By 1959, Senegal and Mali followed the lead of French Guinea by forming the Mali Federation, eventually becoming separate independent states in August 1960.

Like Senegal in the AOF, Tunisia became part of France's "second overseas empire" after its expansion in the nineteenth century into North and West Africa following territorial losses in North America and the Caribbean.[9] After Napoleon's failed efforts to conquer Egypt in the early 1800s, France returned to the region in the 1830s to establish, through conquest, a French colony in Algeria. Later, in 1848, the French named French Algeria a department to be administered as part of France itself. The French penetrated into neighboring regions and planted colonial seeds in Tunisia and Morocco beginning in the mid-1800s. Tunisia's port cities were already home to significant European populations hailing mainly from Italy, Malta, and France. Before falling under French control, Tunisia existed as a province within the Ottoman Empire. The province was administered by a bey, or provincial monarch, who exercised relative autonomy under the Ottomans in exchange for regular tax payments and the promise to conscript armies on behalf of the empire. Following France's annexation of Algeria in 1834, Tunisian beys Ahmad and Muhammad of the Hussaynid dynasty were torn between Ottoman and French influence. Similar to France's efforts to maintain imperial control after World War II with the *loi-cadre* of 1956, the Ottoman Empire granted civil liberties to various ethnic groups in the Balkans and North Africa in 1839 with the *Tanzimat* reforms.[10]

Over the course of the nineteenth century, modernization efforts to enhance infrastructure had severely indebted the Tunisian bey to European powers, including France. Finally, in 1881 French forces took advantage of a border skirmish involving Tunisian and Algerian tribes to invade Tunisia, effectively taking power with the signing of the Treaty of Bardo, which made Tunisia a protectorate of France. The agreement granted Tunisia French protection from military invasion, and France guaranteed Tunisian debt to its European creditors.[11] From this point forward, the French resident general assumed control over Tunisian finances and foreign affairs, with the bey remaining as a figurehead. In spite of its protectorate status, which distinguished it from colonies that faced more direct oversight, such as Algeria and Senegal, Tunisia functioned in many ways as a colony.

Beginning in the late nineteenth century, the French colonial administration encouraged the immigration of French settlers to Tunisia, and by the eve of Tunisian independence, the French population had ballooned from 708 in 1881 to over 250,000 in 1956. Mustapha Kraïem explains the skyrocketing numbers owing to naturalization laws passed in the 1920s specifically to increase the "French population" vis-à-vis the Tunisian population. The French colonial administration began to recognize all non-Muslim residents of Tunisia as French citizens. A 1921 decree granted French citizenship to "all individuals born in the Regency of Tunis, for whom one parent justified with foreign title from a French tribunal of the Protectorate, is himself born in the Regency."[12] A number of Italian, Maltese, and Tunisian Christians and Jews thus became French citizens, and this citizenship was passed down to some of their children who became activists in the 1960s. As an important Mediterranean port city, Tunis in particular was a strategic center for the circulation of goods, people, and ideas.[13]

Tunisians exhibited nationalist tendencies and resisted foreign occupation throughout the Ottoman beylical period, and continued to actively organize against French economic domination. As early as 1924, Tunisian workers created the region's first Indigenous labor union.[14] Modeled after the French General Confederation of Labor, the organization named itself the General Confederation of Tunisian Workers. This name was in place until 1946, when it transformed into its current iteration, the Tunisian General Labor Union (Union Générale Tunisienne du Travail [UGTT]). The Tunisian Communist Party (PCT), which consisted of a mosaic of Europeans and Tunisian Jews and Muslims, was also born during the interwar period. In its early days, the PCT borrowed its structure from and deferred to the French Communist Party (PCF). This placed the PCT at odds with other burgeoning nationalist movements like future president Habib Bourguiba's Neo-Destourian Party (Party of the New Constitution), which ultimately led the nation to independence.[15] Bourguiba changed the party name to the Socialist Destourian Party (Parti Socialiste Destourien [PSD]) in 1964 to reflect new socialist plans to nationalize certain sectors of the economy. By consolidating national organizations under the banner of one political party, a single recognized labor union, and a regime-friendly student organization, Bourguiba streamlined his agenda and mollified political differences to lead Tunisia out of protectorate status. While Algeria was thrust into conflict following the National Liberation Front's declaration of war against France, neighboring states in Tunisia and Morocco enjoyed independent status by 1956.

From Colonial Education to the Creation of the Third World University

For centuries, Tunisia has been a center of intellectual activity, with the heart of Islamic studies shifting from Kairouan to the Zaytuna mosque-university in Tunis in the thirteenth century and producing the famous Muslim historian Ibn Khaldun. Education remained restricted to elites, and, before the protectorate era, educational opportunities were limited primarily to *kuttab* (Qu'ranic studies) or to the Bardo military academy. After 1875, a more secular education was possible at the Collège Sadiki.[16] In the early years of the protectorate, French director of public instruction Louis Macheul began an aggressive assimilation program with the introduction of Franco-Arab elementary schools for Tunisians and Europeans, open to both Muslims and Jews, which included the study of Arabic. Some have argued that this push for inclusion of various ethnic and religious groups influenced the secularism present in Tunisia after independence.[17] Tunisia also proved fertile testing ground for combining France's expansionist cultural and diplomatic initiatives like the Alliance Française, designed specifically to promote French culture and language through education, even in the absence of a large French settler population.[18] By the 1890s, Macheul's increasing influence in curricula at the French Lycée Carnot (a converted Christian school) and at the Collège Sadiki proved a useful recruiting tool for integrating educated Tunisians into colonial/protectorate government positions, many of whom had received portions of their education in France.

Educated Tunisian students were integral to the articulation of Tunisian nationalism and in advocating for independence from France. Habib Bourguiba was one such case, having graduated from the prestigious Collège Sadiki and the Lycée Carnot and then studying law in Paris in the 1920s. Bourguiba and a number of Tunisia's future government leaders cut their teeth in politics in an association of former students of Sadiki. In a 1937 speech to the Association of Muslim North African Students (Association des Étudiants Musulmans Nord-Africains [AEMNA]), Bourguiba pushed for the politicization of students sharing a similar "colonial situation."[19] Given the importance of students to the Tunisian independence movement, Bourguiba, once in power, viewed a strong national education program as crucial to Tunisia's vitality as an emerging sovereign nation. When he assumed the presidency in 1957, there were at least six types of primary schools and four types of secondary schools, including French, Franco-Arab, Sadikian (or Tunisian), Qu'ranic, and various all-girls' schools.[20] One of Bourguiba's first agenda items was to unify education under one national umbrella and to convert the lone secular university in Tunisia, the Institut des Hautes Études de Tunis, founded in 1945 and dominated by the local French population, into the more populist University of Tunis in 1960.[21]

Like Macheul in Tunisia, William Ponty (governor general of the AOF, 1908–1915) pushed colonial education initiatives to stimulate French language and culture in French West Africa. A colonial service training school was founded in 1903 and later set up on Gorée Island in his name.[22] This training expanded to include local elites in the 1920s with the implementation of reforms by AOF governor general Jules Carde and education director Georges Hardy. Influential future African leaders such as Mamadou Dia of Senegal, Félix Houphouët-Boigny of the Ivory Coast, and Modibo Keïta of Mali attended the William Ponty School. New policies were meant to decentralize urban education and offer courses in colonial history and African culture, which corresponded with shifts away from assimilation (to French culture and mentalities) and toward association (increased local autonomy with French oversight). Reforms emphasized Indigenous culture and tolerated the practice of customary law for non-French Africans.[23] Education reforms thus closely mirrored colonial policy on the grand scale. But with the proliferation of early education schools and new opportunities to study abroad—including at the École Coloniale in Paris—came increasing concerns about the quality of preparatory colonial education. Reflecting in the late 1940s on some of the impacts of the French Union, Jean Capelle, French director general of education in the AOF, noted that "ever since the populations of the AOF received the right to send representatives to Parliament, like in France, it has become urgent that the school population that represents the elite benefit from an education modeled on the French system and that these ranks be sanctioned by exams of the same quality and prestige as metropolitan exams."[24] French administrators and African elites alike have historically viewed education in the AOF, and in Senegal in particular, in comparison with the French system.

Like Capelle, many African elites of the late colonial and early independence eras were concerned with achieving and maintaining equivalencies for degrees. Equivalency meant degree recognition in France and the opening of pathways to higher education and employment abroad. To ensure the quality of education in the AOF, the French government established the Institut des Hautes Études de Dakar and a medical school in 1950, which were directly affiliated with French universities.[25] Just as the University of Tunis evolved out of the local French Institut des Hautes Études, the University of Dakar was similarly established in 1957—on the eve of Senegalese independence—to provide higher education to surrounding nations as the first national university in Francophone West Africa.

Higher education had been internationalized in the colonial era, and, after 1956, the independent Tunisian state enacted policies to lure students back to Tunisia. The government committed heavy expenditures to modernize the national public education system. The investment yielded gains, as the number of students enrolled in primary school rose from 213,000 on the eve of independence to over 900,000 by 1969, with the percentage of girls attending schools rising from 29 percent to 38 percent in the same period.[26] Bourguiba's reforms resulted in increased access to higher education as well. With large numbers of Tunisians in institutions of higher learning both in France and at the University of Tunis, opportunities were present for organizational cooperation between communities of Tunisians across the Mediterranean.

Presidents Bourguiba and Senghor, both of whom received advanced degrees from the metropole, engaged in aggressive modernization plans at their home universities. Bourguiba instituted radical changes in national public education; budgetary spending climbed from 12 million dinars in 1962 to 30 million in 1968 (about one-third of the annual budget).[27] Senghor was not far behind, devoting over 20 percent of the 1967 national budget to education in Senegal, though it remained dependent on French subsidies that covered as much as 70 percent of the operating costs at the University of Dakar.[28] More so than its Western counterparts the United States, Great Britain, or Germany, France supported African foreign students at the university level, in large part owing to the relative ease of transition for Francophone Africans who arrived in France with sufficient language training. Still receiving significant French subsidies, Senghor welcomed the establishment of a "Mixed Commission," comprised of both French and Senegalese officials, to consult on Senegalese national education programs and make final decisions regarding university curricula and budgets.[29] Senegalese education minister Amadou-Mahtar M'Bow's 1960s proposals to "Africanize" curricula and teaching corps were balanced with concerns about maintaining French funding levels and degree equivalencies.

Tunisia similarly navigated tensions between education policy and national autonomy in the realm of cultural identity. Driss Abbassi has noted the struggle of Tunisia's education ministers to create, or even invent, a national identity through elementary history manuals. Bourguiba's sociocultural project to establish "the idea of a Tunisian bridge between the two shores of the Mediterranean" included a strong attachment to French language and culture that he thought would propel Tunisia into the modern era.[30] Bourguiba buttressed this cultural bridge with the appointment of the French Jacques Grell as head of the Tunisian Education Commission and inspector of secondary education in Tunisia until 1966.[31] The contradictions of Tunisia's controversial Arabization programs in the 1970s were revealed in the translation of French texts into Arabic as part of a push to promote Maghrebi identity, though the texts still focused heavily on French cultural content. Both Tunisian and Senegalese national education programs faced the postcolonial condition wedging them between the deep roots of the French colonial education system (including continued financial support) and the desire to trumpet national identities and construct national histories.

Intellectual Migration and Student Organizations at Home and Abroad

Before the creation of universities in Tunis and Dakar, the vast majority of colonial subjects in search of higher education had to travel abroad. As subjects of a French protectorate from 1881 until 1956, Tunisian intellectuals had a long history of studying in the metropole. Some also studied in French Algeria, where universities were established earlier, or at theological institutions in places like Damascus.[32] Like Tunisia, sub-Saharan Africa sent its elite to study in France dating from the interwar period. However, this opportunity was reserved for only a handful of brilliant students like Léopold Sédar Senghor, who was one of the "barely 1% of the populations of French West and Equatorial Africa who had any kind of schooling whatsoever" in the 1930s.[33] Yet the AOF witnessed swift transformations in access to education in the first half of the twentieth century. New initiatives to build schools and expand colonial education programs in the following decades increased access to primary schools across the French West and East African federations to 15 percent, though it only became official policy to recruit and organize African students in the metropole after World War II.[34]

In 1963–1964, a total of 3,658 African students were studying on scholarships in France, with 2,662 funded by home countries and 996 by French universities. However, by the mid-1960s, African leaders hoped to gradually reduce the number of students abroad since "their traditional environment was more conducive to control and political recruitment."[35] Simply put, students who studied abroad were more likely to join groups in opposition to home governments than were students who studied in their home countries. These findings came on the heels of the Jeanneney Report, which advocated for a diversion of funding away from operating costs and toward development and trade. The report triggered gradual divestment from France's former African colonies under the de Gaulle administration.[36] The increase in the number of primary- and secondary-educated Tunisians had implications for higher education as well. In 1961, over 50 percent of Tunisians studied at foreign universities (primarily in France), but by 1968, only 31 percent studied abroad, though the total number of students abroad remained relatively consistent. This meant that Tunisian communities in university hubs like Paris remained strong while the number of enrollments at the University of Tunis continued to climb. The Tunisian student population at the University of Tunis rose from 1,908 in 1960 to well over 7,000 by 1968, with an additional 3,275 studying abroad.[37]

The rapid expansion of African student populations created growing pains for new universities trying to meet soaring demands for additional faculty and administration still dominated by French nationals. Training programs for local administrators were still rather weak in 1960 at the apex of the African independence movement. The need for technical expertise led to a period of increased cooperation with France while new nations played catch-up. According to Catherine Coquery-Vidrovitch, "Independence came much more quickly than foreseen, and the pre-existing structures were not sufficient to meet a variety of new challenges in filling political and administrative positions. . . . It was thus necessary to replace them with local 'elites.' These elites were trained hastily and à la française, hence an acceleration of the granting of scholarships and the spike in student immigration to France."[38] While university cooperation between France and its former colonies was at an all-time high in the 1960s, the funding of rising numbers of African students to study in the metropole was untenable. In the early years of independence, most African universities were unable to offer diplomas in certain disciplines and African students continued to seek this training at French universities; however, Africa's national universities had developed sufficiently in the 1970s to maintain the majority of their students through master's degrees. The result was a gradual decline of foreign students in France from Francophone countries abroad.

In Tunisia, Bourguiba's investments led to an increasingly educated population across all sectors of society, including the countryside. Student activists such as Ahmed Ben Othmani and Chérif Ferjani, both of whom came from rural peasant families, excelled in the Tunisian public education system and eventually studied in France, only to return to Tunisia and carry out political action in opposition to Bourguiba.[39] Tunisians continued to study in France in large numbers, and many returned to enroll at the University of Tunis or to pursue careers back home. This created an international community of intellectuals with organizational poles throughout Europe (particularly strong in France) and Tunisia. Sub-Saharan African intellectuals followed a similar trajectory, and, as the flagship university in West Africa, the University of Dakar was home to an extremely diverse body of students from several nations. In 1949–1950, 2,000 African students from French colonies studied in various European metropoles. Ten years later, on the eve of African independence, the number of students from African colonies and Madagascar studying in Europe increased to approximately 8,000 (close to 1,000 of them were Senegalese, with 400 studying in France).[40] At the University of Dakar, French students outnumbered Senegalese until 1965, and, in the 1967–1968 academic year before the explosion of campus protests, the university enrolled 3,826 students: 1,480 Senegalese, 1,351 of various other African nationalities, 892 French, and 103 others.[41] By 1970, the number of sub-Saharan African students in France began to decline as scholarships to study abroad were less readily available and African universities became more equipped to handle greater numbers.[42] This meant that academic and intellectual ties to France had been forged during the colonial period, but also that networks of intellectuals and student organizations were transplanted to home institutions as student populations within the ex-colonies grew. As new institutions developed after empire, they became sites of conflict over the direction of newly independent nations, even as they maintained close contact with French intellectual centers like Paris.

Foreign students who migrated to the metropole often faced hardships related to racism in finding housing, securing proper visa paperwork and travel permits, and maintaining funding for education. As Michael Goebel has shown, interwar Paris became an "anti-imperial metropolis" where increasingly internationalized groups of students and workers cohabited, mingled, and, in some cases, planted "the seeds of Third World nationalism."[43] The first student activist organizations for Senegalese and Tunisian students were actually created in Paris before independence, drawing on a combination of the structural models of predecessors like the National Union of French Students (Union Nationale des Étudiants de France [UNEF]) and Indochinese anticolonial organizations.[44] Students and workers who came to Paris during the interwar period entered into a world with complex and contradictory attitudes about race, cultural identity, and belonging. French republicanism had long promoted theories of color blindness in exchange for assimilation, though these often played out differently in practice. On the one hand, African Americans found 1920s Paris to be a liberating space compared with the Jim Crow South of the United States, and the Algerian resistor Messali Hadj even noted that he received better treatment in France than in French Algeria. On the other hand, Hadj was also well aware that for his services to the French Army during World War I he was paid only one-sixth the salary of his French counterparts, and crime statistics bear out that "colonials entered into conflict with the law far more than native French and foreign immigrants."[45] If views on race emanating from interwar Paris were ambiguous or contradictory, these began to harden in post-Vichy France. Though World War II–era anti-Semitism did not disappear, the postwar increase in North African immigration led many in France to shift xenophobic tendencies from Jews toward Muslim and Arab targets, especially after the Algerian War.[46]

By the 1950s and 1960s, students of color in Paris began to trade the old notions of a color-blind France for one of cold-blooded racism. The embarrassing defeat at Dien Bien Phu in 1954 and the loss of Algeria in 1962 narrowed the parameters of Frenchness and excluded previously "accepted" groups. This extended to sub-Saharan students and students from France's overseas departments and territories as well, who faced challenges when seeking lodging in France.[47] Originally established to help migrating students transition to university life abroad, foreign student unions initially advocated for affordable housing and adequate stipends. In 1952, after French authorities arrested Bourguiba for promoting Tunisian independence, Tunisian students clandestinely created the General Union of Tunisian Students (Union Générale des Étudiants de Tunisie [UGET]) and held its first congress in Paris. UGET hosted illegal meetings in Paris until independence in 1956, at which point it moved its headquarters to Tunisia. UGET was formally recognized by the Bourguiba government after the rival Zaytuna organization was subsumed under its umbrella.[48] The Tunisian student organization also had strong ties to Maghrebi interwar precursors like AEMNA, whose support Bourguiba had solicited. But no organization influenced it more than the largest French student union, UNEF: founders borrowed heavily from UNEF's charter and modeled its bureaucratic structure on its French predecessor, establishing sections in university cities across France. UGET maintained influential sections in Paris, the French provinces, and Brussels. And while UGET and UNEF would take opposing positions on major issues such as Algerian independence, the two organizations were in close contact in the postcolonial era.[49]

Like the Tunisian student groups, the first organizations to represent colonial students from sub-Saharan Africa were also born in Paris. Since at least the early days of the interwar period, when Senghor and the Martinican Aimé Césaire were in Paris, Black students articulated concerns through associations like the Committee in Defense of the Negro Race (Comité de Défense de la Race Nègre), with *L'Étudiant Noir* as their mouthpiece.[50] However, the first official Francophone pan-African student organization, the Federation of Students of Black Africa in France (Fédération des Étudiants de l'Afrique Noire en France [FEANF]), did not emerge until 1950. FEANF linked various national groups of African students in France and held its inaugural congress in Lyon. It played an instrumental role in numerous African independence movements in the 1950s, often working in collaboration with more local sections such as the Dakar-based General Union of West African Students (Union Générale des Étudiants de l'Afrique Occidentale [UGEAO]), many of which were once part of UNEF.[51] By 1958, FEANF had strengthened its ties with North African students and even faced expulsions, reductions in scholarships, and intensified surveillance by French agencies after the publication of *Le Sang de Bandoeng* (The Blood of Bandung), which supported Algerian independence and denounced the torture of Algerians by the French Army.[52]

Student organizations transformed throughout the decolonization process, and the 1960s witnessed the emergence of student groups representing diverse political leanings in Dakar and in Tunis. After independence, their centers of power were transferred from French university campuses to local ones as classrooms became increasingly accessible to Senegalese and Tunisian youth. Many students who previously would have been forced to pursue higher learning in France—as the only available option in the colonial era—stayed home for their education after independence. Growth in education in the early 1960s was mirrored by accretion in government administration. Though governments in Tunisia and Senegal were able to incorporate a number of talented graduates from their national universities into expanding bureaucracies in the early 1960s, the opportunities for employment began to shrink over the course of the decade with restricted budgets.

Aid packages from France were declining at a time when new governments faced the challenges of replacing former colonial administrators and picking up the tab for government and university operations. France significantly cut aid to Tunisia after Bourguiba demanded that France evacuate a former colonial naval base. In what became known as the Bizerte crisis of July 1961, French forces defeated a Tunisian siege and attacked surrounding villages.[53] France finally left Bizerte in 1963 after the base was no longer necessary for operations in Algeria, but Tunisia was forced to look to the United States for aid after the heightened tensions.[54] Bourguiba's modernization policies and investment in education coincided with shrinking opportunities for educated Tunisians as finite positions in the expanding government reached their peak, and as collectivization projects in agriculture produced economic hardship. Beyond questions of employment and foreign assistance, university students lamented the strong French influence in curricular content and in the professoriate.

The Senegalese government likewise confronted the problem of replacing the old colonial bureaucracy with limited resources, which was only exacerbated by a series of poor peanut harvests culminating in 1968.[55] Both nations encountered a burgeoning population of young, educated, and frustrated students concentrated on Third World university campuses in their capital cities. According to Mohamed Dhifallah, by the mid-1960s "the situation became increasingly complicated for the [Bourguiba] regime with the decision of students on the left to no longer expatriate to France for their studies, but to enroll in massive numbers in Tunisian universities with the intention of filling the 'political vacuum' left by UGET, which was servile to the state. These new 'internal activists' energized the student movement, calling into question, for the first time, the legitimacy of UGET."[56] States and students often worked at cross-purposes where emerging state leaders sought to maintain unity within singular national organizations at the levels of politics, labor, and education. These national organizations and parties expanded during the 1950s as anticolonial efforts ramped up. But after gaining nominal national sovereignty, extranational groups of students and intellectuals began to view their role as a check on the power of the state rather than as instruments of state authority. Initially clandestine during Tunisia's protectorate status in the early 1950s, UGET became an integral piece of the national independence movement.

Clement Henry Moore has pointed out that by the mid-1960s, the once plu-ralist UGET had become increasingly dominated by Bourguiba's PSD, and "party control and personal opportunism had discredited the union in the eyes of most students."[57] After independence, UGET transitioned into a talent pool and recruitment center for the growing bureaucracy of Bourguiba's PSD, the lone official Tunisian political party in 1964 that replaced the Neo-Destour.

One of the most important challenges to the PSD came from a clandes-tine leftist group called Perspectives, or the Group of Study and Tunisian So-cialist Action (Groupe d'Études et d'Action Socialiste Tunisien [GEAST]). By October 1963 it had become clear to Tunisian students in Paris that UGET no longer exercised political autonomy. Disenchanted with the PSD's influence and seeking an independent and critical voice, Tunisian students and professors in Paris formed Perspectives, composed of a collection of Tunisians across the po-litical Left. Like many New Left organizations across the globe, Perspectives en-compassed Marxist-Leninists, Maoists, Trotskyists, and Arab nationalists, united in their overlapping anticolonial critiques of the Bourguiba regime. What began in the early 1960s with textual criticism of national economic programs trans-formed into direct conflict with Bourguiba's PSD in 1968, often splitting with other prominent groups of communist reformers in favor of Maoist and Trotskyist theories of cultural or permanent revolution, respectively.

Perspectives' origin story came on the heels of Bourguiba's suppression of the Tunisian Communist Party. In 1963, Bourguiba took advantage of a foiled coup d'état by supporters of opposition leader Salah Ben Youssef to dismem-ber the PCT, in spite of the fact that the PCT denounced the plot.[58] These de-velopments fostered the exportation of political activism to France, where opponents of Bourguiba living in forced or voluntary exile could more freely circulate and articulate oppositional viewpoints. As UGET had done before it, Perspectives expanded from Paris to establish strong sections in Tunis and other Tunisian and European cities with sizable student populations. Perspec-tives had significantly fewer members than UGET, however.[59]

This was certainly not the first time that France provided a space for politi-cal subversion relating to the colonial sphere. Bourguiba himself argued for Tunisian autonomy while studying abroad in France during the interwar pe-riod; in the 1950s, Paris was also a key site of contestation for Algerian resis-tors; and by 1960, French student unions were collaborating with North Africans in support of French withdrawal.[60] Paris continued to function as an important, if ironic, center of subversion after empire, as Perspectives mem-bers across the Mediterranean were instrumental in 1968 mass demonstrations at the University of Tunis. By 1968, Perspectives and UGET's centers of power had shifted from Paris to Tunis, though both maintained influential sections in France. And while French university students far outnumbered those from Tunisia or Senegal, the latter were far more likely to join a national student association (see table 1). Thus, when over three thousand young Tunisians occupied the main campus in March 1968 to demand the release of a student activist, they had robust organizational outposts at home and abroad to sustain their cause.

The Senegalese UGEAO also worked closely with FEANF operatives in France throughout Senegal's struggle for self-determination, yet became a thorn in Senghor's side after independence. Just as Bourguiba outlawed the PCT, Senghor dissolved the UGEAO in 1964 and opened the door for clandestine activism.[61] By the mid-1960s, UGEAO had been replaced by the Senegalese Democratic Student Union (Union Démocratique des Étudiants Sénégalais [UDES]) for Senegalese students and the pan-African Dakar Student Union (Union des Étudiants de Dakar [UED]), made up of non-Senegalese African students. Both of these groups were sympathetic to the Marxist-Leninist African Independence Party (Parti Africain de l'Indépendance [PAI]), which Senghor had been scheming to stamp out since he became president in 1960. Students railed against the continued strong French neocolonial presence in education, especially at the university level, as well as French and Levantine dominance over key business sectors.[62] With a reduced GDP following poor crop harvests and the pronouncement of massive budget cuts to student funding in the spring of 1968, over two thousand Senegalese and African students enrolled at the University of Dakar held a mass general strike that shut down the campus. They were joined by regional high school students and, after facing violent intervention by state authorities, by powerful national labor and teachers' unions as well. While Senghor vacillated in his recognition of the legitimacy of UED and UDES, these organizations maintained contact with FEANF in France, providing mutual support for each other's activism in 1968.

Of course, intellectual migration was not limited to colonial and postcolonial migrants destined for the metropole. In 1967, the University of Dakar was home to nearly nine hundred students of French nationality, and over one-third of the student population was from neighboring African nations. The University of Tunis was more homogeneous by comparison, though there were still significant numbers of French secondary and postsecondary educators in Tunisia. With the creation of post–World War II agencies like the Investment Funds for Economic and Social Development—which had already spent 8 billion French francs on development before African independence in 1959—and the Ministry of Cooperation, created in 1961, France played an active role in supporting development projects, particularly in sub-Saharan Africa, and sent its technicians and teachers abroad. In lieu of mandatory military service, many

Table 1   Estimated number and percentage of adherents to principal national student organizations by country in 1968

COUNTRY	PRINCIPAL STUDENT ORGANIZATION	ESTIMATED NUMBER OF ADHERENTS	TOTAL NUMBER OF UNIVERSITY STUDENTS AT HOME AND ABROAD	PERCENTAGE OF ADHERENTS OUT OF TOTAL STUDENT POPULATION
Tunisia	UGET	3,000	10,715	28%
France	UNEF	50,000	510,000	10%
Senegal	UDES	650	2,500	26%

Source: Figures compiled from multiple sources and estimated for 1968. Table 20, "Effectifs de l'enseignement supérieur," in Bsais and Morrisson, "Les coûts de l'éducation en Tunisie," 83; Moore, *Politics in North Africa*, 170; table 1 in Denis Pallier, "Les bibliothèques universitaires de 1945 à 1975," *Bulletin des bibliothèques de France* 3 (1992): 58–73, https://bbf.enssib.fr /consulter/bbf-1992-03-0058-008; Boris Gobille, *Mai 68* (Paris: La Découverte, 2008), 10; Fougeyrollas, "L'Africanisation de l'Université de Dakar," 42; Fiche no. 354 DAM, 17 July 1968, ADMAE, Afrique: Sénégal (1959–1972), carton 49, Politique intérieure, La Courneuve; Guimont, *Les étudiants africains en France*, 7; Letter of Jean de Lagarde to the Minister of Foreign Affairs, 11 January 1967, ADMAE, Afrique: Sénégal (1959–1972), carton 49, Politique intérieure, Liasse: Université de Dakar, 1967, La Courneuve.

French youth opted to serve as *coopérants*, meaning they would work abroad, often as teachers or in some other development capacity. The number of coopérants working in education in Senegal—which spiked from 594 in 1961 to 983 by 1966—explains the high number of French professors at the University of Dakar.[63] Many of these coopérants would later act as key nodes in the transnational networks of activism that surfaced in the volatile spring of 1968.

The ghosts of the French colonial education system profoundly marked independent Senegal's educational and political landscape in the 1960s. For example, Senghor's appointment of French nationals to key education positions demonstrated his willingness to accept continued French influence. Not only was the chief administrator at the University of Dakar a French rector, but French and Lebanese faculty at the University of Dakar outpaced their African counterparts, who made up around one-third of the total faculty in 1967.[64] Likewise, Senegalese nationals made up less than one-third of total enrollments, while the remaining two-thirds were split more or less evenly between French nationals and other Francophone African students.[65] But if in 1968 Senghor was reluctant to give in to demands to Africanize both university curricula and the professoriate, his reservations were directly linked to the colonial past. Many graduates from back in the days of the École William Ponty found that, in spite of its local prestige, their diplomas were not recognized as the equivalent of the *brevet supérieur* in France, and they were unable to continue their studies beyond *lycée* (high school).[66]

Not only did coopérants, who traveled between France and their overseas destinations, deliver news from abroad to the metropole, but many also engaged directly in local politics. Coopérant Jean-Paul Chabert was politically active in both Tunis and Paris, which led to his imprisonment in Tunisia following 1968 university protests, while coopérant and health worker Jean-Louis Ravel was indicted in Dakar for providing a Roneograph (a rudimentary copy machine) to Senegalese militants who reproduced political tracts calling for violence against the Senegalese state.[67] Intellectual migration was thus multidirectional—bringing large numbers of African and French students to the University of Dakar as well as West and North African students to Paris—and resulted in the circulation of everyday intellectuals from a wide array of nationalities throughout the former French empire. Trans-Mediterranean movement facilitated the creation of complex networks of communication in and around university campuses that could be mobilized for activism.

1968 and the University as Postcolonial Battleground

With growing populations of educated and mobile youth, university campuses captured serious potential for radicalization. Yet with substantial investment on the part of the Senghor and Bourguiba regimes, they were also symbols of progress and modernity for newly sovereign nations. Even before the May explosion at the University of Dakar, at a gathering in April 1968 of the Franco-Senegalese "Mixed Commission," Senghor pointed to "the importance that we attach to the University of Dakar . . . [whose] lineage, by the way, we inherited from the French University."[68] There was an admitted tradition of, and even pride in, French academe. Bourguiba was similarly involved with education programs and made a number of efforts to reach out to student communities at the University of Tunis.

As early as the late 1930s, Bourguiba had shown interest in mobilizing students across the political spectrum, including both Zaytunians (Muslim theology students at Tunis's Zaytuna mosque-university) and the often left-leaning students who studied abroad in France, in order to engage them in the independence movement and to groom them for future ranks in government.[69] Bourguiba viewed it as a great victory that he was able to successfully mediate conflicts between Zaytunians and expatriated student groups during the national independence movement. His relationship to the broader student community began to break down in February 1961, however, when he sided with Neo-Destourian segments of UGET and dispersed crowds of leftists during a ceremony commemorating the life of Congolese activist Patrice Lumumba.[70] Bourguiba, the self-proclaimed "Supreme Combatant," became increasingly frustrated with a fractious Left and lambasted troublesome student elements in a 1965 speech before UGET. "There is no pretext . . . to say that education is more important than the struggle against the group Perspectives and what are known as progressives; you must focus on two primary objectives: the first concerns your studies and receiving a diploma, the second is a concern with national problems so that you can become good citizens."[71] Thus even before campus explosions of the late 1960s, Bourguiba sought to extract the more radical factions from the broader national student movement he attempted to control. Both Bourguiba and Senghor viewed the university as an extremely important symbol of modernity and national achievement, endeavoring to strengthen relationships with student populations. When the students of these nations became frustrated with their governments' failures to deliver on the promises of decolonization—including job creation and the erasure of French influence—they chose university campuses as forums to express their grievances. Indeed, spaces of higher learning became the battlegrounds over which Tunisian and Senegalese state leaders and students meted out their differences over the meaning and structure of a modern, sovereign nation. The university at once represented France's lasting colonial presence and the means for new nations to implement development plans without relying on their former oppressors' technical expertise.

In a sociological study conducted in the summer of 1972 among Tunisian students in both Tunis and Paris, John Entelis found that the increased agitation of students was directly related to the lack of available positions in the public and private sectors.[72] UGET had initially provided fertile ground for Bourguiba's recruitment of bureaucratic administrators in an expanding, quasi-socialist government. Based on findings from a survey questionnaire, Entelis concluded that "socio-economic 'pay-offs' in the form of guaranteed high-prestige jobs, once available to almost every university graduate, are now virtually non-existent. The Minister of Planning envisages the economy's incapacity to absorb more than half of the new recruits into the labour force during the next decade, or only about 23,000 of each year's 50,000 additional entrants to the active population. This further weakens the régime's ability to attract and retain its educated young."[73] In effect, Tunisia's economy could find room for only about half of the qualified people it was training for new positions. As many as nineteen former UGET leaders between 1952 and 1962 held ministerial positions under Bourguiba; yet by the mid-1960s, students sensed that the prospects to work in government were bleak, and the student alliance with Bourguiba had already begun to unravel.[74]

Likewise, Senegalese intellectuals lamented the dearth of economic opportunities and new corrupt classes of Senegalese who had replaced their colonial predecessors. According to one observer, "At the root of the problem is a neo-colonial situation, which is the product of neo-imperialism (French in this case) supported by a 'collaborative' neo-bourgeoisie (Senegalese in this case)."[75] Bloated bureaucracies faced budget cuts and contraction at a moment when the number of graduates was on the rise. In 1964, Perspectives members in France returned to Tunis and began organizing on the university campus. The stage had effectively been set for both youth unrest and transnational communication, as educational networks established during the colonial period were already in place. When the Bourguiba regime violently repressed student dissent and detained hundreds of protesters in March 1968, Tunisians tapped existing lines of communication to France to make calls for political freedoms at home. In Senegal, these intellectual circuits led a number of militants to return to Dakar from Paris in the summer of 1968 to prolong the student protests started in Dakar in late May. The circulation of ideas and the migration of intellectuals to the metropole, and their return home as local universities expanded, produced the conditions for the development and organization of postcolonial networks of resistance that were reactivated in 1968.

The activism of the turbulent 1960s was intricately intertwined with earlier eras of colonial education and intellectual migration. Large numbers of students, especially in the post–World War II era, traveled from the colonies to the metropole to pursue opportunities for career advancement and education. Co-operation agreements and development projects also sent French technicians and educators to the colonies, creating multiple opportunities for transnational and transcolonial cultural and information exchange. The number of North and West African students studying in France at the university level grew alongside rapidly expanding elementary and secondary education programs in the colonies after 1945. These students founded organizations based in France that were designed to assist in orientation and advocate for foreign students' rights. What makes the emergence of new organizations *postcolonial* has less to do with periodization—that many transformed after African independence—and more to do with their historical roots in the era of French colonial education and the ties that bound new nations to the old metropole after empire. The establishment of West African and North African universities in the 1950s and 1960s, a by-product of the independence movement, proved to be a critical step in the creation and radicalization of student groups. Moreover, African university expansion was accompanied by a proliferation of student and intellectual networks of activists. While new nation-states like Tunisia and Senegal began to provide education for their own citizens, their efforts came with highly restrictive political conditions for growing student populations.

African universities located in the former French empire were modeled exclusively after French universities in order to meet requirements for reciprocal recognition in France. They were often governed by French university administrators and featured primarily French faculty for much of the 1960s. Somewhat paradoxically, a large part of decolonization—educating Indigenous youth to replace colonial technicians and bureaucrats—was carried out through colonial education systems. The university thus constituted one critical fragment of empire left over from the colonial era that continued to play an important role in decolonizing nations. Student organizations of North and West Africans founded in Paris were transplanted to home institutions and transformed after independence to advocate for students' rights in the former colonies. The combination of enduring ties to French education and limited freedoms of expression under repressive regimes resulted in a postcolonial condition for students on African campuses.

Whereas universities provided fertile ground for the recruitment of students into new governments to carry out modernization projects, by 1968 these same students had also become an oppositional force. Postcolonial universities in Tunisia and Senegal were thus Janus-faced: backward looking in their persistent ties to the old French system yet also a beacon of light pointing the way toward a brighter future in the developing world. For state leaders like Habib Bourguiba and Léopold Sédar Senghor, the university was a symbol of pride for emerging nations and a potential tool to strengthen national unity and advance development. However, for many young intellectuals participating in the system, the university they experienced in France dating to the colonial era was a safe space for cultivating anticolonial and antiauthoritarian ideas. In developing nations where a university education was rather rare, students possessed a certain cultural capital and prestige beyond their European homologues. In addition to participating in general anti-imperialist global politics, students at universities in Tunis and Dakar were also concerned with decolonizing their universities to extricate French influence and promote Africanization and Arabization of curricula and faculty. Because of the preexisting connections with intellectuals residing in France—of both French and foreign nationality—the university became a site of contestation between states and activist students, as well as a key node in the web of transnational activism.

The shared colonial histories among territories of the former French empire created opportunities for transnational activism in the postcolonial world. For French activists like coopérants Jean-Paul Chabert and Jean-Louis Ravel, identifying with the Third World in Tunisia and Senegal granted an opportunity to distance themselves from the remnants of France's wretched colonial past. Likewise, French activists gained political currency by participating in what 1960s leftists would have considered an "authentic" movement for its Third World relevance and anticolonial political positions. France also became a frequented site of political exile to which numerous activists from the ex-colonies relocated and from which they continued to carry out transnational activism. In cases of authoritarian state repression of student movements in 1968, Tunisian and Senegalese intellectuals could count on sympathetic countrymen and other global activists residing in France to demand increased human rights, freedoms of speech, and democratic principles that rejected the notion of a single-party state.

PART ONE

1968(s) in Tunis, Paris, and Dakar

CHAPTER 2

Tunis

Student Protest, Transnational Activism, and Human Rights

That is what Tunisia was for me: I was forced to enter into the political debate. It wasn't May of '68 in France that changed me; it was March of '68, in a Third World country.

—Michel Foucault, interview with Duccio Trombadori

Tunisian university student Ahmed Othmani and a number of fellow activists found themselves, after receiving vicious beatings the day before, in a torture cell in Tunisia on 19 March 1968. The story of their predicament began on 5 June 1967, when Mohamed Ben Jennet and other members of the Tunisian leftist group Perspectives organized a protest in Tunis against US and British support of Israel in the Six-Day War. Because Tunisia was a predominantly Muslim country and former French protectorate with proximity to the Algerian conflict, anticolonial movements like Algerian, Vietnamese, and Palestinian independence occupied particularly strong positions in the political consciousness of Tunisians across all sectors of society.[1] Yet despite shared anti-imperial positions between students and the Bourguiba regime during the Algerian War—when both condemned French attacks in Bizerte in 1961—the government would eventually clash with university students over its treatment of Six-Day War protesters like Ben Jennet.

With the exception of the Vietnam War, perhaps no other anticolonial cause captured the hearts and minds of politically engaged youth in the 1960s more than "the Palestinian question." This complex issue divided many on the European left, where French students grappled with a post-1945 world forever stained by France's anti-Semitic Vichy past. While Maghrebi and sub-Saharan student groups were generally quick to support Palestinian liberation, UNEF waffled owing to conflicting positions on anti-imperialism and antiracism.

Unquestioned support of Palestinian independence proved difficult for many French who harbored shame at France's inability or unwillingness to protect its Jewish populations in the 1940s. Yet to some anti-imperialists, Israel's Anglo-American-backed military operations in 1967 also smacked of neo-imperialism akin to the American occupation of South Vietnam.

Heightened regional tensions in the 1950s and 1960s—including the rise of Palestinian Fedayeen attacks on Israelis in formerly Palestinian territories and Egyptian president Gamal Abdel Nasser's nationalization of the Suez Canal in Egypt 1956—provided the prelude to the Six-Day War. These developments emboldened Nasser to form a series of military alliances with Israel's neighbors in Syria and Jordan. In the lead-up to the conflict, Nasser ordered the removal of United Nations peacekeepers from the Sinai Peninsula and replaced them with Egyptian soldiers, closing off precious Israeli trade routes through the Straits of Tiran. Israeli forces responded with the first blow in a new hot war, crippling Egypt's air force before it could take flight with air strikes on 5 June 1967. Despite being surrounded by hostile neighbors, the well-equipped Israeli military delivered a crushing defeat to the alliance of Egypt, Syria, and Jordan in just six days. In the Arab world, this embarrassing episode came to be known as *al Naksah*, or "the setback," to describe Israel's seizure of East Jerusalem and the West Bank from Jordan, its takeover of the Sinai Peninsula and Gaza Strip from Egypt, and its occupation of the Golan Heights in Syria.[2]

Whereas French students in UNEF may have been torn on the Arab-Israeli conflict, Tunisian students staked out a much clearer position on the issue. Following news of the Israeli air strikes in June, protesters congregated at the British and US embassies in Tunis to denounce Western imperialism and to reproach Tunisian president Habib Bourguiba for condoning Anglo-American foreign policy. The protest spilled beyond the immediate proximity of the embassies and into popular quarters of the city, finally degenerating into anti-Semitic vandalism of Jewish shops and synagogues. Though protest organizers from Perspectives spoke out strongly against anti-Semitism, their pleas were not enough to stop the swell of anger at Israeli military initiatives.[3] On 8 June, even before the war had come to a close, Bourguiba vowed to "severely punish the troublemakers" who committed injustices against the Jewish population.[4] The state responded with a heavy hand; Ben Jennet was arrested as the ringleader of the demonstrations and sentenced to twenty years of forced labor.

A student at the Zaytuna (the theological school alleged by Bourguiba's regime to harbor Muslim fundamentalists), Ben Jennet became the scapegoat for the regime, which claimed he incited the attacks on Jewish neighborhoods, disrupted the peace, and threatened national security. His sentencing set off a series of political actions led by the student community, culminating in university-wide protests in March 1968. After Ben Jennet's arrest, the Perspectives group laid out its anti-imperial positions regarding Palestine in a famous pamphlet that came to be known as the *brochure jaune*, which answered "the Palestinian Question" by demanding Palestinian independence but also recognizing Israel's right to exist (see figure 1).[5] Perspectives had taken its anti-imperialism from textual form to direct action. What began in June 1967 with a focus on international anti-imperialism transformed into calls for human rights and democratic freedoms at the national level in Tunisia's own version of "1968." Yet these events were not contained to the Tunisian experience, as they included French intellectuals such as Michel Foucault (a visiting professor in the philosophy department at the University of Tunis from 1966 to 1968) and French teachers' organizer Alain Geismar, both of whom spent time in Tunis and witnessed events in 1968. Forever marked by what they observed in Tunis, in particular Foucault, they would both later support Tunisian efforts at human rights reforms after returning to France.

While certain aspects of the Tunisian movement were specific to the local context, the movement contributed to the global story of the 1960s in several significant ways: (1) activists identified with global and anticolonial causes such as Palestinian liberation and opposition to the Vietnam War; (2) actors and organizations involved in the protests frequently crossed national borders, especially those of Tunisia and France; and (3) the Tunisian and French states responded specifically to transnational activism with varying degrees of repression. Furthermore, Tunisia's (post)colonial relationship with France established important Franco-Tunisian networks of students and intellectuals that took on new forms during and after the protests of March 1968. Just as imperial knowledge was constructed in a "web of empire" in which the colonies acted as relays of knowledge transmission, transnational circuits of activists emerged in the postcolonial era to constitute networks of activism.[6]

In the networks explored in this chapter, knowledge was exchanged directly between activist organizations in Tunis and Paris while also circulating within a broader global activist community. These networks of Tunisians moving between France and Tunisia and of French activists who had ties to Tunisia enabled the transnationalization of political activism—and often made it more difficult for states to contain. They provided access to information censored in Tunisia from the comparatively safe distance of the former metropole, and Paris became a meeting place for activists from other former colonies who were sympathetic to the Tunisian cause. The both hostile and friendly ties that linked Tunisians with Paris and the French with Tunis were evidence of a wider global process of building networks of resistance that resonated well beyond the moment of '68 itself.

Publication "Perspectives Tunisiennes" Nº 2

LA QUESTION PALESTINIENNE
dans ses rapports avec
le développement de la
lutte révolutionnaire
en Tunisie

GROUPE D'ETUDES
ET D'ACTION SOCIALISTES
TUNISIEN

Février 1968

FIGURE 1. The *brochure jaune* was originally published as "La question palestinienne dans ses rapports avec le développement de la lutte révolutionnaire en Tunisie," *Perspectives Tunisiennes*, brochure nº 2 (fevrier 1968). Image reproduced with permission from La contemporaine, in Fonds Othmani, Collection La contemporaine/cote OP_43525.

The state's repression of activists fueled unprecedented human rights activism in the region that was initially conducted from afar, making 1968 monumental in the development and articulation of opposition to a Tunisian one-party state. Moreover, Bourguiba's extreme reaction to the 1968 protests contributed to the creation of Tunisia's first human rights group in Paris, which eventually gave way to the first homegrown organization to receive official government recognition, the Tunisian League for Human Rights, in 1976. Tunisia's place in the "global 1968" thus goes far beyond the fact that its movement occurred simultaneously with other movements around the world. Tunisia's 1968 shared a number of aspects with other "68s": anti-imperial politics, revolutionary student activism, convergence and conflict within radical groups like Perspectives, transnational solidarities and border-crossing actors, and, above all, a belief that ordinary people have the power to change the world. All of these aspects of the global 1960s came to Tunisia and followed Tunisians in the world.

March 1968 in Tunis and "the Ben Jennet Affair"

The March 1968 protests of Mohamed Ben Jennet occurred on the eve of Tunisia's celebration of national independence on 20 March. They were not entirely spontaneous, however. The buildup began as early as 17 November 1967 when the Soviet-backed International Union of Students, based in Prague, launched a day of solidarity with Vietnam.[7] After the creation of the Grassroots Vietnam Committees by French activists in late 1966, Slimane Ben Slimane founded the Tunisian Committee of Solidarity with the Vietnamese People in 1967.[8] The committee protested a January 1968 diplomatic visit by US vice president Hubert Humphrey (who was on a tour of nine African countries) and South Vietnamese minister of foreign affairs Tran Van Do to meet with Bourguiba. Slimane cosigned a letter addressed to Humphrey himself imploring the United States to stop bombing in North Vietnam.[9] Student members of Perspectives and the PCT used the Humphrey and Van Do visit to set aside their ideological differences regarding the finer points of Marxism and called for three days of action in solidarity with Vietnam.

Perspectives had historically criticized the PCT for its revisionism and uncritical support of Economic Minister Ahmed Ben Salah's collectivization, and the PCT was known to portray Perspectives as a divider of the Tunisian Left.[10] Yet on 10 January, the two groups jointly organized over one thousand students at the University of Tunis to support the Vietnamese people. Days later, tracts from the Perspectives section in Paris reported highlights of the Humphrey–Van Do protest and called for solidarity with the Vietnamese and the imprisoned Ben Jennet.[11] The Perspectives section in Paris, dating from 1963 and historically rooted in Tunisia's colonial relationship with the French education system, felt compelled to react to events taking place in Tunis, illustrating the role of Paris as a second site of action in the postcolonial web of resistance. Tunisians in Paris participated in transnational communication networks by spreading information and responding to activism conducted by their comrades back home.

In the context of a global 1968, the presence of First World political leaders and imperialist symbols such as Humphrey in a former French colony elicited a strong local response. Likewise, activists located in the West protested the appearance of Third World dictators in the First World. Timothy S. Brown has noted that, in West Germany, the diplomatic visits of Congolese Moise Tshombe (1964) and Iranian Shah Riza Pahlavi (1967) aroused the ire of students.[12] West Germans responded with indignation to the physical presence of US imperialism in their midst, much as Tunisians had done in response to Humphrey and Van Do's visit to Tunis: "The Third World did not make its appearance in the West German '68 in the form of fantasy borne posters of Mao Zedong . . . or the other cliché images of young protesters disconnected from reality and blind to the authoritarian realities of Third World nationalist movements."[13] Engaging in transnational action, West German students, alongside foreign student activists, protested the very real presence of Third World authoritarians visiting Europe.

Resistance to imperialism took on many forms and was often bidirectional. Activists resisted imperialists whether they appeared in the First World or the Third World, and called out neo-imperial collaborators equally, no matter where they originated. In the Tunisian case cited above, First World imperialism appeared in the Third World in the bodies of Humphrey and Van Do (considered a First World conspirator). Yet it was also later identified in the other direction, when French and Tunisian activists protested the physical presence of Bourguiba during a June 1972 visit to Paris.[14] In each case, the international travel of diplomats symbolized collaboration with First World imperialism, whether Third World figures appeared in the First World or vice versa. Their unwanted presence precipitated transnational organization in which acts of contestation occurred in both Tunis and Paris, regardless of the diplomatic destination.

The January protests of Humphrey and Van Do's visit laid the foundation for the March events. While many Tunisians around the country were preparing celebrations to commemorate thirty-two years of independence, the Committee in Support of the Liberation of Ben Jennet swung into action. Activists in Tunis gathered thirteen hundred signatures in a petition to Bourguiba condemning the president's "arbitrary victimization" of Ben Jennet, who had helped organize the June 1967 demonstration at the US and British embassies. Perspectives members distributed tracts at university buildings, on city buses, and in popular quarters of the city demanding his release. By 15 March, at the University of Tunis's Faculté des Lettres, a crowd of over two thousand Tunisian students gathered in response to Perspectives' publicity campaign.[15] The movement spread to the Faculté des Sciences and to neighboring technical and high schools where students held a series of free general assemblies. Student activist Brahim Razgallah declared solidarity with Ben Jennet before a large audience. Cheers roared as he accused the UGET leadership of being apologists for US imperialism and called for a general strike of classes in protest of Bourguiba's repressive dictatorship.[16]

The students linked US imperialism to oppression in the Tunisian government while calling for reform in the students' national representative body. The mobilization on the local level for what came to be known as "the Ben Jennet affair" thus contained claims on a series of other levels. Ben Jennet's original goal—to denounce Tunisian state support of oppressors in Vietnam and Palestine—fit into the broader context of the 1960s anti-imperialist movement. However, Bourguiba's repressive response to June 1967 and March 1968 led to calls for democratic reform at the national level that were not present at the outset. After the March occupation of university spaces, authorities responded with force to student and faculty organizers as police interrogated hundreds of Tunisians and eventually made over two hundred arrests.

No less than eighty-one were incarcerated, most of whom were categorized by the state as either communists, Perspectivists, or Ba'thists.[17] Many were held without trial until September 1968, and reports of torture included pouring acid on the feet, ripping off fingernails, and burning the skin and breasts with ether, electroshock, and cigarettes, which left infectious wounds.[18] Perspectives members Ahmed Othmani, Gilbert Naccache, Noureddine Ben Khader, Brahim Razgallah, and Abdelaziz Krichen received sentences of up to sixteen years for participation in an illegal organization and attempted subversion against the state.[19] Some were charged with the crime of offending a head of state for insulting Humphrey and Van Do during the January protest. One Perspectives member was even indicted for distorting Bourguiba's self-promoting nomenclature "the supreme combatant" (le combattant suprême) into "the supreme hypocrite" (le comédien suprême).[20]

Many of the defendants in Bourguiba's Special Court, created by the law of 2 July 1968 to deal specifically with March 68ers, did not have access to defense attorneys or to evidence that might support their cases. Even though the events in March were produced out of a local context (Ben Jennet's sentencing), Bourguiba's reaction was influenced by fears of international revolution as events in France unfolded during his visit to Europe in May 1968.[21] Because the regime delayed the trials for political dissidents in Tunisia until September 1968, the events of the French May '68 augmented the level of repression and hefty sentences experienced by Tunisia's March 68ers. The Tunisian '68, though originating locally, resonated with other '68s and spilled across national borders as Paris became a site of Third World resistance. Even Bourguiba's repression of activists was shaped by events in Paris, and activism was realized both locally and abroad.

In addition to paying close attention to international events, students also expressed concerns at the local, university level. In its February–March 1968 issue of *L'Étudiant Tunisien*, UGET lamented the French university system that Tunisia had inherited, and called for a swift "Tunisification" of education.

> To be truly engaged [the university]'s teaching programs must be Tunisified to the maximum degree (in each case where this is possible). The applied work must be based essentially on Tunisian examples. A true Tunisification of programs must necessarily include a Tunisification of the faculty of our University. . . .
>
> Moreover, since our system is closely linked to the French university system and since the latter has been modified, it is logical to take into account these French university reforms. It is all the more necessary to preserve the equivalency of Tunisian and French diplomas. We must coordinate the undergraduate degrees granted by the two universities.[22]

Much like students in Senegal who would similarly call for Africanization of the University of Dakar in May and June 1968, UGET pushed for a nationalization of the education system to meet local concerns. Many believed that France's adoption of the Fouchet reforms would propel the university into a new era of meeting increased enrollments and a shifting economy. Yet these specific reforms—designed to limit enrollments in certain subjects based on France's current economic needs—did not reflect realities in the former colonies.

In Tunisia and in Senegal, there was a greater need for educated professionals across all sectors, particularly in education, which was rapidly expanding and still dependent on the expertise of French teachers and professors who often taught culturally French content from a French perspective. Yet as in Senegal, advocates of specific reforms on the national level in Tunisia were forced to balance this issue with maintaining equivalency in the recognition of their diplomas with French granting institutions. At least on paper, Tunisian degrees were equivalent to French ones. Many government administrators also got behind these projects, including Mohamed Mzali, who as national education minister in the 1970s ordered the translation of primary school textbooks into Arabic.[23] These specific claims for Tunisification came not from the oppositional Left, though many likely would have supported this cause, but from the government-backed UGET. And radical groups like Perspectives did not hold a monopoly on anticolonialism. In the same issue of *L'Étudiant* that focused on local reforms, UGET included identification with international causes, pledging solidarity with "peoples and students still under foreign domination [and] reaffirm[ing] its attachment . . . to the students of Palestine, Angola, Mozambique, Zimbabwe, Vietnam, South Africa, and other countries for success obtained against colonialism in all its forms."[24]

In many areas of the Francophone world, such as Paris and Dakar, student strikes in 1968 extended beyond campuses, ultimately receiving the backing and support of workers and national labor unions.[25] However, the lone national labor union in Tunisia, the UGTT, did not challenge the Bourguiba regime until 1978 and actually condemned protesting students in March '68. Efforts by Tunisian intellectuals to recruit workers into the resistance movement initially failed, and the UGTT was allied in many ways with the Bourguiba regime from the early days of independence through much of the 1970s.[26] The Tunisian '68 was thus confined primarily to the university milieu. Calls to liberate Ben Jennet at the University of Tunis certainly symbolized the Tunisian students' desire for democratic freedoms, but they also expressed resistance to Tunisia's complicity with US imperialism in Vietnam as well as its soft position on Israel.

The Ben Jennet affair can be seen as the intersection of an international anti-imperialist movement and a national cry for freedoms of expression and association. Like many anti-imperialist movements around the globe in the 1960s, Tunisian activists primarily focused on Vietnamese and Palestinian liberation. However, the state's repressive response to youth protest caused a shift in the nature of students' claims in a very local context. After Ben Jennet's arrest, students not only reproached Bourguiba's pro-Israel and pro-US stance but also called for the liberation of Tunisia's political prisoners and for rights to free speech and assembly. In countering the repression, students and professors organized an international network of support around the Ben Jennet affair and engaged in a transnational discursive battle over the affair's meaning and the state's heavy-handed response. In fact, the Ben Jennet affair spurred activism from an international community already in place, particularly strong between the French and Tunisian Left, that fought against government repression of human rights.

Transnational Networks of Support and the Struggle for Human Rights

Following Ben Jennet's arrest, Paris was reactivated as a hub for transnational action. Tunisian students held an information session in Paris in November 1967, where they were supported by union representatives from Morocco and Algeria as well as by the principal organization of African students in France, FEANF, and the Association of Muslim North African Students in France (Association des Étudiants Musulmans Nord-Africains en France [AEMNAF]).[27] Paris constituted a central gathering point for activists from various former colonies who were sympathetic to the Tunisian cause and who transmitted information from the metropole back to student groups in their mother countries. The mass arrests and lack of due process for Ben Jennet's March '68 supporters sparked further transnational action, as calls demanding his liberation resounded from Tunis to Paris (see figure 2). On 27 March 1968—the day that the University Council in Tunis broke with legal precedent to definitively expel five Perspectives activists—the International Association of Democratic Lawyers moved to obtain the release of Ben Jennet, along with Tunisian university students and attorneys who had been detained in March.[28]

FIGURE 2. "Mohamed Ben Jennet: victim of the arbitrary in Tunisia." Undated postcard advocating Ben Jennet's release circulated by activists in Paris. Image reproduced with permission from La contemporaine, in Fonds Darmon, Collections La contemporaine/cote ARCH0058/1/5.

Though the majority of the core members of Perspectives—who had re-turned to Tunis in 1964 following study abroad in France—were arrested in the aftermath of the March events, a number of second-tier members were still ac-tive abroad. These members were instrumental in disseminating information on events in Tunisia to the French community. Though there is little evidence that March '68 in Tunis inspired the activism of France's May '68, Tunisian students in Paris certainly expressed their support for the French strikes that followed. Just days after French students erected barricades in Paris's Latin Quarter, Tuni-sians linked the two movements as part of a global revolution: "Comrades, French students, our struggle, whether it be in France, Tunisia, Spain or else-where is absolutely the same. Our respective struggles are inscribed in historical terms, that is to say in terms of the march of humanity toward socialism."[29]

Tunisian students also received invitations to the World Youth and Student Festival held in Sofia, Bulgaria, in the summer of 1968. In spite of the Tunisian media's claims that only regime-friendly UGET delegations went to Sofia, stu-dent members from Perspectives also participated. A Perspectives tract calling for the liberation of Ben Jennet and the March 68ers was signed by over forty delegations, the largest number based in France.[30] Among the signatories were national student unions of the former French colonies Morocco, Algeria, and Senegal, as well as AEMNAF. The French National Student Union, UNEF, re-frained from signing the tract, which may have been because its members were unable to participate after being hassled when passing the Bulgarian border and expelled in the midst of the festival's proceedings.[31]

UNEF had a history of working with UGET dating to the 1950s, but this did not prevent the French student organization from contacting more radical groups like Perspectives, which was invited to UNEF's International Congress in Marseille in December 1968. Presenting before the congress, Perspectives pro-vided an account of the protests against Humphrey and Van Do and described the severe court sentences following the March '68 campus upheaval. The pri-mary goal of the delegation was to inform the global student community of their own national struggle in Tunisia, which they charged was overlooked in French media; however, they also joined the global movement by referencing international struggles in distant lands. "Because our struggle is linked to the struggle of all progressive students of the world, we pay tribute to the students who fight alongside their people against colonialism, neo-colonialism, imperial-ism, and reaction . . . particularly in the righteous struggles of the people of Vietnam, Palestine, Greece, Latin America, and Europe."[32]

Tunisian students invited UNEF representatives to activist meetings in Paris held at the Maison de Tunisie, where UNEF expressed solidarity with the

March detainees.[33] Tunisians thus networked with other students from abroad in order to gain support for their cause and used international student congresses as a forum to spread local news from the ground. Delegations acted as conduits of information that was repressed in Tunisia or ignored by the international press. At the same time, they articulated an internationalist position vis-à-vis popular global movements such as Vietnamese and Palestinian liberation, views for which the imprisoned Tunisians of March '68 paid dearly.

Just as Tunisians made their case in France and beyond, the campus clashes also made an impact on the French living in Tunisia. One of the future leaders of May '68 in France, Alain Geismar, was invited to Tunis by a number of French coopérants who belonged to the French Federation of National Education (Fédération de l'Éducation Nationale [FEN]). Geismar, general secretary of France's National Union of Higher Education (Syndicat National de l'Enseignement Supérieure [SNESup]), was tasked with helping secure the release of detained students and colleagues.[34] Geismar and a number of other French professors and teachers working in Tunis were advised by the French ambassador, Jean Sauvagnargues, not to meddle in local politics since French educators in Tunis were not covered under the same legal rights to strike as those in France.[35] Unable to participate in the strikes, many of the French educators passively resisted by holding vapid classroom sessions in which they did not advance the curriculum, so that detained and striking students would not be punished by missing out on crucial coursework.

Others, such as Michel Foucault, who was a visiting faculty member at the University of Tunis in 1968, resisted more actively. Foucault allowed students to draft tracts from his home in Sidi Bou Saïd, gave sanctuary to student leader Ahmed Othmani while authorities sought his arrest following the Humphrey and Van Do protests, and provided deposition testimony at Othmani's September hearing.[36] Often criticized for his lack of engagement in politics, Foucault plainly stated that his experiences in Tunisia in 1968 led him to finally enter into the political debate.[37] The reported torture of some of his students while incarcerated in Tunisian prisons no doubt influenced his thinking on systematic punishment and societal control in *Discipline and Punish* (1975) and, later, on his concept of governmentality. After returning to France, Foucault continued to support Othmani's liberation—signing hunger strike petitions and requesting testimony from Othmani's former French professors—and later engaged in the causes of North African immigrants in Paris. While events in Tunis transformed the famous philosopher and inspired him to participate in post-1968 activism back home, Tunisia was also a key node in a broader network of global events and intellectual life.[38]

The involvement of FEN affiliates such as Geismar and prominent intellectuals like Foucault in the March events suggests that while the movement's instigators conducted actions at the local level, the Tunisian government's response to March '68 fueled an organized, transnational network of resistance. Geismar's visit to Tunis was no accident; his presence was requested by concerned members of FEN who were stationed in Tunis and had witnessed the government's repressive measures. The efforts of Geismar prompted James Marangé, general secretary of FEN, to obtain a meeting with Bourguiba in order to pressure the latter to look into the accusations of torture and to liberate the detainees.[39] This transnational network applied political pressure to secure the provisional release of a number of the detainees in January 1970, though many were kept under surveillance and later rearrested.[40]

FEN's actions were bolstered by forty-four university professors and intellectuals in France who also showed their support of the Tunisian students. In a telegram addressed to Bourguiba on 31 May 1968, French intellectuals—including Franco-Tunisian writer Albert Memmi, French Communist Party member and historian Albert Soboul, and philosopher Jean Wahl—noted that many of the detainees were either their friends or former students at French universities, and demanded their release and reintegration into the university system.[41] The timing of the telegram is worth noting; it coincides with the events of May '68 in France, just after de Gaulle had issued a national radio broadcast calling for order to be restored following the "intoxication and the tyranny" of the students in France.[42] The day of de Gaulle's speech (30 May), four hundred thousand Gaullist supporters gathered in Paris to give voice to the "silent majority" who denounced the youth movement in France.[43] Thus, at the height of political activity on the French national level by Gaullists, union activists, and students, a group of intellectuals turned their attention across the Mediterranean to implore Bourguiba to liberate detained Tunisians. Yet not all of the transnational activism supported the student movements; at the same time that French intellectuals were reaching out to Tunisian students, a group of coopérants from Alsace working in the textile industry in Tunis asked the French ambassador to send a letter of solidarity to de Gaulle in opposition to the youth movement.[44]

As the September trial date approached, the movement to free the Tunisian 68ers led to the creation in Paris of the first International Committee for the Protection of Human Rights in Tunisia (Comité International pour le Sauvegarde des Droits de l'Homme en Tunisie [CISDHT]). What began as a cause to liberate Ben Jennet had expanded to include the general protection of human rights. The group enlisted members in both France and Tunisia, including the famous Martinican attorney Marcel Manville. Manville, who had defended Algerian activists in the 1950s, was unable to provide similar counsel to Tunisian detainees after being expelled from the country before meeting with his clients.[45] One of CISDHT's most active members, Simone Lellouche, was the fiancé of the Perspectives detainee, Ahmed Othmani. Born on Tunisian soil, Lellouche held French citizenship through her father. After her arrest in Tunis in April 1968, she was expelled to France.

While this was surely a government tactic to rid the country of another nuisance, what resulted was the exportation of a tireless activist who continued her cause from France. Using her intimate knowledge of Perspectives circles and of the prison conditions her partner and other inmates faced, Lellouche acted as a crucial contact point within the resistance network. In preparation for the September trials, she wrote numerous letters to French university professors requesting testimony in support of the moral character of her eventual husband (married 1970) and other detainees. She even contacted French professors in the ex-colonies, such as Jean-Maurice Verdier of the University of Algiers, who wrote on behalf of Mohamed Charfi.[46] Information gathered from prisoners and their families regarding their academic histories enabled Lellouche to locate prominent figures who could write on their behalf. She provided them with the address of the president of the Special Court and recommended that they send copies to foreign attorneys and observers. Upon hearing the reports from the international observers, the International Federation of the League of Human Rights (Fédération Internationale des Droits de l'Homme [FIDH]) joined Lellouche's efforts by applying legal pressure from afar. FIDH wrote to Bourguiba in September 1968 condemning the torture of prisoners and warning that Bourguiba risked "transforming [his] historical image of liberator of Tunisia into that of oppressor."[47]

In addition to orchestrating legal counsel and international observation during the September trials, CISDHT also sought to sway public opinion. It organized meetings at the Mutualité in Paris, giving updates on the trials and discussing strategies for action. CISDHT invited Jean-Paul Chabert, a French engineer who held work contracts in Tunis, to share his experiences in Tunisian prisons. Like Manville, Chabert had been politically engaged long before March '68. Chabert's political education began in his teenage years, as he processed French defeat to the Vietnamese at Dien Bien Phu in 1954 and later, as a member of UNEF, supported independence in Algeria.[48] As early as 1964, Chabert was involved in Perspectives circles as the only French citizen reported to have endured torture for alleged involvement in the March events. He was finally given special clemency by Bourguiba in March 1969.[49] Others, such as French professor and activist Jean Gattégno, carried out a campaign of letter writing to dailies, including France's widely circulated *Le Monde*, in an effort to arouse French sympathy for the political prisoners.[50]

Because the PSD held a virtual monopoly on access to Tunisian media—controlling the content of the daily *L'Action* and frequently seizing international papers like *Le Monde*—one of the most important tasks for organizations such as CISDHT and Perspectives was to act as alternative sources of information. The PSD reported on the March events in the pamphlet *La vérité sur la subversion à l'université de Tunis* (The truth about the subversion at the University of Tunis), widely referred to as the *livre blanc*, which *L'Action* published as a full-page article in August 1968, just in time to influence public opinion before the September trials.[51]

As the March events unfolded, Bourguiba was preparing for the highly anticipated visit of Ivoirian leader Félix Houphouët-Boigny, hoping to quiet the storm of activism and to preserve his reputation in the international community. On 20 March 1968, the day of the visit, the head of national education announced early spring vacation for students and the universities were cordoned off from the rest of the city.[52] Instead of reporting on the student strikes, *L'Action* noted that the Maison de Tunisie in Paris celebrated Tunisian independence by expressing "unwavering attachment to the figure of President Bourguiba, artisan of independence."[53] Much was made of the presidential visit and the commemoration of national independence, while the university strikes and police crackdown were not reported until twelve days later. On 27 and 28 March, *L'Action* published commentary from Defense Minister al-Bahi al-Adgham deploring the recruitment of high school students into the movement and claiming that violence had been limited to student-on-student acts.[54]

To counter the PSD's narrative of events, the CISDHT, with the help of left-wing French publisher François Maspero, released *Liberté pour les condamnés de Tunis: La vérité sur la répression en Tunisie* (Liberty for the convicted of Tunis: The truth about repression in Tunisia).[55] Jean-Marie Domenach, editor of the political journal *Esprit*, penned the introduction, evoking his anticolonialist struggles alongside Tunisian leaders such as Ahmed Ben Salah in the 1950s in order to hold the country's new leaders accountable to democracy.

My anticolonialist past does not grant me any right to intervene in Tunisian affairs. But for the same reasons that I was anticolonialist then, today I must give the same assistance to those who suffer for their people that we gave to the nationalist activists who have since become their persecutors. But first I must give them the voice they are refused in Tunisia. . . . It is not because [Tunisian leaders] became ministers, ambassadors or government officials that we call them out. But it is our duty to insist that they answer us by refuting us, or by re-establishing human rights. Until now they have not spoken; we will not be silent.[56]

Much as the FIDH had claimed that Bourguiba's Special Court risked transforming his image from liberator to oppressor, Domenach called on Tunisia's nationalist leadership to make good on its 1950s rhetoric of independence. He also described activists living in France in 1968 as messengers, suggesting that though Tunisians were intellectually capable of speaking for themselves, they faced severe consequences in their homeland for criticizing the government, which incarcerated them and judged them guilty a priori. The spreading of suppressed information, often conducted from France, became an integral part of the movement. Even the act of free speech had become revolutionary.

The information provided by Domenach and the CISDHT countered claims in *L'Action* that "taking up the 5 June cause of Ben Jennet, who had incited fanatical gangs to burn and pillage in excited racist passion, would constitute a grave offense against civil rights."[57] According to *L'Action*, Tunisian activists were "maniacs under the influence of lying propaganda following orders from abroad."[58] To the contrary, the pamphlet recounts the Ben Jennet affair and the subsequent March movement from the activists' perspective. Letters written from Tunis to the CISDHT in Paris detail prison conditions as well as recorded descriptions of torture and the lack of due process at the September hearings. The contents of the letters illustrate the contradiction of the court's position: defendants were accused of supporting a "fanatical Muslim" (Ben Jennet) who allegedly pillaged a Jewish neighborhood, while they were simultaneously cast as consorting with Jews and questioned regarding their Muslim faith.[59] The pamphlet, published in Paris, presented an alternative truth to the PSD narrative, one that would have been extremely difficult to articulate from Tunis. Individuals such as Domenach, Chabert, and Gattégno developed anticolonial positions as the French empire in Southeast Asia and North Africa began to collapse. Yet even as the empire fragmented into new nation-states, these individuals continued to participate in activist networks when the processes of decolonization in Tunisia revealed human rights abuses.

The PSD went to great lengths to argue that the activists were influenced from afar, whether by Maoists, Jews, French imperialists, or Ba'thists. The fact that March '68 was launched by pro-Palestinian activists in June 1967 did not stop the Special Court or the PSD-dominated media from casting its members as both Zionists and fanatical Muslims when convenient. The *livre blanc* claimed that dissidence stemmed from three major foreign sources: Ba'thists took orders from extremists in Damascus and Beirut; Perspectivists were "zealots of Mao Zedong"; and Tunisian Communists were puppets of the French Communist Party.[60] The PSD falsely linked the Tunisian movement to French riots in May 1968 as part of a foreign plot in which French activist Geismar "traveled to Tunis where he was able to contact Maoists."[61] By creating a three-headed monster, the PSD laid the ground for the September show trials, putting itself and the Special Court in position to condemn diverse members of the political opposition by labeling them all anti-Tunisian (i.e., foreign). French authorities employed similar strategies when identifying May 68ers such as the Franco-German Daniel Cohn-Bendit and Omar Blondin Diop of Senegal—both of whom were denied entry following 1968—as anti-French subversive agitators.

In December 1968, Perspectives pointed out the anachronism of the PSD's charge that Geismar and other French May '68 agitators had infiltrated and influenced the Tunisian March '68, which actually preceded both Geismar's April arrival in Tunis and the events of May in France.[62] In August, Le Monde published an article revising the livre blanc narrative in which James Marangé, general secretary of FEN, asserted Geismar's role as SNESup representative rather than Maoist zealot.[63] The struggle between L'Action and the PSD from Tunis, on the one hand, and various Franco-Tunisian and French sources from Paris, on the other, took on a transnational dimension in which the battleground over Tunisian human rights had spread to France in much the same way that the March '68 protests themselves had resonated across the Mediterranean. The communication networks between human rights groups like the CISDHT and the FIDH, and intellectual-political organizations like Perspectives, enabled activists who had escaped detention to tell the stories of the March events. Observers at the September hearings were able to record details of the trials, and family members and foreign attorneys released information on prison conditions. The contact between activists in France and Tunisia created a web of resistance and information flow that contributed to the international front against Bourguiba's repression.

Drawing historical connections between March '68 and Tunisia's colonial past, and tracing transnational networks in the postcolonial period illustrates that, in some ways, the process of decolonization strengthened certain Franco-Tunisian bonds.[64] In order to successfully articulate a position outside the menacing controls of authoritative governance, activists turned to the former metropole as an information relay center and a hub of political activity. Expulsions of French coopérants and Tunisian activists holding French citizenship did not quash activism; rather, they often led to the exportation of activism to the relative safety of Paris, where it could be carried out in ways that were not possible in Tunis. In addition, the presence of Tunisian students at international gatherings such as the Sofia Congress and UNEF's Marseille Congress in 1968 provided opportunities for young activists to garner support for local initiatives as well as to express solidarity with the global anti-imperialist movement. And while Tunisian workers and intellectuals did not join forces until the late 1970s, Bourguiba's national education campaign leveled some class disparity as an increasing number of rural Tunisians earned university scholarships. Because of the reforms, coupled with Tunisia's colonial ties to the French education system, the university became a space for both trans-class and transnational interaction through established organizational structures and proliferating networks of communication that facilitated activism against authoritarian governance.

From Anticolonialism to Human Rights

Bourguiba's education policies contributed to the expansion of the ranks of a class of educated Tunisians with scarce employment opportunities but with robust intellectual connections in France. Moreover, repression of the international anti-imperialist movement at the local level in Tunis led to its exportation to France and to the merging of its goals with calls for democratic freedoms and human rights. In some ways, as the practice of Tunisian activism became more international, its actual political goals became narrower. March '68 led to the creation of important human rights organizations for penal reform and freedom of expression that remained active in the decades to follow.

If the Ben Jennet affair and its subsequent events can be classified as a "postcolonial," it is not because, as the famous French anthropologist Georges Balandier has claimed, "we are all, in some form or another, living in a postcolonial situation."[65] Rather, it is more localizable and less abstract than that. Unlike histories that focus on a global "spirit of '68,"[66] the Tunisian movement transcended national boundaries in very concrete ways, from the physical presence of Humphrey and Van Do in Tunis to the letters from Simone Lellouche Othmani in Paris to the French ambassador in Tunis. Furthermore, Foucault's experiences in Tunis reveal the power of "decolonizing 1968." Looking beyond events in Paris's May '68, we can see that activism did not merely radiate from the metropole outward, despite the Bourguiba regime's claims. More than any diffusionist or copycat theories that maintain Paris as the center and origin of 1968 activism, Tunisia functioned as a critical cog in the transnational solidarities of 1968 that affected key figures like Foucault, for whom young Tunisians provided the inspiration for his antiracist activism in the early 1970s.

The response to Bourguibist authoritarianism would not have been possible without vast networks in which Tunisians on the ground filtered information to Paris that often made its way back to Tunis via the metropole. What began with a rather general anti-imperialist protest against Tunisia's relationship to the West on 5 June 1967 had, by the close of the September 1968 show trials, transformed to focus more narrowly on basic human rights and democracy. Remnants of empire like the Tunisian university system and the concomitant organizations representing student concerns, which drew directly on French models, constituted the front lines of resistance to the regime. And though the student movement had the wind knocked out of its sails by multiple arrests of key figures and harsh sentences, activists had successfully laid bare the hypocrisies of newly independent Tunisia. The regime's brutality in 1968, including the use of torture, certainly made human rights a primary concern for Tunisian activists. And while influential scholars like Samuel Moyn have rightly pointed to the often nefarious deployment of human rights causes as a justification for post-1970s Western neo-imperial aggression, the Tunisian case calls into question his claim that "no one in the global disruption of 1968 thought of the better world they demanded as a world to be governed by 'human rights.'"[67] For all of Moyn's important interventions, his claim on the emergence of human rights only in the 1970s is based in large part on a Google Ngram reading of the term's increased appearance in English in the *New York Times,* combined with his conviction that human rights in anticolonial or national movements are distinct from "universal" human rights. This methodology overlooks victims of human rights abuses whose very lives depended on important underground pamphlet literature and letter-writing campaigns that do not appear in his analysis.

While human rights were not necessarily the most important feature of the global 1968 writ large, for the hundreds of Tunisians and French activists working to release protesters arrested in 1968, human rights formed a very basic corpus of freedoms on which they could agree, and a cornerstone of the decolonization process. Though the protests of 1968 may not have resulted in political regime change, they moved beyond the physical space of the University of Tunis and beyond demands for university reform, transforming into a more inclusive interpretation of international human rights that sought increased humanity for detained political activists and the exploited immigrant workers of France explored in the next chapter. To be sure, the presence of Tunisians in Paris helped bring the Third World to the metropole.

CHAPTER 3

Paris

Bringing the Third World to the Metropole

And when the rain makes a quagmire,
Of the smallest earth path,
You're splattered with mud from head to toe,
You're never clean in Nanterre.
[Et quand la pluie fait un bourbier,
Du plus petit chemin de terre,
On est souillé d'la tête aux pieds,
On n'est jamais propr'à Nanterre.]

—Michel Murty and Monique Brienne, "Aux bidonvilles
de Nanterre" (In the Bidonvilles of Nanterre [1968])

On 20 March 1968, as the Bourguiba regime
marked the twelfth anniversary of Tunisia's independence from France by
shuttering campus doors and sending students home early for spring break,
activists in Paris "brought the war home" by shattering the windows of the
American Express building in the 9th arrondissement. For the militants in question, American Express was both a symbol of globalized capitalism, promoting consumption with internationally recognized credit, and neo-imperialism
given American disregard for Vietnamese sovereignty. The destruction of the
building's facade by members of the Revolutionary Communist Youth (Jeunesse Communiste Révolutionaire [JCR]) and the National Vietnam Committee (Comité Vietnam National [CVN]) came on the heels of CVN's occupation
of the Latin Quarter in February, during which protesters burned the American
flag in solidarity with the Vietnamese struggle for independence.[1] It also led to
a heightened police response and six arrests, including that of CVN leader
Xavier Langlade, who also happened to be a student at the University of Nanterre. In situating the upheaval that would follow Langlade's arrest in France in
1968, these anti-imperial acts tell a global story of this postcolonial moment in
French history.

The events of 1968 in Paris reveal a French state grappling with radicalism
on the right and the left, new trends in immigration that shifted white nationalist beliefs from anti-Semitism to anti-Arabism, and new forms of *gauchiste*

antiracism with unprecedented outreach to foreign workers. Langlade's connection to the University of Nanterre prompted the student occupation of administrative buildings two days after his arrest, launching the influential Nanterre-based March 22 movement around Langlade's liberation. Nanterre was already a site of activism, owing to a range of issues in 1967 related to the expansion of higher education. These included a library perpetually under construction that forced Nanterre students into arduous commutes to the center of Paris to access alternative libraries, and resistance to sexual repression on a campus that heavily regulated the movements of its male and female students, who were forbidden from entering gender segregated residences. Nanterre was also at the heart of campus brawls between right-wing groups like Occident and the leftist JCR dating to at least November 1966, when JCR assaulted seven Occident members with weapons, prompting retaliation and campus clashes throughout 1967.[2]

Langlade's opposition to the Vietnam War cause linked germinating student anti-authority with hardened anti-imperialism, making Nanterre a focal point in the lead-up to the May events. The crackdown on CVN leadership also provided an opportunity for a robust leftist response to the physical assault of *gauchiste* and North African students in 1967 at Nanterre. Additionally, many university students began to see themselves as intellectual laborers and cogs in the global capitalist machine. In the 1960s' spirit of expanding future possibilities, many students used their status as intellectual laborers as a stepping-stone to identify with the working class. This newfound class consciousness made empathy with Vietnamese peasants particularly attractive, especially as the latter were taking on not just the American empire but potentially the entire capitalist system. Finally, resting on the outskirts of Paris, the University of Nanterre's newly constructed dormitories bellied up next to Paris's most marginalized groups of immigrant laborers. While neighboring students on the left saw these immigrants as victims of neo-imperial consumer society and potential revolutionary actors, many on the right saw them as the new Arab scourge infecting the French nation and stealing French jobs, a foreign disease to be excised as the Vichy regime had done to French Jews a generation earlier.

But it is safe to say that Vichy sympathizers like Occident remained on the margins of wider youth activism. Broadly speaking, May '68 in Paris was about antiauthoritarianism on multiple levels: in the home, in university classrooms, at the workplace, and in government. Students began with cries against paternalism—restricting contact between men and women in campus residences at Nanterre—and transformed them into efforts to reclaim classrooms to address student concerns and educational desires. Student activism eventually spread far beyond Paris when an estimated seven to ten million workers issued an unlimited general strike on 20 May. Workers adopted similar strategies when they challenged employers' authority, occupying executive office spaces and pushing for *auto-gestion*, or self-management, in the workplace. May '68 encompassed all of these antiauthoritarian positions that are now well known, but it was also a postcolonial moment in French history that brought the Third World to the metropole.

The postcolonial dimensions of this radical series of events were numerous. These include the painful memories of French imperial losses in Algeria, Indochina, and French West Africa of the recent past, the prominence of Third World anti-imperialism in the present, and the rising numbers of immigrant workers altering France's future. New postcolonial realities threatened French white supremacy while creating opportunities for progressive groups to build multicultural activist allegiances. Imperial shrinkage called into question white superiority for a nation that was incapable of maintaining rule over racialized others in distant lands. Adding insult to injury for the radical Right, immigrants of color from the very places French whites had once dominated rose rapidly from 1945 until the mid-1970s. Yet for *gauchiste* 68ers on the front lines demanding change, new political projects focused attention on immigrant workers as symbols of authentic revolutionary possibility in and after 1968.

In the plethora of explanations that seek to understand what first united students across campuses, few scholars have looked to France's colonial past in Algeria and Vietnam, or to the wave of postcolonial immigrants that arrived during postwar reconstruction. When administrators announced university closures at Nanterre and the Sorbonne, and authorities entered campuses to arrest student protesters on 2–3 May, the images of police controlling public spaces recalled wartime mentalities from the late colonial era. Riot police were summoned to take back the streets of Paris's Latin Quarter on 10 May, the "Night of the Barricades." To Parisian onlookers peering at the commotion outside their apartment windows, the overzealous crackdowns on France's young people eerily resembled the punishments meted out against Paris's North African populations and antiwar sympathizers during the 1950s–1960s Algerian conflict. Some observers even compared the violence to Nazi Germany's *Schutzstaffel* (SS) that terrorized Parisians in the 1940s. More unconscionable in 1968 was police violence carried out by French authorities directly targeting French-born youth during a time of peace.

In addition to the ways that France's colonial past inflected May '68, a postcolonial reading of events brings into relief more immediate transnational connections. In Tunisia, part of President Habib Bourguiba's crackdown led to the exile of Simone Lellouche to France, from where she continued her political activism and helped launch important human rights groups in Paris.

May '68 also witnessed collaboration from key activists like Daniel Cohn-Bendit (raised in France by German Jewish refugee parents) and Omar Blondin Diop (Senegal), whose relationship linked 1968 movements from Dakar, to Paris, and, after Cohn-Bendit was deemed an undesirable and returned to his parents' native home of Germany, to Frankfurt.[3] During this postcolonial moment, Vietnamese peasants and North African immigrant workers acted as global anti-imperial symbols and key protagonists in the political projects of the New Left. In bringing the Third World home, French 68ers disenchanted with *groupusculisme*—or the splintering off into small groups—on university campuses created alternative outlets for activism by seeking out contact with anti–Vietnam War causes and postcolonial immigrant populations. Likewise, immigrant intellectuals actively engaged in the protests of France's May '68 while simultaneously using Paris as a platform to garner support for causes rooted in their home countries.

Anti-imperialism: From Algeria to Palestine and Vietnam

So what was so postcolonial about May '68 in France? To begin, the recent memory of the Algerian War (1954–1962) and the French police brutality of 17 October 1961 and 8 February 1962 (which came to be known as "Charonne") determined the ways that many participants and spectators experienced and viewed the events of May '68.[4] The Algerian War had driven a wedge in French society that continued to divide the nation even after Charles de Gaulle attempted to answer the "Algerian Question" with the 1962 Evian Accords that brought the conflict to an end. Events and symbols from the war were strategically restaged and redeployed in 1968 by both the Right and the Left. These were meant to either depict negatively a fascistic state (by the Left) or rally French pride against the crumbling of French morals and global prestige (by the Right), demonstrating the lingering pain of the war and the memory of France's last gasp of colonial power.

In October 1961, members of the Federation of France of the National Liberation Front (Fédération de France du Front de Libération Nationale [FF-FLN]) organized a protest against the government curfew imposed on Algerian immigrants, as well as the French occupation of Algeria. Though figures vary regarding the numbers of actual participants, police recorded over twelve thousand arrests on 17 October, and anywhere from thirty-one to two hundred protesters (mostly Algerians) were killed by police and their bodies shamefully tossed into the Seine. A former member of the FF-FLN and 17 October participant, Kader, testified that he was held for thirty-three days and tortured with "hot iron rods to learn the names of leaders," then finally deported to Algeria.[5] Kader's commentary and experiences as an Algerian resister living in Paris reveal a spatial paradox. French oppression of Algerian resistance "extended" all the way to the domestic front, and, according to one member of the FF-FLN, Algerian resistance groups named France the seventh and final *wilaya* (province or division) over which Algerians must fight for independence.[6] A similar postcolonial jumbling of battlegrounds, location of resistance, and boundary busting would re-emerge for Paris's foreign student activists in 1968, who protested in France for home causes and feared both French and foreign authorities. In 1961, the French police force applied torture tactics domestically that the military implemented abroad, right-wing terrorist groups like the Secret Army Organization (Organisation de l'Armée Secrète [OAS]) operated in France and in Algeria, and revolutionary activity likewise extended beyond the political borderlines separating metropole and colony.

The events of October 1961 did not receive wide public attention until they were revealed during a separate 1990s investigation into Vichy crimes. Yet the state-sponsored violence of October would be repeated in various forms against antiwar French activists near the Charonne metro station on 8 February 1962 and on multiple encounters throughout 1968. On 8 February, left-leaning French protesters organized a demonstration against OAS and police violence targeting Algerians in France. The demonstration resulted in the deaths of at least eight French protesters who were trampled by riot police near the Charonne metro station. While the police brutality was relatively mild compared with 17 October, political organizations like the French Communist Party staged a public outcry for the fallen victims of Charonne, forever memorializing the tragedy with a mass funeral procession, which gathered hundreds of thousands of workers, students, and activists across the French Left, to march from the Place de la République to Place de la Nation on 13 February 1962. Charonne displayed a moment of solidarity among a fractured French Left. It also marked a shift in French attitudes away from the radical Right's position on keeping Algeria French at all costs, including now-publicized forms of terrorism: the OAS had killed over sixteen hundred people in Algeria in extramilitary actions in 1961–1962 and brought the war home to the streets of France.[7]

The events of October 1961 and February 1962 established the participation of immigrants in protest movements on French soil, as both direct actors and as symbols. Not only were immigrants from war-torn Algeria heavily active in the Algerian independence movement, but they were also symbols of identification for rebellious French nationals. Jim House and Neil MacMaster's work on the Paris 1961 massacre draws concrete examples of the uses of Char-

onne at PCF-organized commemorations. They argue that French leftist political parties identified more with Charonne than with 17 October. Charonne
represented a united, antifascist Left front, while 17 October witnessed little
direct participation by the French Left.[8] In May '68, Charonne was deployed
as a motif of police brutality in slogans appearing in leftist newspapers and
tracts deploring the national riot police (Compagnies Républicaines de Sécu-
rité [CRS]). The violence of 17 October 1961 became confused with that of 8
February 1962. Before details of 17 October became widely publicized during
1990s trials, the two related demonstrations often merged into one metonymic
event known simply as "Charonne," or, as Joshua Cole has noted, "a kind of
shorthand for evoking the violence of the colonial period."[9] Beyond the suppression of information related to the events at the time, their conflation may
be the direct result of their major commonality: in each case, police used ex-
traordinarily violent tactics to suppress anticolonial protesters. In calling for
public support for their causes, 68ers in France invoked these examples of police barbarism from the early 1960s. They also linked the local police to the
atrocities of the Algerian War, which were laden with tales of torture and rape
by French soldiers and extramilitary groups.[10]

In a May '68 pamphlet signed by the United Bronze Workers, an arm of the
General Confederation of Labor (Confédération Générale du Travail [CGT]),
agitators recalled Charonne when they charged that the state was responsible
for the current violent clashes between police and students. Charonne was similarly cited by leading student activist Daniel Cohn-Bendit as a moment of solidarity for the Algerian cause as well as an early example of "SS tactics" that
were repeated by the CRS in May and June 1968.[11] Moreover, the 3 May Action
Committee referenced Charonne in a document titled "War Gas!" to connect
the government repression of 1968 with the atrocities of the Algerian War.

Material Used by the CRS for Repression of Demonstrators . . .
Combat gas C.N. and C.B. (based on chlorine and bromide compounds
already currently used by Americans in Vietnam; they cause asphyxia
and death).
-Disabling gas.
These devices have been used this week in the Latin Quarter for attacks in cafés, in the subway, buses, stores, and apartment houses.

Now It Is Clear!
We are the guinea pigs for the experiments of a sadistic police who
already has Charonne and the tortures of Algeria to its credit. Thousands
of youth who came to demonstrate have been harried, tracked down,
bestially beaten.[12]

The 3 May Action Committee, based at the University of the Sorbonne, equated the police brutality of 8 February 1962 with French military activity during the Algerian War. This evocation of Charonne also spilled into images of US chemical warfare in Vietnam, demonstrating the malleability of the metonym that evolved into a general trope to express anti-imperialism while denouncing police brutality.

But the French Left was not the only group to place greater emphasis on the violence of Charonne over 17 October, or to reference it to condemn state violence. One Tunisian student who was active in 1968 while studying in France described how important Charonne was to the Tunisian political consciousness, stating that Tunisians participated in, and were injured at, Charonne in support of Algerian independence.[13] This student clearly identified with Charonne while making no mention of the far more fatal events of 17 October. By 1968, Charonne symbolized a moral victory for anticolonialists over police brutality as well as leftist solidarity against fascism. It also evoked the power of the masses, as estimates of as many as five hundred thousand people gathered on 13 February 1962 to mourn the dead.[14] While historians have uncovered many of the complexities of 17 October, Charonne, and their "afterlives," it should not be overlooked that Charonne also acted as a symbol of the power of the people to organize and was not simply a slogan to depict a repressive police force. Underlying the recollections of Charonne was an implied challenge to state-sponsored violence and right-wing terrorism through mass organization. When French or Tunisian 68ers recalled Charonne, they were rejecting the violence of France's colonial past in its postcolonial present. The events related to the early 1960s' conflict in Algeria had polarized French society, reenergizing the Right while galvanizing the French Left in unprecedented displays of unity, however brief.

Beyond the memories of the Algerian War, May '68 drew on the anticolonial language of the anti–Vietnam War movement and the struggle for Palestinian liberation. The confusion and division among French students on the Algerian question transferred directly to the Palestinian question just a few years later. UNEF, France's largest national student union, failed to take a position on Algeria until six years into the conflict, when it called for peace and a vague diplomatic solution.[15] The same can be said for Palestine when, in 1966, UNEF faced extreme criticism from competing international organizations—like the Prague-based International Student Union on the left, and the moderate Leiden-based International Student Conference—for abstaining from a vote on Palestine.[16]

This type of indecision contributed to the proliferation of new student groups with firmer anticolonial positions on such issues, and instances of double affiliations with both UNEF and more self-assured, often left-leaning groups. But with the June 1967 Arab-Israeli War, UNEF felt it necessary to order a special commission named from within its ranks to report on the issue. Under pressure from the pro-Palestinian international network of student groups such as FEANF, AEMNAF, and UGET, as well as internal pressure from strong UNEF sections like Lyon, the report called for the coexistence of Israel and Palestine. It cautioned against giving in to pressures from Jewish student organizations or to the general French population's pro-Israeli sympathies based on France's own sordid World War II anti-Semitism under the Vichy regime.[17]

But perhaps most interesting in the report's argumentation was that it called for a removal of race from the Palestinian question. The UNEF commission claimed that antiracist sympathies for Israel would cloud objective readings of "the imperialist character of [Israeli] interventions" and concluded that UNEF "must maintain its staunchly anti-imperialist positions, whether this be in Vietnam or in the Middle East."[18] This reading of events cautioned that racializing the conflict in the Arab world would lead to a more favorable reading of two of the most egregious practitioners of neo-imperialism: the United States and Israel. Interestingly, in this case UNEF's devotion to anti-imperialist causes like Vietnamese independence trumped other concerns, including antiracism.

After the 1954 French defeat at Dien Bien Phu and the loss of the imperial crown jewel Algeria in 1962, joining the anti–Vietnam War movement was a chance at redemption for young generations of French activists. They could finally and unequivocally denounce the French imperialism of the past as well as its new American form in Southeast Asia. As Daniel Gordon points out, the French Left's turn to Third Worldism in the 1960s was in many ways a reaction to the French Communist Party, which "had been ambiguous in its relationship to French colonialism, failing to make a clear stand in support of Algerian independence until it was too late."[19] These political positions on international events were a far cry from the material concerns—for example, housing and funding—to which leaders in Tunisia and Senegal attempted to limit their national student unions. UNEF's role extended well beyond advocating for the immediate financial needs of its members or issues only affecting students. After grappling with Algeria, UNEF inserted itself, however reluctantly, into international-political debates. By finally taking a position on Algeria, UNEF not only firmed up its commitment to anti-imperialism but also created opportunities for coordinated efforts with Palestinian-friendly student unions like UGET, AEMNAF, and the General Union of Palestinian Students, which identified with Arab and anti-imperialist causes.

Whereas UNEF was hesitant to declare support for Palestinians, many on the radical French left were not. Ali Mehrez, an Egyptian activist in the Arab

League, successfully forged ties with French radical leftists during the events of 1968 in Paris. With the participation of Trotskyists from the JCR, Marxist-Leninists, and anarchists, Mehrez incited a pro-Palestinian protest outside of the Israeli embassy in Paris on 5 June 1968.[20] The general sentiment of contestation and political action in Paris spread to immigrant neighborhoods like Belleville—once known as a multicultural community living in relative harmony—where North African Jews and Muslims violently attacked each other in early June 1968, and when segments on the left supported North African communities during the intervention by French riot police.[21] Given the large populations of North Africans brought to France's borders by what they deemed a neo-capitalist system, it is not surprising that students on the radical left would find affinities with postcolonial immigrant causes and view a pro-Palestinian position as part of an international, anti-imperialist cause.

Even more so than the Palestinian question, Vietnam preoccupied the minds of France's activist youth. If the consensus on Palestine was tenuous, anti-imperialist positions on Vietnam were much easier to establish. These sensibilities were evidenced in the Grassroots Committee on Vietnam (Comités de base du Vietnam), created in 1967 by French Maoists to break from the PCF's comparatively soft position calling for peace in Vietnam, as opposed to outright national independence and victory. Protest against war in Vietnam was generalized through UNEF's newfound anti-imperialism. These sentiments rested at the heart of early calls for student action in Cohn-Bendit's March 22 movement, which had been set off at the campus of Nanterre following Xavier Langlade's attack on US imperialism in Vietnam.[22]

Activism to end war in Vietnam created common ground and opportunities for contact with foreign student groups like FEANF, which held film screenings of *Vietnam Vaincra* (Victory in Vietnam) while protests swept the streets.[23] Yet while opposition to the Vietnam War and pro-Palestinian statehood were important features of 1968 mentalities, these were not omnipresent in May '68. Indeed, Romain Bertrand argues that the March 22 movement shifted away from anti-imperialism as it expanded: "The 'nationalization' of the protest agenda came about rapidly, the international struggle against American imperialism transformed into a domestic struggle against 'consumer society' and the Gaullist regime."[24] The major claims of 68ers from across the former French empire thus vacillated between more internationalist, anti-imperialist, and postcolonial ambitions and issues at national, regional, and even local levels.

For the French workers who decided to join forces with students on 13 May for an intersyndical strike tallying over one million in Paris and reaching France's provinces, their protests had more to do with the local impacts of global imperialism. While urban industrial workers may have been less likely to don "Vietnam Vaincra" signs than their student counterparts at the picket lines, they were far more likely to encounter postcolonial laborers in their daily lives, owing to the over 255,000 Algerian immigrants working in construction and metalworking industries.[25] Whereas students were brought to immigrant causes through a combination of Third World mentalities, global events, and the physical location of places like Nanterre, French workers interacted with immigrants on a daily basis, as networks of anticolonial activist laborers had been established during the Algerian War. And though French workers' activism had a much longer history than that of students, even predating the French Revolution, it is undeniable that students sparked the uprisings that would overcome the country in 1968.

Unlike in Tunisia, where workers actively undermined student protests, French workers took advantage of the momentum generated by Parisian students. They found their own symbols of authority to attack on 14 May when two thousand workers occupied the Sud-Aviation aircraft factory in Nantes, sequestered the plant manager, and demanded workers' self-management.[26] What students sparked at Nanterre and the Sorbonne spread beyond campuses and transferred to other social classes. A mixed bag of grievances against various forms of authority provided enough fodder to fuel intergenerational and cross-cultural discontent. Shortly after Sud-Aviation, Renault auto workers went on strike at several factories across the country in Billancourt, Flins, and Cléon and were ultimately joined by millions of workers in all sectors in an unlimited general strike on 20 and 21 May: postal, railroad, and public transportation services, banking, clothing, teaching, and construction.[27] At least for a brief moment, the largest student union (UNEF) held press conferences with one of the largest workers' unions, the French Democratic Confederation of Labor (Confédération Française Démocratique du Travail [CFDT]) to announce that "the workers' and students' struggle is the same."[28] Without the politicization of students witnessing the unfolding of a devastating war in Vietnam and informed by the recent memories of conflict in the colonies, it is difficult to imagine that workers could have mobilized the largest strike in France's history.

Anti-imperialist affinities dating to the Algerian War had politicized both French students and foreigners living in France and informed their positions on postcolonial conflicts in Vietnam and Palestine. If their targets shifted from distant US warmongering politicians to the authoritative figures standing in front of them, like university administrators, parents, and protest-busting riot police, these initial anti-imperial mentalities certainly contributed to an identification on the left with what Frantz Fanon termed the "wretched of the earth": in this case immigrant workers.[29] For many French students invigorated by the unwavering rebellious spirit of the Vietnamese peasants who stood their ground against the world's greatest military superpower, taking up immigrant causes in France provided a way to atone for their nation's own past colonial abuses. May '68 was a postcolonial moment not simply because it occurred "after" imperial collapse in North Africa and Indochina; rather, it was "produced by" the end of empire.[30]

The University of Nanterre as a Postcolonial Space

Founded in 1964 and constructed as a new campus by 1966, the University of Nanterre was in many ways an experiment in modern higher education. It was designed to uncork the bottleneck created in Paris by the rapidly expanding populations of university students in France, which surged from 175,000 in 1958 to over 500,000 by 1968.[31] Just outside the inner walls of Paris, the university was built in a northwest *banlieue* (suburb) in the heart of working-class immigrant populations. The law of 20 September 1947 granted French citizenship to Algerian colonial subjects, allowing for free movement between France and Algeria. The law led to an increase in the Algerian population in France from 20,000 in 1946 to 210,000 in 1954 at the onset of the Algerian War, and another upsurge of Algerian immigrants resumed again between 1962 and 1975, when the Algerian population in France reached 758,000.[32] In addition to Algerians, the French government recruited workers for postwar reconstruction in large numbers from Morocco, Tunisia, Spain, Italy, Poland, Portugal, and West Africa, among others. This immigrant labor contributed to a long period of economic prosperity in France after 1945 known as the Thirty Glorious Years (1945–1975).

The number of North Africans residing in France had swelled to almost one million by the late 1960s, with many residing in segregated semi-urban *bidonvilles* (shantytowns) like those that cropped up in Nanterre. With dorm-room vistas overlooking some of the poorest ghettos on the outskirts of Paris, the Nanterre campus directly confronted the harsh realities of working-class and immigrant life. French anti-imperialist sentiments and student awareness of immigrant living conditions converged in the state-produced space of Nanterre. With horrifying inequalities in plain sight, the French radical Left began to sympathize with postcolonial immigrant communities, ultimately paving the way for solidarities with the antiracism and immigrant workers' movements of the following decades. At the same time, these postcolonial projects and immigrant solidarities enabled the Left to further antagonize their anti-immigrant rivals like Occident on the right.

The cultural and societal intersection created by the physical location of the University of Nanterre played a significant role in student politicization. Henri Lefebvre, the famous Marxist sociologist at Nanterre, remarked on the profound impact of the bidonvilles on his students. "The suburbs and their shanty-towns are more than a sad spectacle—they constitute a void. . . . Nanterre is marked by a two-fold segregation—functional and social, industrial and urban. Functionalized by initial design, culture was transported to a ghetto of students and teachers situated in the midst of other ghettos filled with the 'abandoned,' subject to the compulsions of production, and driven into an extra-urban existence."[33] Nanterre was situated in a bizarre urban but not-quite-Parisian setting, which made for an interesting meeting point between France's university students and its most underprivileged classes of workers. A new state project (the university) to help meet France's economic needs, Nanterre was also emblematic of the melding of industry and education. In the postwar 1960s, higher education was increasingly open to a cross-section of social groups, from France's most privileged to working-class and rural students, many of whom related to the struggles of the laboring classes residing next door. With Daniel Cohn-Bendit's launching of the March 22 movement, Nanterre had become the locus of student activism that would soon envelop Paris and spread throughout several of France's provincial centers. As Kristin Ross has noted, because of this student–immigrant worker dynamic in Nanterre, "May '68, in fact, marks the emergence onto the political scene of the *travailleur immigré* (immigrant worker) in French society."[34] It is not surprising, then, that Nanterre provided the headquarters for the first bidonvilles Action Committee in the Paris region in 1968.[35]

The construction of the University of Nanterre adjacent to immigrant-populated *banlieues* coincided with intellectual currents of the New Left moving toward subalternism and Third World causes. As the French Communist Party lost a number of prominent intellectuals for its support of the Soviet invasion of Hungary in 1956, including anticolonialists like Aimé Césaire, many leftists turned away from traditional bureaucratic structures. Frustrated with the many failures of the decidedly unrevolutionary positions of the French Communist Party with respect to French workers, many "New Leftists" looked to society's most repressed groups (postcolonial immigrant laborers) as sources of true revolutionary potential.[36] At the same time, the waves of immigrant workers from ex-colonies that entered France during postwar reconstruction altered French demographics and created new social and cultural interactions.

Increasingly visible bidonvilles in Paris intersected with French New Left philosophy. Althusserian-influenced Western and urban versions of Maoism, Henri Lefebvre's and Guy Debord's neo-capitalist urban "situations," and Alfred

Sauvy's Third Worldism all produced a strong interest in actively engaging with immigrant issues. Indeed, what Sauvy articulated in his 1952 article in *L'Observateur*, "Three Worlds, One Planet," theorized the revolutionary action put in practice a few short years later by Third World leaders at the 1955 Bandung Conference in Indonesia. According to Sauvy, the oppressed peoples residing in Africa and Asia constituted a powerful revolutionary force, the Third World, akin to France's Third Estate in 1789.[37] Like this social group of "commoners" that made up the vast majority of the eighteenth-century French population—but which held far less wealth and fewer political rights than the clergy (the First Estate) and the aristocracy (the Second Estate)—the Third World harnessed revolutionary potential and strength in numbers. It also leveraged moral high ground over competing Cold War systems in the First (Capitalist West) and Second (Communist East) Worlds. New Leftists in France needed only peer onto immigrant ghettos north of Paris or visit the Renault auto factory in Boulogne-Billancourt to find present-day revolutionaries from its former colonies. With the Third World being brought home, they came to view metropolitan France as a site of global protest.

For postwar Europeans horrified by the Cold War's evolving nuclear threats to humanity, the nonalignment positions of Third Worldism further provided an attractive alternative to US-led global capitalism or Soviet Communism. While Afro-Asian leaders expressed Third World solidarity at Bandung—just one year after France's embarrassing defeat at Dien Bien Phu in 1954—Vietnamese populations began preparing resistance to the new US presence in South Vietnam. Responding to the surprising resilience displayed in the Vietnamese Tet Offensive of early 1968, as Salar Mohandesi has argued, "If Vietnamese peasants could defeat the most powerful military machine in human history, then anything was possible."[38] Inspired by these extensions of possibility, radical French 68ers actively sought ways to adapt the Third World revolution to their own context. The New Left engaged in anti–Vietnam War activism and consumed contemporary French philosophies alongside those of Third World intellectuals like Mao Zedong, Che Guevara, and Frantz Fanon.

Others found revolutionary symbols in the victims of global capitalism in everyday life: the French working class and postcolonial immigrant laborers. The March 22 movement began at Nanterre with anti-imperialist solidarities in support of Vietnam, but it also generated momentum for a number of related causes as it moved through Paris to the provinces. Among the multiple causes that brought protesters to demonstrate was support for immigrant workers. Given the 1968 convergence of anticolonial New Left philosophy and the expansion of the French university into immigrant neighborhoods, the contact zones between the French New Left and immigrant workers can be seen less as "improbable encounters," as some have argued, and more as actively sought connections by actors living in a particular historical moment that produced them.[39] Unlike some of their predecessors from the 1950s and 1960s whose goals remained rather circumscribed, 1968 opened possibilities for French radicals to envision revolution beyond Algeria or Vietnam.[40] France could be reimagined as a site of revolution as well, where French militants worked alongside workers and intellectuals from elsewhere.

The Postcolonial Immigrants of May '68: Symbols and Activists in Their Own Right

Though only a short physical distance of less than 15 kilometers from the bidonvilles of Nanterre, the glistening hallways occupying 45 Rue d'Ulm in the heart of Paris's Latin Quarter seem as if from another dimension. There rests one of France's finest institutions of higher learning, the École Normale Supérieure de Paris, where philosophy professor Louis Althusser's reinterpretation of Marxism-Leninism influenced a young generation of activists. Althusser's critique of bourgeois society and the inaction of the PCF prompted a group of his students, known as the *Ulmards*, to form the Union of Marxist-Leninist Communist Youth (Union de la Jeunesse Communiste marxiste-léniniste [UJC(ml)]), which transformed into the Proletarian Left after its dissolution in June 1968.

The *Ulmards*, led by prized student Robert Linhart, were enchanted by Mao's Cultural Revolution. In the summer of 1967, Linhart and other UJC(ml) leaders were invited to the People's Republic of China, where they experienced the Cultural Revolution firsthand.[41] Upon their return in the fall of 1967, they searched in France for their own authentic experience with the working and peasant classes as part of a subset of activists called *établis*. Initially drawing intellectual inspiration from coursework with Althusser, the établis charted their own course by combining his ideas on Marxism-Leninism with other ideological currents. The name *établis*, borrowed from Mao's speech "Let One Hundred Flowers Bloom," had several meanings: *établissement* referred to both the factory as a site of class struggle and the installation of a movement; *établi* invoked the artisan's workbench; the verb *s'établir* referred to the action of establishing oneself and settling into a new environment.[42] Equally enamored by the Chinese Cultural Revolution, these men and women went into the factories in France to put their philosophical beliefs into practice and to engage and organize the French and immigrant working class. Recalling his établi motivations, Pierre Delannoy noted that after May '68, "for most of us, with bourgeois roots, we wanted to learn about 'the people,' to discover their way of life, language, relationships, it was a worldview."[43] For Delannoy personally, who came from humble beginnings, the goal was to glorify and celebrate the working condition.

By applying Maoist principles to the French context, the établis found a way out of Althusser's diagnosis of consumer society: that it was impossible to avoid bourgeois ideology emanating from the ruling class of the state apparatus. To alter the "imaginary relationship of individuals to their real conditions of existence," they would launch an "investigation" (enquête) by purposefully changing their habitat and environment and "settling in" with the working classes.[44] The change in the real-life conditions of their daily routines would first mirror, then become integrated into, the lives of the working class and, hence, of the revolution. It led établis outside of Althusser's study sessions to the assembly lines of France's industrial factories, oftentimes alongside France's most oppressed immigrant laborers. This direct engagement also satisfied the Leninist component of their UJC(ml) identities since they would act as a vanguard group helping to awaken the revolutionary consciousness of their fellow workers.

The établis were rather significant in number—it is estimated that between two thousand and three thousand établis entered into factories in the 1960s and 1970s—and continued their activities investigating, infiltrating, and "settling into" French factories into the 1980s.[45] Their participation in immigrant workers' struggles spilled over into other elements of the French Left. After the dissolution of UJC(ml) in June 1968, its successor, the Proletarian Left, engaged in a number of antiracist demonstrations and frequently sought contact with international student groups like FEANF and, after its creation in 1970, the Arab Workers movement.

The établis influenced other groups as well, such as the Cahiers de mai, which formed in 1968 and would later be instrumental in organizing immigrant workers in Rothschild-owned metallurgy factories across France in the early 1970s. Activists Daniel Anselme and the Algerian War resister Henri Fournié launched Cahiers de mai out of frustration with the ineffectual PCF and, more importantly, to tell workers' stories. As Donald Reid has pointed out, Anselme was concerned with "the importance of inclusive politics, of the defense and assertion of the interests of 'all the men of the second zone,' whether the colonized, Blacks in America, or Jews in Europe."[46] Anselme and Fournié wanted to steer attention away from students and link up with workers' causes. Similarly, for the Nanterre students, who witnessed the Third World conditions of the neighboring immigrant slums, and the Ulmards, who returned from China to seek authentic experiences in the industrial trenches, the engagement on the radical left contained both postcolonial and transnational dimensions.

For the former, the Third World was visible in France in the figure of the post-colonial immigrant of the bidonvilles, while the latter brought Third World sensibilities back to France from actual experiences in Maoist China.

It seemed only natural, then, for activists like Roland Castro, a former member of the UJC(ml), to move to Nanterre to carry out post–May '68 activism.

> I moved to Nanterre,
> there where it had begun.
> The sons of the bourgeois
> in the middle of the bidonvilles,
> on the other side of the tracks,
> in the depths of the banlieue.
> At [the train station] Nanterre-la-Folie
>
> You look around, there where it's real,
> in the noise, revolt.
> And at Nanterre there is no shortage
> of subjects of revolt.[47]

For French radicals like Castro, the train tracks of the Nanterre–La Folie station marked the meeting place of the university and the shantytowns, or what Daniel Gordon calls the place where the "sons of the bourgeois found the revolt and the authenticity they were seeking."[48] The quest for authentic revolt, whether at Nanterre or in the factories, was an attempt by radicals to reeducate themselves in the Maoist sense, stepping away from privilege and into a pair of workers' boots. Women like établi Juliette Campagne, who spent years in and out of labor-intensive jobs, joined the cause "to leave behind our 'privileged' milieu."[49] Others, such as Pierre A. Vidal-Naquet, joined the établis when they became frustrated with the limits of a student movement. Vidal-Naquet found that rather than in the campus quads or the streets of the Latin Quarter, "the real fight is in the factory."[50] With reforms to the French university system leading to a 180 percent increase in the student population between 1961 and 1968, it is certainly true that working-class students had greater access to higher education. Yet compared with the poor conditions of laboring immigrants next door, they still stood in a position of relative circumstance. In a highly industrialized society and in the absence of a down-to-the-countryside movement for intellectuals, Nanterre was a logical venue in which to engage with the most oppressed, and therefore legitimate, revolutionary class of immigrants.

The level of actual immigrant participation in France's May '68 has produced a certain level of discord among scholars. Early analyses point to a limited role, with claims that "foreigners in [Mai '68] did not appear center stage" or that the participation of immigrant workers was "unequal: active in some sites, followers more often . . . without necessarily belonging to the groups of leaders."[51] Others have gone even further in minimalizing their role, declaring that "immigrants seemed somewhat marginal" and viewed strikes as "a French work stoppage in which they played only a passive role."[52] While immigrants might not always have been at the forefront of the May events, a few clarifications need to be made regarding their activity.

First, the evidence used to support their lack of participation, which has appeared in multiple historical accounts, comes from one police report focusing largely on Spanish and Portuguese workers who fled factories because of their "fearful mentality" and an "apolitical nature."[53] Second, the police report ignores the fact that many of the tracts disseminated during worker strikes were translated into several languages and made claims for pay equal to that of French nationals. The report leaves out that foreign workers demanded better treatment and decent lodging; but it also fails to distinguish Spanish and Portuguese workers from those of France's former colonies, who had a different relationship with both the French state and their home countries. Thus, while the source of the document is not sufficiently problematized, neither are its contents.

What did not make it into the report is that out of more than two hundred arrests following a violent rally on 24 May in Lyon, over fifty Algerians were detained.[54] Nor does the police account take into consideration the foreign CGT members who were deported following their involvement in strikes at a Citroën factory. Indeed, French authorities reacted to events by immediately expelling well over two hundred foreign students and workers and incarcerating others, all linked to "public disorder," curtailing much of the potential participation of immigrants who feared reprisals.[55] Even if immigrants made up a proportionally small percentage of participants in the events of May–June '68, they faced a disproportionate level of police repression and brutality, not to mention the scorn and violence of right-wing groups still yearning for the glory days of colonial France. Many believe that police were given specific orders to target foreigners in crackdowns, with foreigners making up as much as one in six arrests during the heightened period of protests, even though they made up one in nineteen of the overall population in France in 1968.[56]

As in Tunisia and what would later happen in June 1968 in Senegal, the de Gaulle government attempted to externalize the revolts. This was a much more difficult proposition for de Gaulle given the extent of the strikes, which quickly spread from Paris to other large university centers like Lyon and Bordeaux and even to parts of the countryside, eventually involving as many as ten million striking students and workers.[57] Gaullist expressions of postcolonial nationalism were in many ways a reaction to the issues raised for national debate by the events of May '68. French whites feared losing supremacy to shifting demographics of postcolonial laborers and mobilized to prevent radical changes proposed by a youth they viewed as possessed by the foreign influences of Maoism or Marxism-Leninism. In his famous radio broadcast of 30 May, de Gaulle declared the dissolution of the General Assembly and announced a referendum and new legislative elections. He denounced the movement for blocking French workers from working and students from studying, suggesting Soviet influence through methods of "intimidation, intoxication and tyranny exercised by organized groups for some time, and as a result of a party that is a totalitarian enterprise, even if it already has rivals in this regard."[58] The broadcast was welcomed news to the tens of thousands of counterdemonstrators, many of whom feared another national economic shutdown, gathered in Paris at the Champs Elysées to support de Gaulle on 31 May.

The socialist François Mitterrand had announced his candidacy for president in the event of new elections just days before the Gaullist demonstration. While the students of Nanterre and the Sorbonne declared solidarity with immigrant workers, Gaullists at the counterdemonstration chanted such slogans as "Send Mitterrand to Moscow," "Right to Work," and "France for the French."[59] This placed Gaullists in stark opposition to students donning posters from the Atelier Populaire of the ex–École des Beaux Arts declaring "French and Immigrant Workers United." And while many French workers continued to strike throughout June, the wind had been taken out of their sails after many refused to accept serious gains negotiated by CGT leader Georges Séguy. Indeed, more radical elements of CFDT and Force Ouvrière unions were not impressed with 35 percent minimum wage increases and 10 percent increases across the board that Séguy secured from the government in late May through the Grenelle Accords.[60] The goodwill they had generated by supporting students against police violence was lost in the early weeks of June, when much of the continued opposition began to smack of opportunism. This public sentiment shown through at the polls, when voters overwhelmingly supported the de Gaulle government at the 30 June referendum, stamping out the possibility of political revolution.

Perhaps even more prominent than the participation of immigrant workers in 1968, which increased significantly in the 1970s, was that of students from the ex-colonies. One of the results of intellectual migration was that it brought Tunisian Mustapha Khayati to the University of Strasbourg for his postsecondary studies. Khayati worked closely with Guy Debord on a number of key texts for the Situationist International, including "Address to Revolutionaries of Algeria and of All Countries," which was clandestinely distributed in Algiers in July 1965 and published in 1966 in the *Internationale Situationniste*. Khayati was perhaps most well known as the supposed ghostwriter of an anonymous 1966 pamphlet, "On the Poverty of Student Life," which diagnosed the alienation felt by many 68ers. The essay encompassed the frustrations of France's 1968 generation, setting forth a critique of the merger between capitalism and the university that resulted in the student's direct subjugation "to the two most powerful systems of social authority: the family and the state."[61]

The provocative text sparked the "Scandal at Strasbourg," during which the Situationist International challenged UNEF leadership at the university. A sociology professor, deemed a promoter of an oppressive system, was pelted with rotten tomatoes in October 1966. The text further influenced the *Enragés* at the University of Nanterre in February 1968 and the eventual March 22 movement. The pamphlet declared that students were intellectual laborers and made the connection between the exploitation of university students and the working class. Bridging Third Worldist and Marxist leanings, activists looked to France's immigrant workers, who faced related oppression from French neo-imperialism. In an expanded definition of colonialism comparing France's past colonial practices overseas to the home front, the pamphlet proclaimed that "student poverty is merely the most gross expression of the colonization of all domains of social practice."[62] Given his interest in the Tunisian situation back home, and as a close follower of revolutionary events in Algeria—the standard-bearer for Third World revolutions—Khayati was sensitized to the colonial dimensions of university life and the French state. He later left the Situationist International to join the struggle for Palestinian liberation in 1969, only to renege on some of his pan-Arab nationalist positions in the 1970s to promote an end to war and the unity between the Israeli and Palestinian proletariat.[63]

Yet the pamphlet also included a diagnosis of the emotional and sexual alienation experienced by students, which no doubt influenced pre-May grumblings at Nanterre regarding strict limitations on gender-divided campus dorms. The power of the pamphlet was not lost on Daniel Cohn-Bendit, who identified with its recognition that the university had become "a sausage-making machine which turns out people without any real culture, and incapable of thinking for themselves but trained to fit into the economic system of a highly industrialized society."[64] The Strasbourg pamphlet had traveled to the hallways of Nanterre, speaking to a number of university student concerns and pointing a finger at scores of authoritative figures that would be challenged in 1968: university administrators, professors, religious leaders, police, parents, agents of the state, and politicians.

Other young Tunisians living in France actively participated in May '68, especially those who would have preferred to engage in their own national student movement but who found themselves in France either for studies or to escape repression from their own government. *Jeune Afrique* noted the massive support of French students emanating from the 115 blvd. Saint Michel, the headquarters of the Maison d'Afrique du Nord, following the "Night of the Barricades" of 10 May. Police crackdowns on North Africans helped cement Franco-Maghrebi solidarities after French activists helped obtain the release of four Tunisian students who had been arrested during clashes with authorities. As one Tunisian student recalled, "Thanks to the actions of our French comrades, [the Tunisians] were released the next day. . . . What is happening here holds great importance and the experience of this struggle will prove useful for us, even if the situation in our country is extremely different."[65] Simone Lellouche, who was exiled to France in April 1968 after student strikes at the University of Tunis, likewise continued her political activism in Paris. Despite an ardent political education in anticolonialism and Third Worldism, Lellouche found herself in solidarity with the French movement owing to circumstances outside of her control.

While depressed by news of the imprisonment of her Tunisian colleagues, Lellouche happened upon a large protest in front of the Sorbonne when attempting to access the Saint-Geneviève Library in early May 1968. After a policeman struck her with his club, Lellouche began attending protests regularly. According to Lellouche, "It was the first time that I found myself in-sync with the French, the children of those who had colonized us and with whom I was hurling the same slogans."[66] Lellouche's experiences in Tunisia had already politicized her. Yet while actively seeking the release of detained Tunisian comrades back home, she felt a certain connection with the spontaneous French crowds in May. Not long after her realization in the Latin Quarter, she again coordinated with French and other Tunisian activists.

During the Tunisian minister of tourism's speech at the Maison de Tunisie of the International University campus, Lellouche and company asked the minister to give tours of the prisons of Bizerte, where Tunisian activists were being held without trial. "Our French friends helped us organize a certain disorder in the uniformity and order of the speech that was about to be given. . . . [The cops] rounded up everyone on the spot. We didn't know that on rue Gay Lussac that same night that the students were building barricades against the CRS."[67] Her experiences speak to both the spontaneity and the global reach of the events. Her confrontation with police brutality in early May had placed her in the same camp with French protesters, yet in her own right she was already actively organizing against the capitalist and neo-imperialist tourism industry of Tunisia that served the French. After learning of the simultaneous protests in the Latin Quarter, Lellouche made it a point to participate whenever possible in Parisian activism, viewing her struggle against Tunisian authority as part of the larger movement of her French counterparts. This odd rejoining of old colonial foes was a major part of the healing process often overlooked in analyses of decolonization.

While Spanish and Portuguese immigrants made up a sizable portion of the foreign population in France in 1968, they did not experience the same postcolonial relationship with France, or with the French population, as did immigrants hailing from France's former colonies. For those southern European immigrants who joined workers strikes or student protests, their references as either political or material activists differed from those who had directly experienced, or had been sensitized to, French colonial authority. Immigrant workers certainly shared a number of common characteristics in often deplorable working and housing conditions and shared the desire to find gainful employment to support their families. Yet the political concerns of Portuguese and Spanish immigrants centered on their own local experiences with dictatorship in the figures of Salazar and Franco, rather than French colonialism or decolonization. Thus, when Yvan Gastaut cited immigrant communities that fled in "panic" during the course of May '68, he was referring to a certain set of immigrants from southern Europe.[68]

Some May participants, such as the Senegalese Omar Blondin Diop, had already been active since the March 22 movement at Nanterre alongside Daniel Cohn-Bendit. Blondin Diop frequented leftist circles and even landed himself a prominent role as a Maoist revolutionary in Jean-Luc Godard's film *La Chinoise* (1967). Far from being a passive participant, as some historians would suggest regarding immigrant involvement, he, along with Lellouche, was on the front lines in May '68. The activist couple Marie-Angélique and Landing Savané also participated, having already exhibited Maoist tendencies before the protests. They used the backdrop of French activism strategically to make claims in support of university protests in Dakar, and even organized the occupation of the Senegalese embassy in Paris on 28 May 1968 in denunciation of government repression of the Senegalese movement.[69]

Just as the radical Left in May '68 carried posters calling for the unity of French and immigrant workers, immigrant students held their own banners proclaiming, "Students of the Third World in solidarity with their French comrades."[70] UNEF arranged for foreign student organizers to operate out of the fourth floor of the occupied Sorbonne as their headquarters. African students of FEANF responded to the police invasion of the Sorbonne on 2 May when it was shut down by administrators, and supported French students against the generalized police violence of May. FEANF further expressed "total support to UNEF and its militants for the democratization of the University. . . . The savage repression of which French students are victims recalls the massacres perpetrated by the colonialist and neo-colonialist forces in our countries against the masses and African students in their struggle against pro-imperialist regimes installed by French neo-colonialists. In their struggle against imperialist domination, African students from Abidjan and Dakar (reunited under UED: the Dakar Student Union) as well as those of France (organized under FEANF) etc., lead the fight against neo-colonialist education."[71] FEANF thus engaged directly with the French student movement and linked French events to anticolonial student movements in West Africa. Though these activists did not reference historical events like Charonne, they established a clear connection between the police repression of 1968 in Paris and the savagery of violence committed by colonialists and neocolonialists in both West Africa and France. And like Simone Lellouche, whose group of Tunisian activists used May '68 to protest Tunisian authority in France, African students participated in the French movement in part to leverage support for events in their home countries.

May '68 took on a plethora of meanings for multiple different actors and spectators: Gaullists felt that it undermined French values the 1940s *résistance* had fought so hard to regain; French Maoists viewed it as an opportunity to reach out to the most oppressed classes of French society as part of their own reeducation; and many immigrant students and intellectuals felt that solidarity with the French validated their own anticolonial struggles. Only taken together can these fragmentary experiences fully capture the essence of May '68, which was not merely a cultural revolution, a political one, or a purely French one. Postcolonial relationships were important for each of these perspectives, as well as integral elements of May '68, from the lingering memory of the Algerian War to the postcolonial politics of the French établis. If Algerian freedom fighters and Vietnamese peasants came to represent Third World power in the face of neocolonialism for many on the French left, the postcolonial immigrant was its most visible embodiment at home. And if the loss of French Algeria marked France's most recent failure for those on the right, they also found new targets on which to project their ire in the figure of the immigrant and the morally depraved youth activist.

Imperial Fragments and Postcolonial Nationalisms

The postcolonial dimensions set forth in this chapter do not attempt to encompass the entire story of May '68; rather, they are intended to tell an important piece that has not been systematically or sufficiently treated in the existing literature. From the imperial fragments of May '68 emerge a desire for authenticity and a willingness to engage with the non-Western world. Indeed, a certain orientalism reveals itself in the efforts of French Maoists to reproduce the down-to-the-countryside aspects of the Cultural Revolution and to experience the existence of, and revolt alongside, the wretched immigrant worker.[72] Armed with Lefebvre and Althusser, some members of the radical Left, like Roland Castro, actually moved to Nanterre to be at the site of revolt, and among the revolted and revolting. The struggles for Vietnamese and Palestinian liberation, coupled with the construction of Nanterre in working immigrant neighborhoods, brought the Third World to French students in the figurative and the literal. By joining anticolonialist causes abroad and at home, French activists in 1968 could directly participate in the decolonizing projects of 1968.

Observing the commotion at Nanterre, Henri Lefebvre proclaimed, "This fragment of a broken, rejected, and marginal university regains a kind of universality. Among the students *all* tendencies manifest themselves, especially *all* those which oppose the established society. Even the institution called university [*sic*], which has in fact already exploded, and which thought that it could regain strength and autonomy in a marginal location, is dissolving. The crack, the outlet for tensions and latent pressures, is widening."[73] The physical environment at the University of Nanterre forced French youth to confront the difficult conditions of working immigrants living next door. This proximity fed their double desire for contact with the outside world and for the political righteousness of Third World anticolonialism. The anti–Vietnam War movement and the Palestinian struggle for independence offered opportunities to redeem UNEF's original deference to the "Algerian Question" by putting forward an unequivocal anticolonialist position.

If the university was one battleground among many in 1968 (others being factories and urban streets) and the postcolonial elements of May '68 a fragment of its entirety, they encapsulate a certain "kind of universality" of anti-authoritarianism, anti-Occidentalism, anticapitalism, and anticolonialism. These features were all recognizable to both participants and observers of May '68, from the *Enragés* of Nanterre and the *Ulmards* of the École Normale Supérieure to the intrepid Tunisian and Senegalese everyday activist intellectuals who combined their support of protest in France with homegrown anticolonial causes. The degrees of cooperation between French and immigrant workers, and between workers and students, varied significantly. In some cases, Maoist and other leftist students experienced successes in connecting with workers. But unions like the CGT had complicated histories with immigrants whose membership and needs they did not always consider since they lacked voting status. It was not until the 1970s that labor unions began to seriously reach out to immigrants, and that immigrant workers began to engage in their own autonomous organizations.

Both the aftermath of May '68 and its immigrant activists reveal an expanded notion of a postcolonial situation beyond that of its chronological implications. By concretely tracing the historical fragments of the once-connected empire as they transformed during postwar processes of decolonization, May '68 emerges as the beginning of the politicization of immigrant workers, rather than the last breath of the French student movement before de Gaulle's intervention. Immigrant activists communicated with broader French activist networks, but also with organizations in the former colonies. Many of these networks were historically rooted in the colonial period out of the French structures of student and worker unions, taking on new forms after 1968. The end of empire altered demographics in both the metropole and the colonies, with the proletarianization of France's immigrant population and mass emigration from the former colonies. Yet it is clear that the fragmentation of the empire did not result in the clean severing of ties between metropole and colony. Indeed, webs of transnational resistance, including those connecting France with Tunisia and Senegal, emerged alongside international networks of state control. Gaullist isolationism—fearing the invasion of foreign bodies and ideologies—and French students' Third Worldism can be viewed as two opposing forms of postcolonial nationalism. Each was a domestic ideology taking root in France at this time in reaction to the forces bringing the world to the metropole.

CHAPTER 4

Dakar

The "Other" May '68

Shouts—who knows if it is hate?—
Shot from the faces of rebellious adolescents.
Dust and sweating back, enthusiasm, panting.
Painful envelopes with landscapes of baobab trees,
Single-file duty patrols and vultures on the blue backdrop.
And many more secrets.

—Léopold Sédar Senghor, "Sadness in May"

Has our cultural expansion just received a definitive blow?
I don't think so.

—French ambassador to Senegal, Jean de Lagarde, in a
    12 June 1968 telegram

Léopold Sédar Senghor's poetic description
above evokes his dismay and confusion at the groundswell of student discontent that erupted at the University of Dakar on 29 May 1968. For Senghor, it
was a moment of heightened anxiety due to persistent threats since his acces-
sion to the presidency in September 1960. In the next decade, he would dismantle, abrogate, or subsume rival political parties. He even overcame an
attempted coup by his prime minister, Mamadou Dia, whom he later imprisoned. But in 1968, Senghor faced political challenges from African students.
This was particularly perplexing for Senghor since his government had allo-
cated enormous budgetary resources to fund generous university student stipends and expand national education. For French observers like ambassador
Jean de Lagarde, the moment constituted a challenge to France's status in Senegal. With student demands to Africanize curricula and teaching corps at the
University of Dakar—buttressed by support from the largest national labor
union that resented French presence in other industries—de Lagarde wondered
whether it was time to recalibrate the degree of France's long-term cultural
influence in Senegal.

Senghor's handling of the student movement was directly related to the importance he placed on the university, and the African students it educated, as a symbol of Senegalese progress and modernization. Himself a product of the French education system, Senghor sought to replicate it in his homeland and to eventually replace French technical experts with local talent. With youth unrest brewing on the campus at the University of Dakar, students were bound to clash with the new Senghor government, which they felt was an extension of the old French colonial regime. As a reflection of both the lasting French influence and the future of independent Senegal, the university became a postcolonial battleground where youth and the state struggled over the nature of decolonization more broadly. Drawing on Senghor's Francophilia—including his adoration of Charles de Gaulle and his friendship with French prime minister Georges Pompidou—students easily transformed anticolonial slogans once aimed at France and redirected them at the Senghor regime. Their denunciations presented an alternative postcolonial nationalism, one that rejected Senghorism, which called for a one-party state and deferential student and labor unions.

The events of 1968 in Senegal highlight the importance of colonial history to postindependence student and worker activism during which both national and global perspectives were critical. Though much of the existing scholarship on the Senegalese student movement rests at the national level, its transnational dimensions were indeed numerous.[1] At the root of the protesters' claims in Dakar lay a grave disappointment in the Senghor regime's inability to shed the French colonial yoke. Furthermore, Senegalese students abroad in France participated in France's May '68, and campus activism in Dakar precipitated responses abroad, including a protest by Africans at the Senegalese embassy in Paris.

Like their counterparts in France and Tunisia, these activists identified with anticolonial causes in Vietnam and Palestine. And as in France, Senegalese labor leaders joined forces with students to leverage their own claims against the Senghor regime, ultimately expanding the student strikes into a generalized social movement beyond campus grounds. Moreover, the regime's expulsions of foreign students and Chinese "subversives" call into question strictly national studies of the events. Global forces like Maoist ideology and international communism linked students in Dakar with ideas emanating from—and events in—Paris, Prague, Beijing, and Moscow. These transnational connections informed the expressions of postcolonial Senegalese nationalism in 1968, without which it would be impossible to understand this event. Far from simply an(other) example of student protest in the image of France, 1968 in Senegal reflected extreme tension between national context and global decolonial forces. Decolonization was multifaceted with iterations at the local and transnational levels. Colonial relationships had welded Senegalese institutions to French ones all while 1968 agitators sharpened the tools to sever those bonds.

From Student to Worker Activism: Indépendance Inachevée and May–June 1968 in Dakar

The legacy of the French empire-building projects left lingering traces in the educational and political landscapes of independent Senegal. For example, Senghor's secretary general, the Frenchman Jean Collin, who had married into Senghor's family, embodied an enduring French presence. French faculty at the University of Dakar far outnumbered African faculty, who made up only 31 percent of the total professoriate in 1967, and the university was run by a French rector, Paul Teyssier.[2] Senegalese students railed against the presence of French students in the university, with whom they competed for resources. In 1967, Senegalese nationals made up only 32 percent of the total enrollment, while the French made up 27 percent, and the remainder were mainly African students from neighboring countries.[3] The University of Dakar mirrored the Senegalese government, employing Frenchmen to occupy primary leadership positions even eight years into the independence era. With the university serving nearly as many French students as Senegalese, many sought to expedite the processes of decolonization. Even without piling on currency devaluation and a national budgetary crisis with ramifications at the university level at the end of 1967, students at the University of Dakar had plenty of reasons to contest the institution.

In an effort to rein in rising education costs and to offset state revenue reductions from low peanut-crop yields, the Senegalese Commission on Higher Education decided to cut student scholarships in October 1967. Monthly stipends would be reduced to either two-thirds or one-half, and they would no longer be distributed over twelve months, but over ten. The commission never consulted with student representatives and refused to give in to student demands made in March 1968 to reinstate the original value of the scholarships. When confronted directly by leaders from the primary Senegalese student union (UDES), university officials argued that several other African nations made similar cuts without protest from students.[4] This prompted a "warning strike" from UDES on 18 May at the University of Dakar. After an unproductive meeting with the office of the minister of national education, UDES, with the support of the organization of non-Senegalese African students of the UED, called for an unlimited strike of exams and classes on 27 May.[5]

But what began as an initial protest to maintain funding levels quickly developed to encompass the notion of an *indépendance inachevée*, or incomplete independence, of Senegalese society more generally. Students demanded more immediate decolonization absent continued foreign influence in education, government, and industry. Senghor's general secretary was French, as was the university rector Teyssier. It was only in 1969 that student strikes finally ushered in the appointment of the first Senegalese rector, Seydou Madani Sy. Beyond the realm of education, Senghor had appointed several French civil servants to decision-making positions in industry. When the Ministry of National Education cited the dire straits of the national budget as a cause for the reductions, students lamented the increased spending on military instead of education and reported census findings that only 16 out of 320 businesses in Senegal were operated by Senegalese management. Questioning why the head of Senegal's chamber of commerce was French, students castigated "[a] regime that has been rotting since nominal independence and which has been hitherto maintained by corruption and repression"—citing national unity measures that "have thus served only to augment the internal contradictions of the regime, whose eight years of rule have proven its incapacity to resolve the problems of the country."[6]

The university had become a key front in the broader struggle over decolonization. UDES insisted that the University of Dakar was "in reality nothing but a French university installed in Senegal," and placed their grievances "in the general realm of the claims of the Senegalese people."[7] With similar complaints about French dominance in business and management from the powerful National Union of Senegalese Workers (Union Nationale des Travailleus Sénégalais; UNTS), students felt that their anticolonial demands represented a national movement to democratize Senegalese society. Adding to this already tense context was a general uncertainty of the future following the deaths in 1968 of prominent national politician Lamine Guèye, president of Senegal's National Assembly, and the famous Mourid leader, Cheikh Mohamed Falilou Mbacké. If students could win resources otherwise destined for military or foreign enterprise, achieve recognition of key student organizations, and Africanize teaching corps and intellectual content, then the process of decolonizing the university might spread to other sectors of society.

Yet while the movement grew beyond the campus, the student strikes started on strictly material grounds for those most affected: students of Senegalese nationality. As one Senegalese 68er recalled, "There was practically unanimity among Senegalese students. The reticence was on the part of non-Senegalese students from Benin, Togo, Guinea, Mauritania, Mali, Chad, Niger, nearly all of the ex-AOF was present at Dakar. . . . What I intended to do was to protest against a policy of *my* government. The others said 'okay, you have the right to protest but that causes problems for us. We came here for our studies too.' There was a long negotiation . . . that facilitated the arm-twisting of other national organizations to join in the strike."[8] After initial apprehension, non-Senegalese African students at the university were brought on board gradually but crystallized their support after police encircled the campus and prevented students from leaving. High school students at prestigious institutions like Lycée Blaise Diagne and Lycée Van Vollenhoven (Van Vo), whose elite students stood to face scholarship reductions once they entered the university, also joined the movement.

The energetic eighteen-year-old Mamadou Diop Decroix, a senior at Lycée Van Vo in 1968, played a critical role in the strikes. Diop Decroix became politicized in the 1960s during the Dia-Senghor split, when he sided with Dia because some of his friends' parents were imprisoned, and following the Arab-Israeli War of June 1967, when he sympathized with Arab causes in support of Lebanese friends in the Dakar community.[9] His political education included bearing witness to an elder role model, Landing Savané, who led the first strike ever to occur at the prominent Lycée Van Vo, before Savané left for Paris to continue his studies (and activism). Diop Decroix worked alongside UDES leaders such as Mbaye Diack, Abdoulaye Bathily, and Moussa Kâne and cited the "mythical influence" of the unifying, supranational organization UED, led by the Guinean medical student Samba Balde. As Diop Decroix would recall, "When [UED] seized upon a problem and convoked a General Assembly, every student understood that the hour was grave."[10]

Diop Decroix and other high school student leaders found themselves at the university campus attending a meeting of delegates in support of the May strike, and awoke the morning of 29 May to the sounds of police brutality on the campus grounds. As Diop Decroix recalled in 2010, "The regime was scared; I don't know why, I was too young to understand, but in any case the regime was scared and Senghor promised to destroy the university, which was really saying something for a great intellectual like him."[11] Like Bourguiba, whose decision to quash student strikes was influenced by witnessing other campus protests in the West, Senghor drew on the tactics employed by Columbia University to swiftly repress student uprisings, but expressed fears that these might breach Franco-Senegalese accords.[12]

French rector Teyssier persuaded Senghor to negotiate a solution in spite of Senghor's desire for immediate intervention and university closures. Teyssier declared that the regime would be willing to negotiate if students were to pronounce their goals as apolitical in nature. But students reported that there were no university or government representatives on hand through which to hold any negotiation, having been convoked by Senghor and unavailable on campus. Their absence was by design, as Senghor kept earlier promises to use force if pushed by students, ordering the Special Armed Forces onto campus to break up the protests.[13] At 10:30 a.m. on 29 May, Senegal's fiercest fighting forces breached the sacred university grounds to disperse protesters, just as the authorities had done at universities in Tunis and in Paris. According to UDES students,

> The Senghor regime's forces of repression were ready for war, and armed head to toe. . . . The Special Armed Forces, reinforced by the police, charged and invaded the pavilions one after the other. They had orders to remove the students by any means necessary. They used billy clubs, rifle butts, bayonets, tear gas, even breaking doors and windows, looking for students in their rooms. The guards and police behaved like real thugs. They stole everything and smashed anything in their way, tearing clothes, and books. Pregnant women were mistreated and workers abused. At the pavilion of married students, women and children were beaten.[14]

Students on campus were likely emboldened to occupy the university since they believed, along with their counterparts at the Sorbonne and the University of Tunis, that university grounds were protected from state intervention. This thinking was clearly a mistake, with even the most vulnerable student populations targets of state-sponsored violence. The French ambassador reported that "students, armed with clubs, hurled insults at the brigades of police who had encircled the campus. Despite warnings from the Rector on the eve [of the campus occupation], they were convinced of the inviolability of academic freedoms and seemed to believe that they were untouchable on campus grounds."[15] Students in Paris and Tunis also cited breaches of law that require special permission from the attorney general before authorities may enter university grounds, suggesting the application of French precedent on university campuses in the former empire.[16]

The clashes on 29 May resulted in eight hundred arrests, seventy injured students, and the death of one protester, a Lebanese student, Salmon Khoury, who, according to authorities, was killed when a Molotov cocktail exploded in his hands.[17] Four hundred to five hundred students were sent to the Archinard military camp. According to Mamadou Diop Decroix, who was detained that day, Senghor's forces attacked students and secluded them in military camps to discourage future actions, whereas labor leaders were sent to work in the flax fields of Dodji and to sweltering camps in Ferlo.[18] "We were prisoners. . . . Once a guy is out there, several hundred kilometers away, the problem is solved. They dispersed us in police stations while things calmed down and then let us go. That was the situation in '68."[19] Senghor announced publicly on 30 May that the university would be closed indefinitely, and privately stated that "the conflict called into question the existence of the Senegalese state."[20] He further expelled forty-eight student leaders from the university for protesting and forced the expatriation of foreign participants.[21] In Senghor's eyes, a seemingly simple budgetary act regarding scholarship reductions—which had been passed at other regional universities—escalated to become a threat to the entire existence of independent Senegal.

Leo Zeilig has argued that "Students were not immediately galvanized into political action in 1968 to effect revolutionary change, or because they had been reading Lenin. On the contrary, it was the reduction of the grant, or more specifically its *fractionnement* (splitting up), that triggered the action."[22] Yet, when given the opportunity to limit their demands to funding issues, protesters declined and maintained their attacks on the broader political system. And while Zeilig is correct that the grant reductions ignited the protest, this interpretation downplays the influence of oppositional groups like the Maoists and the African Independence Party (PAI), whose membership was predicated on a theoretical engagement with the texts of Marx, Lenin, and Mao. Recalling her experiences, one 1960s activist noted that "we learned; we had weekend political education sessions, we had to read so many books," while another stated that many PAI sympathizers sought "a return to the original texts of Marx and Lenin."[23] Thus while funding cuts catalyzed the movement, the intellectual political education of activists was also a significant factor in the student radicalization.

Much to the chagrin of the regime, and unlike in the case of Tunisia, the movement was not contained to the university milieu. Meetings between students and labor leaders in UNTS added another dimension to the protests and increased repression. Yet the Senegalese case is unique in that, whereas large labor unions like the CGT and CFDT in France had a historically contentious relationship with government, UNTS was comparatively more subservient to Senghor's Senegalese Progressive Union (Union Progressiste Sénégalaise [UPS]). Senegalese labor only officially broke with the party line during the student strikes in spring 1968. Indeed, the minister of public service, work, and social laws, Magatte Lô, advocated a "responsible participation" and integration within the government dating to 1963, though he pushed for Africanization of middle management positions and the limitation of *petits blancs* in intermediary positions that could easily be occupied by salaried Senegalese.[24]

The UPS integration of political parties and consolidation of power over the course of the mid-1960s led to increased pressures to work in tandem with, and exert control over, labor unions like UNTS. The paradox of the regime-labor relationship revealed itself when UPS pressured UNTS to mobilize a number of autonomous organizations under an umbrella of collective action. This inclusion of progressive groups backfired, ultimately bringing about a number of demands as early as 1967. From within the structures of power, consolidated groups called for autonomy from political parties, increases in minimum wages, and reforms in education; they even called for "workers to join their action with that of the people for total decolonization and social and economic improvement."[25] Françoise Blum astutely observes that, after Senghor arrested Mamadou Dia and incorporated political rivals into government, "the only remaining audible voices of contestation were those of the students and labor union members."[26] In the case of labor, UPS's efforts to exert control actually led to collective action against the state.

Though student strikes certainly tossed fuel on the flames of union activism, workers were displeased with their conditions before the campus erupted. Regional UNTS affiliates in Cap Vert met ten days before the student strikes to deliberate their own claims against the government. Already with long lists of demands and complaints of continued French influence in education and commerce, UNTS and other progressive labor unions like the secular teachers' union and the union of dentists and surgeons joined the students in calling for a general strike on 30 May 1968.[27] The government ordered police to occupy the UNTS headquarters in Kaolack and Dakar and sent a number of detained leaders to military camps in Dodji. Over nine hundred workers were apprehended for protest participation, including UNTS secretary general Alioune Cisse, and thirty-six labor leaders were condemned to sentences of eighteen months to three years for pillaging or the edification of barricades.

Once it became clear that national labor unions were backing students, Senghor laid out tough sanctions in Circular no. 47, threatening striking state employees with their jobs or even imprisonment if they did not return to work on 5 June. In a propaganda ploy akin to de Gaulle's supporters convening en masse in Paris in late May, Senghor organized UPS militias and regime-friendly peasants from the countryside in counterdemonstrations.[28] Interestingly, while Muslim religious leaders, particularly in rural areas, generally supported Senghor, who was Catholic, a strong contingent of Dominican brothers and Catholic student groups sided with the opposition.[29] Police statistics show wide participation outside of Dakar, with 364 functionaries on strike in Diourbel, 28 percent of teachers in Kaolack, and 160 teachers out of 260 in St. Louis. As Omar Guèye points out, "Workers thus led a struggle in parallel with students, but of shorter duration, as they entered into the movement later and left earlier."[30] Growing national support for both students and workers led the Senghor regime to release all detainees from military camps and prisons on 9 June and to enter into negotiations with labor leaders and businesses shortly thereafter. These talks resulted in a series of eighteen measures, including significant wage increases, regulations on the duration of workdays, and employer contributions to employees' health care.[31] UNTS eventually obtained substantial gains, such as a 15 percent increase in the minimum wage and assurances from the government that it would consider Africanizing, through nationalization, certain foreign-dominated industries. As in France, the workers' movement ultimately exceeded what students had set in motion, and mirrored the significant gains of the Grenelle Accords for French workers.

French ambassador to Senegal Jean de Lagarde noted the dynamic relationship between labor and state politics that was unique in the region. "In Mali and Guinea, as in Mauritania, Tanzania, or in Algeria, the national labor union is an extension of the Party and an instrument of the state over the masses. On the contrary in Senegal, UNTS, outside of the fact it only represents a portion of the workers, distances itself from the Party and the government and the problems of 31 May violently proved this."[32] Even after negotiations and significant gains, the once-loyal UNTS lambasted the government's failure to recognize union autonomy in August, promising to safeguard the interests of the people against French imperialism. And while the use of torture was not as widespread in Senegal as it was in the Tunisian case, UNTS recollections suggest that Senegalese authorities adopted similarly repressive tactics developed during French colonialism. "Under the direction of French experts Senegal ushered in modern methods of torture (by electricity). A heinous law on organizations declared 'seditious' was voted in. A special jurisdiction was created to judge summarily and to condemn patriots with heavy prison sentences whose sole crime is to have said no to the exploitation of their people."[33] It is clear that UNTS did not buy into the regime's insistence on party control in the name of national unity. State repression only led to widening the divide between labor and government, and amplifying the outcries for political rights. Not only did Senghor use his own troops trained by the French government to quell domestic resistance, but he also called on the services of French paramilitary forces that were still stationed in Senegal after independence.[34]

Senghor's reliance on a system of education designed by French educators and backed with French military support incensed the students of Dakar, who joined the chorus of labor leaders in denouncing his neocolonial regime.[35] Students decried the lack of opportunities that awaited them at the end of university study. Reflecting on the aftermath of the events of 1968, Hassan El-Nouty—a Franco-Egyptian professor of French—captured the bleak future for Senegalese students facing scarce economic prospects and a new corrupt class. "At the root of the problem is a neo-colonial situation" in which "opportunistic elders . . . high-jacked the fruits of independence for its profit . . . [running] Senegal in order to fill the coffers of French neo-imperialism."[36] Tunisians polled in the early 1970s at universities in both Tunis and Paris cited this same frustration as they faced the crisis of increased competition and dwindling economic opportunities.[37] Third World universities faced growing pains owing to rising numbers of educated youth with limited available positions in a squeezed financial system, coinciding with freezes in government hiring after an early period of expansion. Using the University of Dakar as a litmus test for how decolonized Senegal had become after liberation, students and workers alike found that after eight years of Senghor, they had not yet achieved full independence from French influence. Ironically, cutting ties from France also meant that Senegal could lose up to 70 percent of its university funding to pay instructors and grant scholarships. In this regard, the students' dual aims of Africanization and increased (or sustained) subsidies were incompatible. Even the government solutions to the strikes reflected Senegal's ongoing postcolonial relationship to France, as French rector Teyssier initially tried to appease students angered over the funding reductions by offering three hundred supplementary scholarships to study in France.[38]

In addition to workers' gains, joint protests with students forced Senghor to hasten the Africanization of the university. Classes had been canceled for the year, but Senghor reopened discussions with UDES leaders in September 1968. At first, he tried to take a hard line and close the university indefinitely until strict reforms were put in place; however, under pressure from Paris and his own university administrators, classes resumed in the fall after students were granted the opportunity, as in France, to take exams that had been canceled in spring. All who showed up received passing grades. Negotiations with UDES reaped benefits for the students; UDES leader Mbaye Diack signed an accord in which funding was reinstated, expelled students were finally allowed to return, and, somewhat surprisingly, student representatives successfully obtained a seat at the table in future discussions on reforms.[39] While campus clashes would continue into the 1970s, other immediate gains included Senghor's naming of the first Senegalese university rector, and African faculty members at the university skyrocketed from 34 percent in 1967 to nearly 50 percent by 1971.[40] With striking similarity to the unfolding of events in Paris, students in Dakar initiated broader participation beyond the campus, where collaboration with labor leaders resulted in some degree of government capitulation in both labor and education. A major win for student empowerment, these reforms far outpaced outcomes for their counterparts in France.

Exploring the Transnational Dimensions of Dakar's 1968

Trouble at the University of Dakar began as early as 1966 and coincided with the populist Ghanaian president Kwame Nkrumah's ouster. In Dakar, the organizers led students in a 28 February march on the US and British Chancelleries. In protest of those governments' roles in the Ghanaian coup, UDES declared that "there was no doubt that the champion of pan-Africanism was victim to Anglo-Saxon imperialism."[41] Students went on strike in March 1966 to protest the expulsion of five student leaders from French Upper Volta (now Burkina Faso) and Benin, who had organized the pro-Nkrumah and anti-US protests.[42] The anti-imperialist and pan-African leader Nkrumah thus had wide support in FEANF and UED. Fearing loss of control of the youth movement, Senghor issued directives to increase the influence of his party's affiliated student organization, UPS Youth Movement (Mouvement des Jeunes Union Progréssistes Sénégalais, MJUPS). This plan did not fare well, however, with the majority of students opting for more radical organizations like UDES or the UED. A year after its inauguration, the French embassy in Dakar reported that Senghor's MJUPS consisted of a meager 30 student members, while the more radical UDES maintained 650 adherents.[43]

French ambassador Jean de Lagarde noted Senghor's frustration with "the vain efforts of the students affiliated with the UPS, whom the authorities had asked to calm the movement, only served to underscore the powerlessness of the single-party state."[44] MJUPS, like the Tunisian student group UGET, began to lose legitimacy in the eyes of the majority of university students for its close ties to government forces and its failure to appeal to the growing anger of the student body. In a 1966 effort to counter the strong recruiting power of international associations like FEANF, many African and French leaders assisted in the promotion of the moderate, ostensibly apolitical Student Movement of the African and Malagasy Common Organization (Mouvement des Étudiants de l'Organisation Commune Africaine et Malgache [MEOCAM]). Senghor and Ivoirian president Félix Houphouët-Boigny were particularly instrumental in the creation of MEOCAM, which held its first constitutive congress in January 1967 in Niger. Congressional members criticized FEANF's political preoccupation with the Sino-Soviet split, war in Vietnam, and capitalist and Marxist doctrines. MEOCAM's founding charter called on its new order to "accept to work with the leaders of their countries" and conduct "a radical disengagement with Marxist-Leninist doctrine to support the heads of state in their effort to unify Africa and Madagascar."[45] MEOCAM further declared itself "ready to fight any other association, old or new, which systematically denigrates their countries and heads of state."[46] With headquarters in Paris, Abidjan, and Dakar, MEOCAM provided an alternative organization to advocate for African students, which French and African state officials hoped would erode FEANF's overwhelming influence.

FEANF and its affiliates in Africa responded by condemning US involvement in Ghanaian politics and Senghor's pro-French trade policies. Senghor's refusal to recognize the existence of the UED in 1967 further exacerbated tensions. In Paris—just after MEOCAM's constitutive congress—FEANF members backed the UED in a tract denouncing the association as an "instrument of French imperialism in Africa, in its attempt to create a French commonwealth," and claimed that Senghor would prefer "to spend millions stripped from the Senegalese people to sustain and uphold puppet groups that comprise bogus student groups."[47] The MEOCAM-FEANF confrontation and the coup in Ghana thus had implications for groups in several locales in France and West Africa.

But perhaps most interesting in FEANF's tract was its indictment of the persistence of a French model of university education in Senegal. "Education throughout all of the colleges follows word for word the same curriculum as those in French colleges. . . . The University of Dakar [remains] a French University established in Senegal; it is a [French] state in the Senegalese state."[48] In an era of ubiquitous nationalist and anticolonial sentiments, students wondered not only why Senegalese institutions borrowed constitutional language from French ones, but also why independent Africans continued to study French poetry and history under French tutelage with French evaluation systems. As early as January 1967, the Senghor regime sought to reclaim influence with failed parallel organizations like MEOCAM, while local groups like UED responded on international issues but attached local university concerns to their global anti-imperialist outlook. The claims against the Senghor regime and efforts to decolonize the French curricula—articulated in both Dakar and Paris by pan-African organizations—foreshadowed the May 1968 student uprising and undermined later charges by the regime that Senegalese students were only mimicking their French counterparts.

Back in Dakar, students vehemently contested MEOCAM's first congress and Senghor's intransigence regarding UED's right to exist. On 4 January 1967, UPS leader and MEOCAM supporter Moustapha Niasse was roughed up by audience members when he tried to speak at a campus basketball game.[49] The ensuing mayhem resulted in antigovernment calls for a university strike on 5–6 January that were supported by FEANF in Paris and in Abidjan. Students in Dakar drafted a resolution after the basketball brawl in protest of the Ministry of the Interior's refusal a month earlier to accept UED's status as a student organization, attacking both MJUPS student leaders and MEOCAM.[50] If these acts of contestation at the university presaged the larger protests in May 1968, so too did Senghor's response during the lead-up. Already upset with the pro-Nkrumah UED activism that coincided with the First World Festival of Negro Arts in April 1966—when he evacuated the university campus and sent foreign students home—Senghor was now frustrated by possible perturbations and negative press on the eve of an international congress of jurists to be hosted in Dakar in January 1967. In a rather menacing threat, Senghor stated, "We will let them have fun for a few days during the congress; but then, if they take as weakness what was meant to be a desire for dialogue, they will have to confront our commandos."[51]

Senghor's failure to recognize UED incited students to forge broader global aims. UED's cause was taken up in the summer of 1967 at the 9th Congress of the Prague-based International Student Union (UIE), held in Mongolia. There, in addition to denouncing Senghor's position on UED, international students also called for action in support of the Vietnamese people against US aggression.[52] The UIE had direct connections to the Senegalese movement through PAI sympathizers like Amath Dansokho, who, though past his days of student activism, was stationed in Prague while working for the communist organ *Nouvelle Revue Internationale* in the late 1960s. According to one Senegalese 68er, "All of these international movements of solidarity came [to us] through the UIE because we had a presence there; orders from the UIE reverberated to our movement by the way of student members of the PAI."[53] The international protest against US involvement in Vietnam was set to take place on 17 November 1967, which was headed by UED in Dakar, Perspectives in Tunis, and FEANF and many other sympathetic groups in Paris.[54] As in Tunisia and France, Senegalese students created the Grassroots Committee in Support of Vietnam, with members on university campuses in both France and Senegal.

Though in smaller numbers, women played critical roles in transnational activist networks. Student leaders Marie-Angélique Savané and her husband, Landing Savané, were active in the movement while living in Paris in the late 1960s. Marie-Angélique was the first woman elected to lead a delegation of students at a university general assembly upon her return to Dakar in 1969. And although trailblazers like Senegalese women Marie-Angélique and Fatou Sow participated in activism in Paris and Dakar, and there exist some exam-

failures to the weak national economy and accused the Senghor regime of corruption. An 18 March strike elicited an intervention by authorities, and by April UED had joined the action, calling for a joint struggle with Senegalese workers and making contact with labor leaders.[56] In the buildup to May 1968, Senghor had faced multiple challenges to his authority from students and political foes like Mamadou Dia to the PAI, and he even survived an assassination attempt. He also progressively hardened his responses to provocations, ordering the execution of would-be assassin Moustapha Lô and threatening student agitators that he would not hesitate to send special forces to the university campus. The creation of puppet international organizations such as MEOCAM only served to drive a wedge between the regime and the student body. Likewise, the mechanisms of political mobilization around international movements like Vietnamese independence were redeployed for national causes like official recognition for UED and an end to the corruption of the pro-French Senghor government.

If the context precipitating the campus uprisings of 1968 in Dakar consisted of several postcolonial and transnational dimensions, so too did the responses of both activists and the Senghor regime in their aftermath. Just as Bourguiba had done in Tunisia, likening Simone Lellouche Othmani to a so-called foreign agitator, Daniel Cohn-Bendit (a Franco-German Jew), Senghor likewise framed the student movement as "subversion by foreigners." He accused Senegalese students of "aping" their French counterparts, whom they allowed to "control them by remote."[57] By undermining the Dakar movement as French mimesis, Senghor attempted not only to delegitimize the Dakar students' claims but also to justify the use of violence in ways similar to the French state. The negative connotation of the colonial past led student leaders to associate Senghor with French imperialism, and it led Senghor to cast the Dakar student movement as juvenile mimicry of privileged French students. This desire to create distance from Frenchness was shared—on both sides of the protest fault lines—in a veritable postcolonial situation.[58] Both camps were tied up in the knot of postcolonial tension pulling students and government leadership in national and transnational directions. On the one hand, French students (for Senghor) or the politics of French cooperation (for Senegalese students) were established as boogeymen to be resisted through acts of patriotic postcolonial nationalism. For the former, this meant national unity against seditious students; for the latter it meant resisting corrupt leadership. On the other hand, the persistence of postcolonial ties enabled Senegalese students to advance their causes with international groups in Paris and Prague, while these same ties informed and enhanced Senghor's means of repression. After initial negotiation with some student groups, Senghor reneged on his prom-

ises to work with students. By February 1971, Senghor had dissolved the cata-
lysts of Dakar's May 1968, UDES and the UED, which were among the last
vestiges of Senghor's long-despised political opposition, the PAI.

UED president Samba Balde was exiled to Mali's capital, Bamako, after the
May campus raids in Dakar. There, he organized a group of Malian activist
students to provide UED's version of events by distributing copies of its "Mem-
orandum on the Events at the University of Dakar" en masse.[59] Back in Paris,
the Senegalese branch of FEANF, the Association of Senegalese Students in
France (AESF), outlined its steady support of the struggle in Dakar. In addition
to organizing meetings and circulating L'Étudiant Sénégalais, AESF "also occupied the Senegalese Embassy in Paris on 28 May 1968 with all of the African
students of FEANF in solidarity with our comrades in Dakar. We sent a telegram vigorously protesting the government and supporting UDES and UED."[60]
Landing Savané, who had led the first protests at the prestigious Lycée Van Vo
in the mid-1960s, helped orchestrate FEANF and AESF students' occupation of
the embassy in Paris. Activists entered the premises, implored the ambassador
to send a telegram to Senghor in protest of police intervention on the campus
in Dakar, and demanded the release of all the detained students and the re-
opening of the university.[61] These pan-African efforts not only were important
in giving Africans back home the confidence to sustain the movement, but they
also contributed to providing a counternarrative to the Senegalese state.

It is worth noting that not all students were supportive of the campus disruptions. UPS youth leaders Moustapha Niasse and Baro Diène rebuked the
antigovernment elements of the protests. Diène echoed Senghor's claims of
mimicry, noting, "There was a May '68 in Dakar because there was a May '68 in
France. There was a contagion. The university was in effervescence. It was
contestation. In France, there was Cohn-Bendit, here, there was Mamadou
Diop Decroix, Bathily and others. . . . For us it was a conspiracy against our
government and we needed to defend it. We [in MJUPS] considered ourselves
patriots because we brought the country to independence and now we had to
preserve the regime."[62] Of course, these comments likely represented only a
fraction of students based on MJUPS's weak membership compared with other
groups. And though there may have been sympathy for the student cause from
groups in Prague and Paris, there was little support from the local French student population. They were concerned with school closures that might jeop-
ardize the year's work, and worried about potentially losing the recognition
of degrees in France if the University of Dakar were "Africanized."

Learning from the French case—in which twelve thousand unionized radio and television workers occupied France's largest state-controlled program-
ming agency, Office de Radiodiffusion Télévision Française, which regulated

and limited media coverage—Senghor protected national broadcast centers and released several broadcasts from Radio-Dakar.[63] He ordered the seizure of foreign newspapers that conflicted with the state's positions and announced to the nation as early as 30 May that the movement was being led from abroad.[64] Senghor further charged that "yesterday morning's troubles were organized by African students from FEANF, having come [to Dakar] specifically from Paris," and quipped, "It is curious that the students who abhorred us for succumbing to the will of French imperialism have waited for the student revolt in Paris to copy French students without changing a single comma."[65] Given Senghor's attempts to undermine the national character of Senegalese students' and workers' claims, it is not all that surprising that historians like Abdoulaye Bathily and Ibrahima Thioub would insist on its local characteristics.[66] Sixty-eighter Mbaye Diack asserted in a 2000 interview that "there was no relationship linking the leadership of UDES and the French students. No contact existed at the time between students based in France and their counterparts in Dakar."[67] Mimicry in this sense went beyond Homi Bhabha's understanding of it for the colonial era, in which it could be used as a tool of resistance and even as a way of differentiating from the object of mimicry (i.e., British or French imperial culture).[68] Here, charges of French mimicry were launched by both the Senghor regime and youth activists as an accusation and indictment against an internal, Senegalese enemy (each other). To adopt French culture, as in the case of student depictions of Senghor, or to imitate frivolous French youth activism, as in Senghor's accusation of students, was to undermine Senegalese nationalism.

Despite Diack's claims, students indeed had contact with organizations outside Senegal as seen in the international support from the UIE in Prague and FEANF and other French organizations in Paris. Even Bathily, who was adamant about the national character of the protests, identified key postcolonial activist networks that supported the cause. The UIE sent its Moroccan vice president, Abdel Malek, on a clandestine mission to Dakar in early June to report on events and, upon his return to Prague, to launch an international campaign in support of UED.[69] Apart from chronology, there is little evidence to suggest that the Dakar student strikes were a mimicry of the French movement. Yet there was certainly an exchange of information with and mutual support from Paris-based groups, especially through Senegalese students with membership crossover in French organizations. For example, Landing and Marie-Angélique Savané, as well as Omar Blondin Diop (the Senegalese activist famous for his appearances in Jean-Luc Godard films), ran in the same circles as the Paris-based Maoïst group, the Proletarian Left (la gauche prolétarienne).[70] One Senegalese female activist studying in France described how events in Dakar inspired a revival of transnational activism in which Senegalese students in France became more engaged politically after what they experienced in Paris.

> In the summer of 1968, we decided that everyone who could take vacation back in Senegal had to do it in order to connect with the student movement [in Dakar], and to see then how to coordinate the movement in France as much as in Senegal. Why? Because in France, we could carry out the work of explaining [the movement] to the French authorities as the former colonial power, et cetera. But most of all we could solicit the support of organizations like the French Communist Party and all of its democratic splinter groups on the left.
>
> You see back then the radical French left was extremely dynamic and popularized the Trotskyists and all of that, and popularized the movement. It was also a way to recruit students. Many of them were not necessarily members of AESF and it was a way to create a strong movement. And in fact, it was thanks to the movement of '68 that the Senegalese student movement was revived and propelled in France. The following year in 1969, people responded in large numbers and the AESF had representation in all the large French cities.[71]

While it is difficult to assess the degree to which French students were broadly interested in Dakar, it is evident that events in Senegal influenced ongoing communication. Africans studying abroad became more engaged following May '68, when activists reestablished transnational networks—which lay dormant after independence—and formed new connections with French leftist splinter groups like the Proletarian Left.

Landing Savané participated in multiple activist organizations at the national, international, African, and French levels. Many of the debates taking place within the global New Left, particularly regarding the Sino-Soviet split and disillusionment with centralized communist parties, were reenergized in 1968. Both the dynamism and the fragmentation of the New Left were transported to Dakar when activists like Savané returned from Paris in the summer of 1968. Competing groups of socialists, democrats, Marxists, and Maoists in UED and UDES (often returning from study abroad) joined forces in 1968 to reclaim their education and demand systemic change at the national level. Political differences were at least temporarily overlooked as Senegalese students bonded over anticolonial nationalism and shared a common disdain for the cultural essentialism of Senghor's Negritude, or pride in Blackness and celebration of African heritage.[72] What separated 1968 from previous activism, according to one participant, was the "political realization that occurred. In the movements of 1966, with the Nkrumah coup d'état and all that, there was a pan-African consciousness but it was vague. Now, concretely, the students saw that we had to defend our university."[73] With an injection of new energy arriving from Senegalese students who experienced the May events in Paris, networks within France proliferated and students in Dakar had never before exercised such agency, ultimately negotiating participation in decision-making processes at the university.

The Senghor regime had difficulty comprehending the audacious claims that privileged youth made against the state, and made several attempts to undermine the movement's national character. On 13 June 1968, a group of technical assistants working at the Lycée Van Vo—linked to *coopération* programs between France and Senegal—signed a petition repudiating police violence and forced evacuations at the university and lycée. Senghor in turn declared them undesirables and announced numerous expulsions from Senegal following summer vacation.[74] In a study of the demographics of expelled persons from Senegal from 1948 to 1978, Momar-Coumba Diop found a spike in 1968, when the government expelled professors from the African Institute of Economic Planning and Development and the College of National Applied Economics, as well as a number of foreigners from China.

According to Coumba Diop, "The Chinese were the primary scapegoats of May 1968. The state declared over and over that students at the University of Dakar in May 1968 were manipulated by the Chinese. . . . On these occasions, the state expels foreigners to justify its argument of 'foreign intervention' in Senegalese domestic affairs."[75] Just as Bourguiba had done in Tunisia, the Senghor regime took advantage of the crackdown to eliminate perceived threats from Maoists and communists. Senghor did not hesitate to expel forty-seven Chinese people from Taiwan residing in Senegal and rescind permits to correspondents from a Chinese news agency.[76] His xenophobic assertions about foreign subversion transcended France to include China, perhaps influenced by his knowledge that FEANF had sent a delegation of African students there for a two-month visit in 1960.[77] Senghor's failure to distinguish between Taiwanese and Chinese nationals when meting out punishments suggests a disturbing racial motivation transcending a simple fear of communist influence.

The concurrent protests in the spring of 1968 fostered a number of transnational networks and communities of activists. Paris was a key site of information exchange and a central node connecting various groups. Closely tracking the movements of the German national Daniel Cohn-Bendit, Richard Ivan Jobs details how, in June 1968—after being accused of organizing a series of protests in and around Paris—Cohn-Bendit, under threat of deportation, was not allowed reentry into France after he returned to West Germany.[78] Similarly, Cohn-

Bendit's Senegalese coconspirator during the March 22 movement, Omar Blondin Diop, was expelled from France in October 1969 after being interrogated by French authorities for participation in a May protest in the Latin Quarter.[79] While Blondin Diop and Cohn-Bendit are particularly important for illustrating the importance of France's colonial past in connecting activists in 1968, they represent only two of hundreds of foreign students and activists arrested and either deported or imprisoned, many of whom were from France's former colonies.[80] And it was not only in France where activists faced the threat of deportation, as Senghor clearly employed these same strategies in Senegal. Given Cohn-Bendit's and Blondin Diop's mutual participation in the March 22 movement and their presence at the front lines of the Latin Quarter protests, it is highly probable that their relationship contributed to Cohn-Bendit's awareness and support of students in Senegal.

Upon his return to West Germany, Cohn-Bendit brought his passion for revolutionary activism to the Socialist German Student League (Sozialistische Deutsche Studentenbund [SDS]) when he reproached the group for being "a boy-scout movement" that "in its pitiful state had forgotten international politics."[81] In September 1968, shortly after making these comments, Cohn-Bendit was instrumental, along with Senegalese foreign students within the SDS, in organizing two thousand students in a more globally conscious action in protest of Senghor's presence. The acclaimed poet was set to receive a peace prize from the German Book Fair in Frankfurt just months after unleashing Senegalese authorities on protesters in Dakar. Cohn-Bendit provoked a situation in which the rejection of Senghor's authoritarianism prompted yet another act of state violence against students in Frankfurt. German authorities used tear gas and mounted police to disperse students from behind barricades, and arrested Cohn-Bendit on the spot.[82]

The Frankfurt protests received rather wide press coverage from those reporting on the book fair. By the summer of 1968, many press agencies were aware of the activities of "Dany the Red," Cohn-Bendit's activist sobriquet (see figure 3).[83] Cohn-Bendit's connections with global movements while in France—through key figures like Omar Blondin Diop—reverberated even outside the boundaries of the former French empire. The French authorities effectively labeling him a persona non grata led to the exportation of the Francophone radical Left's particular anti-imperialist causes. Protesters even likened Senghor's Negritude to the racial essentialism of Nazism.[84] Though the driving force behind the SDS student protest was Senghor's brutality toward Senegalese students, his past connections and his continued economic reliance on France, coupled with his intellectual ties to Germany, accented the demonstration in Frankfurt.[85]

FIGURE 3. Daniel Cohn-Bendit, also known as "Dany the Red," inciting German protesters in Frankfurt to charge the gates of St. Paul's Church on 22 September 1968, the site of the German Book Fair where Senghor was set to receive an honorary literature prize. Photo by Gus Schuettler. Reproduced with permission from Stars and Stripes. © 1968, 2020 Stars and Stripes.

Immediately after Cohn-Bendit's arrest, the executive committee of UDES in Dakar sent a letter to the president of the German Federal Republic, Heinrich Lübke, and demanded the release of Cohn-Bendit and the other protesters.[86] Though it is unclear whether Lübke ever responded to the students, it is quite evident that they were aware of events in Frankfurt and expressed solidarity with Cohn-Bendit. In fact, the UDES members made certain to justify the actions of the SDS by educating the German president on events in Dakar. In an act of associative historical memory, they also drew parallels between Senghor's imprisonment of protesters and the prison camps under the Nazi regime. Senghor's selection as winner of a German peace prize was "the expression of a flagrant contradiction which unmasks the hypocrisy of neocolonialism."[87] Comparing Senghor's authoritarian reactionism to Nazism effectively accomplished what the French Left sought with recalling Charonne: each group created a series of symbolic images that linked oppression to groups of violent perpetrators (Nazis, CRS, OAS, or Occident), and associated these groups with the state. And while the Senegalese and French students' conjuring of historical memories during acts of protest took place at the local level, students shared certain global referents, such as a vilification of imperialism, neocolonialism, and fascism. To be sure, local resistance can have global resonance, and global events happen in localizable places.

Protesters from afar employed historical memory when responding to local events like Senghor's visit to Frankfurt. UDES even claimed that the SDS protest of Senghor "symbolizes the most pure internationalist spirit by acting for an altruism and rich human depth that have been unfathomable for privileged minorities who tend to accumulate material wealth unjustly acquired on the sweat and blood of the masses."[88] In spite of UDES's anti-French stance and Bathily's claims to a purely nationalist student movement, the UDES letter to Lübke illustrates that even very local causes were not restricted to the national borders of Senegal, or even those of France for that matter. In this regard, the creation of "undesirables" by French authorities actually exported transnational activism to other parts of Europe. Much as Paris had been for the protest of a Bourguiba visit, Frankfurt also acted as a site of Third World protest in which the presence of a Third World authoritarian elicited a transnational response.

The Senghorian Paradox: Between Negritude and Francophonie

Senghor's identity politics are crucial to understanding acts of subversion by his countrymen in 1968, particularly for student intellectuals who had access to the cultural criticism of the day. Before his life in politics, Senghor had made quite a name for himself as a celebrated poet, becoming the first African to be named to the illustrious French Academy in 1983. But his cultural stances revealed a paradox. Senghor was a Francophile, opening himself to anticolonial critiques from opponents. Yet he was also a proponent of Negritude, a cultural movement valorizing African heritage that was coming out of vogue in the 1960s in favor of more direct political action.[89] By 1968, the practice of (neo-)colonialism had taken on racialized characteristics. During heightened tensions, both the regime and the students accused each other of succumbing to French imperialism. Activists viewed their rejection of the Senghor regime, with its ties to France, as antiwhite as well as anticolonialist. According to journalist Vieux Savané, analyzing 1968 in Dakar forty years later, "Activism against the regime was risky, perilous, anti-militaristic, anti-white in the sense of the color of colonialism, imperialism, and oppression."[90] Senghor's background in French literature and his close friendship with Pompidou made it easy for students to associate him and his party with "whiteness," or at the very least, "Frenchness."

The president-poet's identity crisis—identifying with two cultures without being fully accepted by either—emerged in dynamic ways during his confrontations with student and worker activists.[91] The politics of 1968 led activists to view Senghor's subjectivity through the refracted light of an anticolonial lens, heavily scrutinizing his relationships to both Frenchness and Africanness. Perhaps Senghor himself, whose wife was French, best described his liminal position: "For me, French is no longer a foreign vehicle, but the natural form of expression of my thought."[92] French not only permeated his consciousness, but his subconscious being as well. "From time to time I would dream that I was white. Each time, I was so tormented that I awoke suddenly. Not because I'm racist—as you know my wife is French—, it's just that, if I were white, I had the impression that I would no longer know pain and suffering, nothing to struggle for. I prefer, in spite of it all, to remain in contradiction and suffering— to have the joy of struggle, action, and creation."[93] Senghor's own fragmented identity may explain his conflicting relationship to Francophonie and Negritude, in which he simultaneously sought to promote both French and African culture. By 1968, many of his opponents were less than understanding of his policies of continued cooperation with France.

Criticisms at the personal level affected Senghor to such an extent that he felt obliged to publicly address his identity and to deploy colonial history to defend his politics. During a July 1968 visit to Paris, Senghor asserted that three hundred years of French presence had marked his nation, and that "if there hadn't been a May crisis in France, there would not have been one in Senegal." He further expressed a desire to solve the Dakar crisis through dialogue to "find a balance between Francophonie and Negritude."[94] The university crisis forced Senghor to face these somewhat contradictory dual state projects. On several occasions he made public reference to both concepts in the aftermath of the May–June events. On the eve of campus disruptions, Senghor claimed that "[Francophonie] is about obtaining cultural assistance that enables us to reinvigorate our national and continental values by incorporating scientific technology and French techniques. . . . This explains the high standard to which we hold ourselves which, by the way, we inherited from the French University."[95] On the one hand, Francophonie suggested participation in a larger community based on shared French language and cultural values, of which the university was part and parcel. On the other hand, Negritude was not reflected within the university, which still drew heavily on the French system and employed primarily European instructors in 1968.

Senghor's hybrid notion of Francophonie, with cultural and technological exchange between the Third World and the West, was thoroughly rejected by protesting students who clamored for Africanization. He openly admitted his fondness for the racial theories of the German anthropologist Leo Frobenius, who deduced that both Europeans and Africans possessed faculties of reason; the European was analytical while the African was intuitive and emotive. Senghor even admitted the appeal of the prideful racialism of Nazism for Negritude. "Unconsciously, by osmosis and reaction at the same time, we spoke like Hitler and the Colonialists, we advocated the virtues of blood."[96] Senghor defended his duality when he declared to the French ambassador in March 1969, "In truth, we never stopped identifying as 'Negroes,' but we started identifying, at the same time, for two centuries, as men of French culture and, since independence, as activists for Francophonie."[97] At least six times in public addresses between 1969 and 1971, he referenced the *cahiers de doléances*, or "grievance lists," destined for the French king on the eve of Revolution of 1789 and a major forum for the expression of popular dissent in the twilight of the ancien régime.[98]

Senghor imagined a long Senegalese history of merging Francophonie and Negritude dating back to the late eighteenth century. He interpreted the representatives from the colony of Senegal in 1789 as "militants" and "veritable precursors to Negritude and Francophonie" who "declared their double quality as 'Negroes' and 'Frenchmen.'"[99] There seems to have been some merit to Senghor's claims about the dual identity in the *cahiers* of the French Revolution. The inhabitants of St. Louis in Senegal indeed wrote to the delegations in Paris to outline problems in the colony in April 1789. "Negroes or mulattos, we are all French since French blood runs in our veins or in those of our nephews. These origins give us pride and lift our souls! No other people showed more patriotism and courage! In 1757 when Senegal was handed over to the English, we wanted to defend it in spite of our colonial leaders. . . . We viewed it as the best day of our lives when, in 1779, we had the pleasure of seeing the French flag fly on the port of St. Louis. We greeted the French as our liberators, as our brothers."[100]

Though he did not acknowledge that the mixed-race St. Louisians of 1789—many of whom were merchants—were likely employing an obsequious strategy to achieve material gains by claiming French allegiance, Senghor identified the complicated historical relationship between France and Senegal dating to the seventeenth century, when France first occupied the slave-trading island of Gorée. He also leaned on historical rhetoric to support his claims for the mutual compatibility of Francophonie and Negritude.

Senghor faced no lack of challengers to this notion. A giant of anticolonial thought, the Martinican and key Algerian freedom fighter Frantz Fanon found two foundational problems with Negritude. First, the constant comparison to

Western culture produced a rage-filled inferiority complex in "colonized intellectuals" like Senghor, whose efforts to overcome their present condition led them on a "passionate quest for a national culture prior to the colonial era," often neglecting contemporary real-world solutions.[101] Second, Fanon found a certain irresponsibility in the false equations produced by Negritude that forced connections between disparate national cultures along racial lines. According to Fanon, "Every culture is first and foremost national, and [the] problems for which Richard Wright or Langston Hughes had to be on the alert were fundamentally different from those faced by Léopold Senghor or Jomo Kenyatta."[102] In short, the bards of Negritude like Senghor spent far too much time either glorifying mythical cultures of the past or forcing racialized connections with disparate cultures in distant lands, neither of which had any chance of solving the problems of the day. Although Senghor fully embraced the racial and historical essentialisms that were the subject of Fanon's critique, he attempted to solve contemporary issues by melding Negritude with Francophonie through linguistic, cultural, and technological cooperation with France and the French-speaking world.

Another critic, Hassan El Nouty, likened the cultural movement to a form of neocolonialism in which "the African himself subscribes to the thesis of his ethnic specificity, different from the European, such that technological mastery and world domination are reserved only for the West. . . . This neocolonialism provides an ideological alibi that is disguised as symbiosis (the word reappears in almost obsessive fashion beneath the pen of Senghor) between Africa and the West."[103] Senghor did not passively receive these criticisms. In a 1969 speech in Kinshasa, he responded to charges leveled by Anglophone African intellectuals Wole Soyinka (Nigeria) and Ezekiel Mphahlele (South Africa)—who viewed Negritude as a form of cultural imperialism emanating from Francophone Africa and an extension of Rousseau's "noble savage"—and urged the "diasporic world to end the Anglo-French rivalry . . . and focus on universalism."[104] But even outside of intellectual debates about the merits and origins of either Francophonie or Negritude, it is worth noting that Senghor found the two concepts inseparable, commonly referring to them in the same speeches, and even in the same sentences. These concepts were foundational for Senghor's approaches to Senegalese politics and social life. Francophonie and Negritude buttressed his notion of African Socialism. Combining them justified the continued reliance on the French university model and the need to maintain reciprocity and mutual recognition of advanced degrees. Given the importance he attached to Negritude, his position paradoxically precluded Africanization of university curricula. While some academics have recently revised historical narratives that depict Senghor as lacking in authentic revolutionary anticolonialism, defenses of Senghor's international and domestic politics would have fallen on deaf ears among students in 1968.[105]

The student protest in May can thus be viewed in part as a rejection of Senghor's tethering of Francophonie and Negritude to "modernity." In his mind, modernity would be best brought about through unity emanating from his political party down to union levels in labor and among students. "The Party must, in its triple role of direction, control, and animation, be the principal instrument of our development. . . . As for objectives, it is our duty to construct a modern nation, where citizens will rejoice in democratic liberties, on the level of a developed nation."[106] For the university, the modernization project involved the Franco-Senegalese "Mixed Commission," through which all decisions passed.[107] For its part, the French Ministry of Education sought to "safeguard its privileged ties by working to preserve and uphold our values in the name of a certain type of civilization, and to be able to help the African of tomorrow make his way through the modern world."[108]

While there was no shortage of paternalism in these remarks by the French Ministry of Education, Senghor seemed to echo this view. He sought creative ways to navigate the gradual increases in Senegalese budgetary responsibility in education. Education would be the vehicle carrying his young nation into a modern future. In consultation with the Mixed Commission, the Senegalese government decided to undertake "education reforms from pre-school to the university, from linguistics to mathematics, in which the ultimate goal is the creation of a new Senegalese man ('l'homo senegalensis'), solidly rooted in Negritude to open himself up to modernicity [sic]."[109] The Senghor regime squarely tied Francophonie and Negritude to modernity, citing Senegalese education as the key to unlocking a new, modern African man worthy of a Latin appellation. Protesting students, on the other hand, had an altogether different version of a modern university and criticized the "inauguration in Senegal, under the direction of French specialists, of modern methods of torture by electricity," that the Senegalese state used to suppress the PAI and its supporters.[110]

Anti-French sentiment surfaced at opportune moments well beyond 1968, especially when Senghor publicly drew connections between Africa and France. Charles de Gaulle died on 9 November 1970, after which Senghor issued a statement that his passing "has shocked Senegal as much as it has France," and gave homage "to the decolonizer of Africa, to the Father of Senegalese independence."[111] While these comments were made through diplomatic correspondence, Senghor also stated in a public address to the Senegalese nation that "without [de Gaulle], we would not be independent today. It is he who allowed us to finally realize our ideal of national independence and friendly cooperation with France."[112] It is worth pausing to remark that Senghor planted the roots of African independence at the feet of de Gaulle rather than an African. Even if it were a politically strategic move to attain a particular end, this seemed a far cry from Senghor's anticolonial stance from the pre-independence era and undermined his status as a mouthpiece for Negritude.

The Senegalese journalist Jean-Pierre N'Diaye explained that, "during this era when the continent was emerging from the pain of colonialism, the 'Francophonie-Negritude' coupling was unacceptable . . . the recognition of Francophonie was inseparable from the development of Negritude."[113] Whatever revolutionary content that Negritude contained at its inception in the interwar period had been removed by 1968, when it became inseparable from Francophonie. But perhaps N'Diaye summed it up best in a 1971 article on the state of the African university: "In effect, how can the university promote scientific and technological development—one of the components of national liberty—and depend on a capitalist metropole to give it direction? Therein lies the dilemma! The same problem continues to be posed today in all of the African national universities."[114]

Though the protests at the University of Dakar began after those in Tunis in March and shortly after the wreckage of the Night of the Barricades in Paris, they arguably yielded the largest gains in terms of government negotiations with both labor and student movements. Unrest struck both Paris and Dakar almost simultaneously. Both movements were ignited by students, violently suppressed by state authorities, and then supported by workers' unions. In the wake of economic crisis due to peanut crop failures and a falling currency, Senegalese students faced cutbacks in university funding and housing access. Dakar 68er Abdoulaye Bathily characterized the unrest as both nationalist and antigovernment since, he claimed, students instrumentalized the university's financial woes to criticize the presence of an overwhelming number of French professors, as well as the relatively large number of foreign French students occupying limited university seats.[115] Even President Léopold Sédar Senghor, acclaimed for a particularly African Socialism, had named the University of Dakar "a French University in the services of Africa."[116]

As a result of the country-wide economic crisis, Senegalese students faced a reduction in the number and amount of scholarships, which were slashed anywhere from one-half to two-thirds of their pre-1968 values. Yet on the basis of this material issue, students demanded the Africanization of the faculty and the subject matter. While Senegalese students felt that French immigrants received access to education that should be reserved for Senegalese, workers faced similar limitations regarding coveted high-level positions in government and industry that were dominated by foreigners. Similar to portions of the French Left who grafted their anti-imperialist causes onto the question of immigrants' rights, protesting students at the University of Dakar couched their demands in the context of the persistence of colonialism. The postcolonial elements—or specific historical links to the colonial period—reveal themselves in (1) the University of Dakar's continued reliance on French subsidies; (2) Senghor's numerous references to Francophonie and his rhetorical use of the *cahiers*; and (3) both the students' and Senghor's labeling of each other as servants of French imperialism. For students, part of being modern meant supporting an African university independent from France, whereas for Senghor, the modern Senegalese citizen would be born of the synthesis between French reason and African intuition. Nineteen sixty-eight also marshaled in an era of postcolonial nationalism in which students deployed anti-imperialist claims that had once been designated for the French state and repackaged them for Senegalese leadership. In this regard, the strikes in Dakar should be considered as part of the larger decolonization process in which activists railed against an unachieved, or incomplete, independence in Senegal.

Like Tunisia, the Senegalese state created a Special Tribunal to deal with subversion. Yet reports of torture and the decennial imprisonments were much more common in Tunisia than in Senegal. While students and labor leaders spent time in military camps just after the May strikes, the vast majority returned to their homes in June during labor negotiations. As a result, the increased transnational communication after May 1968 between Senegalese activists in Paris and Dakar was not focused on penal reform or basic human rights; rather, they were able to successfully increase student representation and argue for inclusion in university decisions. This increased power would have been unthinkable in Tunisia, where rebellious students never achieved this degree of agency in university politics. It is all the more surprising given that Senegalese students were not even in the majority at the University of Dakar, which was heavily populated with French and non-Senegalese African students—whereas the student population at the University of Tunis was nearly three times larger and quite homogeneous. Despite these challenges, Senegalese students succeeded in forging joint efforts with other African students in Dakar, and with the broader student community in France, Germany, and Czechoslovakia.

While certain aspects of the movement were specific to the local context in Dakar, students also identified with larger international causes, beginning with Algeria, and later shifting their gaze to Ghana, Vietnam, and Palestine. In many ways, despite its locally rooted issues, May '68 in Dakar actually invigorated transnational activism abroad rather than being catalyzed by it. As evidenced in the memories of Senegalese activist "Mariane," the AESF gained membership and expanded beyond Paris following widespread African student support in other French universities. And if levels of solidarity on the French left is rather difficult to gauge, this is due in part to their preoccupation with their own national movement.[117] Senegalese students located in France returned home in the summer of 1968 to coordinate efforts with students in Dakar and to develop a plan of action to take back with them to France. This level of organization among activist networks had been absent since the independence movement and also rejuvenated FEANF.

Preparing Senegalese youth to undertake Senegal's modernization was at the heart of Senghor's political project. The university was the mechanism through which he hoped to achieve cultural synthesis and technological advancement for Africa. And though student strikes spilled into the streets and grew to encompass a national labor movement, the university remained the key to Senegal's future, its link to the French colonial past, and a reflection of Senegalese political institutions more broadly. It is no surprise, then, that as it increasingly opened its doors to the ranks of African students, professors, and subjects, so too did the government integrate a multiparty system and gradual decentralization. With decolonization in the university came democratization in government in the 1970s.

PART TWO

Activism after 1968

CHAPTER 5

From Student to Worker Protest in Tunisia

> *In a country where history has so often been falsified, we must be conscious of the importance of written documentation, especially since our generation, the last of the colonized, has passed from oral tradition to written form.*
>
> —Simone Lellouche Othmani, "Conversation avec Simone," *Mémoire & Horizon*

The 1968 protest theaters of Tunis, Paris, and Dakar shared a number of characteristics, and, in some cases, activists communicated directly with each other. The children of the World War II generation transformed into a dynamic youth that ignited social movements in each case. This group constituted a rapidly expanding global university population, whether in France or in its former colonies, that bottlenecked on campuses ill equipped to accommodate such influxes. What is more, students from these regions lamented similar university reforms, though for different reasons, based on their shared experiences under, and grievances against, the French higher education system. Many student activists also shared international and Third World sensibilities such as identification with revolutionaries in Vietnam and Palestine that were seen as extensions of their own national independence movements. In each case, the demands specific to student groups—such as Africanization/Arabization of the professoriate or increased student participation in administration—were accompanied by larger political claims that often included a denunciation of an oppressive head of state and a neocolonial relationship to France.

The transnational networks created out of 1968 enabled the articulation of counternarratives to state-controlled media in 1970s Tunisia, France, and Senegal. These transnational networks served as a check, albeit with limited degrees of power, to these states' monopolies on public information. The movements referenced each other, and each city became fertile ground for rising discontent with global events from the Vietnam War to rallies of solidarity with local issues by diasporic communities in France. In this regard, Paris acted as a site of Third World protest as North and West Africans abroad transmitted valuable information to immigrant communities and mobilized in support of homegrown protests. Significant numbers of Tunisians and Senegalese students were living in France, and many participated not only in France's May '68 but also in their own national student movements as well. Each movement also articulated a "postcolonial nationalism" combined with transnational action, and pushed for democratization in both local and international institutions. Yet in spite of these shared characteristics and transnational connections, movements in Tunisia, France, and Senegal took decidedly different turns in the 1970s.

In Tunisia, the 1970s witnessed the emergence of an Islamist movement that was hardly present in March 1968, when religious elements began to fill the void after the Bourguiba regime decimated the Tunisian Left. Heavy state repression prompted the proliferation of human rights organizations and a strong Franco-Tunisian network of activists. After 1968, Tunisian students launched another campus-wide strike in February 1972 in protest of the prolonged incarceration of activists and the sentencing of one exiled protester in absentia. And while Tunisia's national labor union did not strongly support student protests in 1968, unlike both Senegal's and France's national labor unions, by 1978 workers led their own general strike against the state. Tunisian authorities predictably employed violent strike-breaking tactics against workers just as they had against students in 1968 and 1972. This time, the transnational networks of human rights activists resulted in a successful international campaign to secure the release of student and labor leaders.

Tunisia's Mai 68? The Korba Crisis and February 1972

Contrary to France and Senegal, where students and workers joined forces, at least momentarily, the student protests of 1968 in Tunisia did not reflect the apogee of activism in the long 1960s there. In fact, in February 1972 an even larger Tunisian student movement struck university campuses and lycées extending beyond the capital city. Though March '68 did not eclipse the activism of February 1972, it provided the networks and infrastructure necessary to produce nonstate sources of information and, perhaps most importantly, the language of resistance to the authoritarian regime. Prolonged state repression produced revolutionary tremors that finally ruptured on campus grounds, when the arrest of activist Simone Lellouche Othmani sparked university-wide demonstrations demanding her release. The student strikes set off a state-run media smear campaign in 1972 in which officials friendly to the regime cast protesters as foreign threats to the well-being of the Tunisian nation.

Webs of activists spanning the Mediterranean were reactivated to engage in the production of alternative information about state violence and incarcerations. The sustained and hardening position of authorities led the movement to transition from a student identification of global anti-imperialist causes (as seen in Ben Jennet's June 1967 demonstration) to much more narrow goals on the national level. Tunisian leftists faced several challenges in defining their political scope, causing the splintering of groups originally linked to Perspectives. However, the concrete realities of the Bourguiba regime's oppressive measures—using tactics of intimidation, militia violence, and even torture—pushed activist groups to finally crystallize around issues they could agree on: core basic human rights for all Tunisians.

On 10 January 1972, Tunisian police arrested Simone Lellouche Othmani to serve out a sentence she received in absentia during the trials that followed the eruptions of March '68. Lellouche Othmani had been expelled to France in April 1968 and later received permission to return in the summer of 1970.[1] Prior to her 1972 arrest, she was never served notice of the verdict, which was especially odd since she had freely entered Tunisia in 1970, when she married Ahmed Ben Othmani. She had even been detained in April 1971 in Tunisia, only to be released shortly thereafter with no indication of the pending sentence.[2] After her arrest, she was put on trial and received a suspended sentence of two years. The massive protests that followed led to what Lellouche Othmani later deemed "the first democratic movement in Tunisia on a national level," albeit with "the university as its point of departure and a provisional student organization that was only established for the student masses, and whose existence was constantly contested by the authorities."[3]

News of Lellouche Othmani's trial launched protests in which over four thousand students at various colleges at the University of Tunis went on strike. The February events—viewed by many as Tunisia's equivalent to France's May '68—quickly spread to high schools and even beyond Tunis, again leading the regime to close down the university.[4] This time, students called for the liberation of Simone and Ahmed Ben Othmani, as well as for increased democracy within the major student association. Tunisian authorities expelled Lellouche Othmani to France for a second time on 5 February 1972. Though authorities claimed that her husband played a key role in the February protests, this would have been quite unlikely from his prison cell. Ahmed was arrested in April 1971 for allegedly having edited works published in the journal *El Amel Tounsi* (*The Tunisian Worker*), and remained in prison without trial at the time of his wife's expulsion.[5] With renewed attention to his case, activists created a committee for the liberation of Ahmed Ben Othmani, as they had done for Mohamed Ben Jennet before him, to advocate for his release. This time, however, they made fewer references to Palestine or Vietnam and focused mainly on Ben Othmani's release, freely elected student representation, and freedom of expression.[6]

Where the '68 movement began as a general anti-imperialist protest and ended with narrower goals of liberating Ben Jennet and company, February 1972 took the reverse order in that it started as a liberation movement and grew to a national democratic one. Much of the global anti-imperialism that accompanied calls to release Ben Jennet in 1968 had been replaced with more circumspect objectives on the national level in 1972. The PSD's increased interference in the national student union (UGET) led many students to demand autonomy and the creation of alternate organizations, and to petition for the removal of political parties in university affairs. The PSD's influence on UGET had waned significantly after the repression of 1968, and Bourguiba supporters were on the verge of losing control of executive offices at the student elections set to take place in Korba in August 1971. When it became clear that opposition groups, collectively termed "Progressives," held the majority, the PSD helped orchestrate a coup of the elections to place its own partisans in positions of student leadership.

Student accounts of the Korba Congress suggest that Progressives denoted a short-lived leftist alliance between members directly affiliated with Perspectives, communist holdovers from the defunct PCT, and socialist students disillusioned with the Bourguiba regime. While this alliance outnumbered regime supporters, it had its own internal conflicts, where self-proclaimed communists and Perspectives members disputed which of their groups held the greatest support at the congress.[7] Students' calls for better representation in university organizations were directly linked to divisions over the future of UGET, where some hoped to reform it from within while others sought to eradicate it. Many denounced the PSD-friendly coup from the Korba Congress, when PSD leadership usurped student elections despite being heavily outnumbered by the Progressives coalition. Already in December 1971, "mobilization in the university had reached peak levels."[8]

Cries against infringements on the democratic rights of the student body at large dovetailed with students' disgust at the violations of individuals' rights following news of Lellouche Othmani's arrest. Protesters occupied the steps of the courthouse and took to the streets in solidarity on the day of her trial. Lellouche Othmani also staged an individual protest by refusing to wear the traditional sefseri, a full body covering. "I demanded to wear civil clothes for the trial. They wanted to put me in a sefseri, but I said, 'in my entire life I've never worn a sefseri, and it's not today that I'm going to start.' They told me 'but you'll be ashamed' and I said, 'no, it's them who should be ashamed for having put me in prison!'"[9] Just days later, thousands of students gathered at the Law School in Tunis on 2 February 1972 to demand new elections. They even challenged Bourguiba's self-proclaimed role as the nation's "Supreme Combatant" by chanting "the people alone is the Supreme Combatant."[10]

According to one student who was present at the Korba Congress, the February movement resulted in the marginalization of UGET, exacerbating rifts between communists and Perspectivists on the issue of democratizing the student union.[11] While March '68 led to an alignment between the leadership of UGET and Bourguiba's PSD, it was Korba in 1971 that resulted in the Left successfully isolating pro-regime students. Ultimately, as Mohamed Dhifallah argues, Korba brought about the "total effacement of the union, precipitating a rupture between the student movement and the Bourguiba regime. From this point forward, the university theatre became a refuge for all of the illegal political currents, while the party in power was nearly absent."[12] After Korba, students were divided among Perspectivists who sought to work outside of UGET (or through alternative organizations), communists seeking to reform UGET from within, and a minority of PSD loyalists who supported the new executive office. Divisions were later reflected in February 1972, when communists and other reformers abstained from, but did not denounce, the protests. Many young communists still supported Ahmed Ben Salah, who had been cast aside as a scapegoat by Bourguiba for the country's failed collectivization project.[13] This camp hoped to "win back" UGET through political reform rather than create parallel organizations like its more radical counterparts.

In many respects, the friction on the left between communist reformers and more radical currents mirrored tensions within the French New Left of the same era. Critics of both the PCF and the PCT viewed them as subordinate to bureaucratic structures within the international communist scene (with the PCF taking orders from Moscow, or the PCT as subservient to the PCF), whereas Far Left Marxist-Leninist or Maoist tendencies often gave way to *grousculisme*.[14] Despite tensions, by February, the majority of the student population shared a distrust of the Destourian elements of UGET. And while the University of Tunis had become the center of political contestation, UGET was no longer seen as a potentially oppositional force to the regime. Activity within UGET represented alignment with the PSD, while non-UGET activists were targeted as dangerous to regime stability.

Bourguiba's crackdown on students, coupled with UGET's lack of credibility, led to a significant decrease in union membership among Tunisian students at home and abroad. Students fled UGET for proxy organizations like the Provisional University Committees and the Committees of Action and Struggle–General Union of Tunisian Students (CAL-UGET), or to organizations that had long been banned by Bourguiba, such as the PCT and Perspectives, with some crossover. In an analysis of the February events, one France-based proxy organization noted that UGET experienced "massive desertion"—its total numbers in Paris were under five hundred, though there were more than three thousand Tunisians studying there.[15] Of a sample of Tunisian university students surveyed in 1972 in both Tunis and Paris, only one-third supported the present system while just over three quarters did not feel they could express opinions freely in Tunisia, including a surprising nearly one-third of respondents who identified as "Destourian."[16]

Contrary to March '68, the February '72 movement spread beyond the university halls of Tunis to the interior of the country, where high schoolers went on strike in Sfax, Jendouba, le Kef, Mateur, Tabarka, Sousse, Kasserine, and Gafsa. The regime struck hard in 1972, launching tear gas at protesters and intimidating sympathetic French coopérants. Authorities engaged in mass arrests targeting many of the March participants who had since been released from detention.[17] Others, like Ahmed Ben Othmani, were implicated in the February events even though they were in prison at the time. As in 1968, the regime arrested citizens of undesirable political persuasions en masse and employed similar torture tactics. Many imprisoned activists faced the common "balançoire," where victims were suspended from a rod with their hands tied behind their legs and beaten in the genitals.[18]

One activist and Perspectives member—who had evaded arrest in March '68 but was apprehended after February '72—recounted in an interview that after eight months in prison, "I then spent 2 and one-half months in the hospital after being tortured because my anus had been penetrated—with the bottle system and all."[19] Fighting back against these breaches of basic human rights proved particularly challenging, as many were denied attorneys, though the majority of the accused were liberated without trial between September and December 1972.[20] However, the Bourguiba regime never relented on its attacks against opponents, and several of the original Perspectives leaders remained unlawfully imprisoned for most of the 1970s. The Tunisian student movement may have reached its zenith in February 1972, but it also precipitated sustained international activism against government repression throughout the next decade.

On 8 February 1972, Tunisian students in Paris called a general assembly at the headquarters of the AEMNA, during which they denounced the administrative commission "elected" at Korba.[21] They recognized the results of a separate extraordinary congress held in Tunis and elected a provisional group of CAL-UGET representatives for the Paris section to replace the illegitimate Korba results.[22] Students overwhelmingly supported the special congress convened in February 1972 and voted to nullify Korba's proceedings, after which point Neo-Destourian adherence became anathema in the university setting. Students' demands reverberated from Tunis to Paris, as the extraordinary congress in Tunis of 2 February was emulated in Paris less than a week later. Tunisians in Paris reflecting on the situation a year later noted that "our movement responded to an objective local situation, linked dialectically to that of our comrades in Tunis regarding calls for a democratic, representative, and autonomous UGET. Our combative claims were ignored equally in Tunis as in Paris."[23] Yet while the liberations of Simone Lellouche and Ahmed Ben Othmani were only part of the larger democratic goals for February activists, the PSD-dominated media reports focused almost exclusively on this aspect, completely omitting student demands for free elections in major media coverage.

Lellouche Othmani, who was born in Tunisia to Jewish parents, was labeled by PSD sympathizers as French and Jewish. She was designated as the Tunisian version of Daniel Cohn-Bendit, the famous student leader in France's May '68 who had Jewish parents and German citizenship, though he was born and raised in France. The PSD, UGTT, and even UGET acted as a pro-government tripartite front against Lellouche Othmani and any other "agitators." Leaders from each of these organizations, through *L'Action* and *La Presse*, published a series of scathing critiques, alleging the incoherence of a movement led by foreigners with no attachment to the university or to student life. On 2 February 1972, *L'Action* stated that Lellouche Othmani was a French national who had, along with her husband, been sentenced by the Special Court for crimes against the state, and that neither one was actually a student at the University of Tunis.[24] While the claims on student status were accurate, they lacked important context. Lellouche Othmani had long finished her studies, and Ahmed Ben Othmani had been denied access to any Tunisian university after March '68.

UGET asserted that the February strikes were nothing more than a "campaign orchestrated from abroad to propagate subversion in the heart of the university," while UGTT released statements that the strikes were led by "destructive Zionism, embodied as much by Simone Lellouche Othmani as by Cohn-Bendit, from the children of former collaborators of the colonial regime . . . and from all sorts of anarchist rings."[25] The Destourian youth group issued a statement expressing its total support of the "Supreme Combatant" and Prime Minister Hédi Nouira. The minister of national education, Mohamed Mzali, called for a counterprotest on 9 February—the day after announcing university closures—to combat the directives he alleged emanated from Ba'athists from the Middle

East and Europe.[26] Whether coming directly from the regime or from its minions in the UGTT and UGET, there was a clear strategy to paint antistate claims first and foremost as anti-Tunisian. The regime's narrative, and the activists' counternarratives, in fact reflected debates about postcolonial nationalism in independent Tunisia. When agitators expressed their desires for a modern nation where free speech and a wide array of political currents are accepted, they were denounced as foreign threats to Tunisian independence: Jewish, Maoist, European, Communist, or Ba'athist. Though the objects of vilification may have shifted depending on the national political terrain, both the de Gaulle and Senghor administrations would deploy similar tactics when undermining their opposition.

In addition to smearing Lellouche Othmani, PSD leadership also used the events of May '68 in France to deflect any notion of a homegrown movement in Tunisia. The accusations came despite the anachronism that the initial 1968 Tunisian protests occurred months earlier than in France. In a March 1972 interview with the PSD's Arabic news journal, Minister of Foreign Affairs Mohammed Masmoudi noted the possibility of a "contagious phenomenon" following the French events and denounced "'the absolute mayhem' produced in the heart of the university and the petty and shameful imitation of agitators in the Latin Quarter by our students."[27] Two days later, Masmoudi was cited in *La Presse* stating, "Thankfully, neither extreme leftism, nor Trotskyism, nor anarchism, nor Ba'athism can, under any circumstances, resonate in our country. . . . By agitating alone, practicing verbal terrorism, and seeking to change everything all of a sudden, outside of existing structures and disciplines, without method, without organization, without programs and without allies, they will only succeed in creating fear and regression that will end by disappearing into folklore."[28] Here Masmoudi used rhetorical tools to create the imagery of an exterior threat when he referred to all forms of opposition as existing outside of, and in opposition to, *our country*. Reports from *La Presse* and *L'Action* attacked the Tunisian and French activists alike in an effort to frame them as radical agitators acting in unison. Ignoring the continuum of Tunisian events linking March 1968 and February 1972, the regime attempted to exteriorize the causality of the latter, blaming external forces couched in unfounded claims of imitation or contagion.

Shortly thereafter, *L'Action* proclaimed the dangers of rampant Maoism. The article, "Maoist commando," detailed how the French CEO of an automobile factory was taken hostage by radicals after the death of French militant Pierre Overney, who was killed by plant security on 25 February 1972 during a protest.[29] The regime sought to discredit student demands by stating that they were unrealistic and went far beyond the university, presumably risking criminal actions similar to those in France. This was an effort to render UGET like the UGTT, where orders were taken from above and claims were relegated to material issues like increased wages (for UGTT) or scholarships and housing (for UGET). According to the regime, the current student demands were outside that which was even relevant to Tunisian national realities, much less the University of Tunis. It was also a way of internationalizing the student movement in such a way as to deflect antidemocratic practices in Tunisia. By claiming that youth protesters were following orders from abroad, or influenced by distant and foreign political currents, the regime attempted to disqualify the national character of their demands.

Reactivating Transnational Activist and Policing Networks

Activists in both France and Tunisia reacted to the negative characterizations of the student movement by Tunisian media. The regime's lopsided reporting impelled the creation of the Information Group for Struggles in Tunisia (Groupe d'Information pour les Luttes en Tunisie [GILT]). GILT was made up primarily of Perspectives members who had escaped persecution in 1968. Founded in February 1972 in Paris, the group sought to spread news of the February events in Tunis to the university milieu in France, though their larger goal was to eventually reach Tunisian workers.[30] While GILT had limited success in connecting with Tunisians outside of intellectual circles, their reporting contributed to the organization of a hunger strike at the Maison de Tunisie in Paris. The hunger strike was completely ignored by the Tunisian press, however, with PSD-friendly media claiming that "the Maison de Tunisie at the University of Paris was the only building among all of the student dormitories that was not covered with graffiti and slogans."[31] On the contrary, the Maison de Tunisie had become an important *point de rencontre* for students to debate issues from the future of UGET to possible courses of action, which often resulted in anything but a consensus. Attendance was not restricted to Tunisian students, as FEANF, UNEF, AEMNA, and others were regularly invited.[32]

At the same time, GILT helped keep Tunisian ex-patriots informed on developments back home. As François Maspero had done after March '68, when he published *Liberté pour les condamnés de Tunis* (Liberty for the Convicted of Tunis), Tunisians abroad again published their own texts to counter the regime's account of the February strikes. In July of that year, Perspectives produced a pamphlet detailing the ensuing police repression including clubbings, illegal university occupation by police, and mass arrests.[33] The pamphlet outlined the usurpation of UGET at the Korba Congress, stating that despite majority opposition, "UGET's leadership, composed of agents of the authorities, resorted to the lowest tactics (stealing the elections, violence following union meetings, etc.) in order to maintain its puppets at the head of the student confederation."[34] The Korba moment marked the serious decline of UGET for Tunisian students, both at home and abroad, who had once thought it might be reformed to effect positive university change. As with March '68, Paris provided a comparatively safe distance from which to publish counternarratives and base operations for human rights awareness. Yet the safety of Paris was limited owing to cooperation between Tunisian and French authorities, namely joint surveillance of activities at the Maison de Tunisie.

GILT not only relayed and published news of events in Tunis but also oversaw international outposts and printed information on activist organizations such as CISDHT. On 15 February, students in Paris held a meeting in solidarity with Tunisians attended by Maghrebi activists in AEMNA, the national student unions of Morocco and Algeria, members of the General Union of Palestinian Students, and UNEF, with attorney Marcel Manville appearing as a special guest. Revived by the February momentum, CISDHT gained the support of Tunisian communist students in Paris who sought the release of 68ers and published advertisements seeking contributions from the readership of *Tribune Progressiste*.[35] Other Tunisians studying in Paris likewise called for the liberation of Ahmed Ben Othmani. Through student channels in France, news spread to Tunisians in the French provinces who denounced the Korba coup and demanded syndical autonomy from UGET.[36] GILT helped garner support from abroad by reporting that French coopérants had thwarted National Education Minister Mohamed Mzali's effort to break strikes when they refused to hold classes—ostensibly for nonstriking students. GILT further reported that a teacher was arrested and tortured in Gafsa and accused of being "a Zionist agent on the payroll of a foreign embassy."[37] While repression spread beyond Tunis, so did the news as GILT noted that Mohamed Ben Jennet—amnestied in 1970—was again arrested while with his family in Kelibia despite not participating in the February events. GILT was still active in September 1972 when it denounced trials of the Special Tribunal that heard the cases of February activists, as well as those who had been arrested without cause.[38]

Another important oppositional media outlet surfaced in the spring of 1972, the Paris-based Tunisian Committee of Information and Defense of the Victims of Repression (Comité Tunisien d'Information et de Défense des Victimes de la Répression [CTIDVR]). Made up exclusively of Tunisians, CTIDVR included members who were holdovers from the international CISDHT that was created after March '68. They joined CTIDVR to narrow the group to *Tuni-*

sian efforts for *Tunisian* human rights causes. They also sought to reduce political tensions within the group following the Ben Salah affair, which had divided many along ideological lines related to state-sponsored socialist projects.[39] CISDHT members remained split between those who denounced Ben Salah as a corrupt Bourguiba operative and architect of a completely failed agricultural collectivization project, on the one hand, and reformers who viewed Ben Salah as an oppositional socialist unfairly blamed for economic factors outside his control, on the other. CTIDVR's main goals were to alert the public of events in Tunisia and provide legal, moral, and material support to victims of repression. To facilitate the creation of CTIDVR, former French coopérant Jean Gattégno acted as the primary contact for the association, though the organization was run by Tunisians. As a French citizen, Gattégno was a convenient frontman and eased the process of receiving mail, creating a bank account, and obtaining publication and distribution authorizations. This may have been a common practice at the time, since Simone Lellouche Othmani used her French citizenship to provide similar cover for the publication *El Amel Tounsi*, even though she did not write for the organ.[40]

CTIDVR launched a media campaign by sending "information letters" to various press agencies. After sustained efforts from 1972 to 1974, it contributed to the appearance of articles on Tunisian repression in important French outlets such as *Le Monde, Libération, L'Humanité, Politique-Hebdo,* and *Afrique-Asie,* as well as foreign publications *El Bayane* (Morocco) and *El Hadef* and *El Balgh* (Beirut), and obtained German television and radio interviews with Tunisian hunger strikers and PCT activists.[41] Members worked closely with CAL-UGET to organize hunger strikes at the Maison de Tunisie in February and December 1972. They also communicated regularly with Amnesty International and assisted in setting up the "adoption" of a number of prisoners. In the fall of 1973, CTIDVR reported that twenty-five students at the University of Tunis were forced to enroll in military service as a result of political activity, while Tunisian immigrant workers in St. Etienne and Lyon had been expelled by the Tunisian Consulate.[42] This shift beyond student activism and toward the plight of Tunisian workers was further emphasized by efforts to work with the Paris-based Arab Workers' Movement (Mouvement des Travailleurs Arabes [MTA]) during the same period.[43] Their goals thus centered on defending against repression occurring on both sides of the Mediterranean while they advocated for both students and workers.

In spite of certain successes in the defense of victims, CTIDVR was not immune to internal strife. Friction dated to the accord reached between Perspectives and the PCT in the formation of the Committee for the Liberation of Ben Jennet in 1968. Perspectives' desire to push the political agenda beyond

Ben Jennet's release jeopardized the committee's ability to reach consensus. Perspectives sent representatives to Paris specifically to carry out orders from Tunis, led by Hachemi Ben Fredj—in part to keep watch on rogue members like Khémaïs Chammari, who frequently disobeyed orders regarding content of publications—while Chérif Ferjani became the voice of Perspectives within the CTIDVR after Simone Lellouche Othmani proclaimed her independent position.[44] Similar divisions could be seen within CISDHT regarding Ben Salah, who was generally defended by communist party sympathizers and vilified as a vulgar Marxist and regime collaborator by the more radical Left.

Moreover, CISDHT, whose original purpose was to defend those arrested in 1968, was forced to evaluate whether it had the means and desire to also defend prisoners arrested during the protests of February 1972. Eventually, CTIDVR fulfilled this function after the former waned in influence.[45] Simone Lellouche Othmani recalled that CISDHT's role was no longer clear following the release of many of the prisoners. "We were seeking liberation [and] it was not a question of overthrowing the government. It was not a question of engaging directly in politics."[46] As another former member put it, "In the absence of a clear political line for defending victims, we have oscillated between opportunism, dogmatism, and sectarianism. . . . All of the difficulties we've faced came from confusion between defense of democracy and a political program."[47] And although CTIDVR was in many ways created as a reaction to CISDHT's fracturing, it eventually succumbed to similar disputes. While international action was essential to reaching a public audience and providing support to detainees, CTIDVR's internal conflict reflected similar challenges of other leftist organizations attempting to organize activists under a large umbrella.

Just as international groups of support located in France—with contacts on the ground in Tunis—provided vital assistance to political prisoners, authorities maintained their own Franco-Tunisian networks. While the PSD-friendly UGTT and UGET were busy publishing newspaper articles castigating the student movement, French police conducted surveillance across the Mediterranean that included Tunisian activists and others sympathetic to the Palestinian cause. French authorities monitored the activities of individuals such as Khémaïs Chammari, whom they linked to Mahmoud Hamchari, the leader of the Parisian section of the Palestinian Liberation Organization. Hamchari, with whom Chammari was suspected of having ties, was eventually assassinated by the Israeli secret service on French soil.[48] Palestinian liberation was a key element of the student movement in general, and especially for Tunisians; however, it was equally a point of emphasis for the national security of a number of countries, including France. After May '68, French police created new surveillance programs to follow students' activities and kept records of student meetings and protests, originating with concerns about the commencement of the fall semester in 1968.[49] Chammari, a founding member of Perspectives who was indefinitely expelled from the University of Tunis and later active in Paris, made it onto the "List of Arabs of various nationalities suspected of supporting Palestinian terrorists" in the Paris region.[50] It is unclear what, if any, relationship Chammari had with Hamchari. Though Chammari was in and out of Tunisian prisons throughout the Bourguiba and Ben Ali periods, he has never been directly linked to terrorist activity. His surveillance following involvement in March '68 by both French and Tunisian police points to collaboration on the part of state authorities that mirrored the transnational activity of opposition groups.[51]

During the February 1972 hunger strike at the Maison de Tunisie in Paris, French police intervened at the behest of the Tunisian embassy in Paris. They interrogated 105 students and asked them to complete a questionnaire, provided by the prefecture, in which they were asked if they were affiliated politically with Ba'athists, communists, or Perspectivists. In some cases, French police reported confusion regarding the nature of these groups, and even asked the interview subjects what the terms meant.[52] This suggests a high probability that police interrogators were working with information provided by the Tunisian embassy—which had solicited the intervention—about groups they deemed dangerous, yet another form of transnational cooperation at the state level. At the same time that antigovernment activity was organized through transnational networks at the Maison de Tunisie in support of detainees, French police worked in concert with intelligence information emanating from Tunisia.

From Student to Worker Protest: January 1978 ("Black Thursday")

Just as national education systems in Senegal and Tunisia drew on French models, so too did Tunisian nationalized industries in energy and public transport mirror their French counterparts. Like in France, these sectors were vulnerable to the power of a strong national union that often had a monopoly on the supply of labor. Though the student protests of 1968 in both Senegal and France sparked general strikes with the participation of flagship national labor unions, workers did not participate en masse in Tunisia until January 1978. Labor unions were an integral part of the Tunisian independence movement, and the national labor union, UGTT, had been allied with Bourguiba's

Neo-Destour since 1946.[53] These ties between labor and the state persisted into the independence era, and labor leaders backed the regime in its suppression of students in both 1968 and 1972.[54]

Union secretary-general Habib Achour publicly stated of Simone Lellouche Othmani in February 1972 that "[UGTT] will never tolerate a strike in favor of a Zionist woman. . . . I affirm that the 'Red Guard' of the Party is the UGTT, which will always assume full responsibility for the defense and safeguarding of the fruits of the nation."[55] This was a reference to Mao's Red Guard, a paramilitary group deployed in 1966 to protect the Chinese Cultural Revolution. Of course, the irony of Achour's statement is not lost as he was mobilizing workers to suppress communist and Maoist students. Yet state-labor relations eventually soured as the PSD encroached on workers' rights. At the moment of Tunisian independence in 1956, workers numbered between 150,000 and 200,000 and were often divided by nationality. By the mid-1970s, the working class was much more homogeneous and had ballooned to approximately 500,000, almost one-third of the active population.[56] This rising class became more demanding as it grew. Between 1970 and 1974, salaries increased 35 percent thanks to worker strikes. These gains came at a high price, however, when, in 1974, the state put in place a repressive law allowing the requisition to cease even legal strikes and up to one-year prison sentences for strikers who refused to adhere to state orders.[57]

Tensions were temporarily mitigated in a January 1977 labor agreement (termed "the Social Pact") that was designed to augment wages in exchange for the state's authority to withhold the workers' right to strike. Yet already in September 1977, authorities seized the UGTT's organ, *Ech-Chaâb* (The People), which had become increasingly critical of the regime. Meanwhile, the head of the UGTT, Achour, faced death threats in November 1977, allegedly from PSD henchmen.[58] Formerly a party loyalist, Achour distanced himself from the Bourguiba regime when, in a symbolic act demonstrating his desire for syndical autonomy, he resigned from the PSD at the union's national council meeting of 8–10 January 1978. Authorities retaliated by arresting another prominent labor leader and agitator from Sfax, Abderrazak Ghorbal, on 24 January. Achour completely severed ties with the regime when he called for a general workers' strike to be held 26 January 1978, the first of its kind since Tunisian independence. Borrowing a slogan from the student movement, he exclaimed before a crowd of union members gathered in Tunis, "The only supreme combatant is the people."[59] The violent state response led to the first instance in postcolonial Tunisia in which students and labor leaders agitated for similar causes. It also marked the crystallization of a previously disorganized and nascent Tunisian Islamic movement and mobilized transnational human rights activist networks on behalf of detained labor leaders that had been forged during the previous student movements.

Observers of the regime's crackdown on striking workers later dubbed the events of 26 January "Black Thursday."[60] On the eve of the strike, authorities encircled UGTT headquarters, effectively blocking in two hundred of its leaders who had ordered workers to stay home to avoid provocations by authorities. Upon the arrest of their leaders, thousands of workers took to the streets and clashed with police, military, and PSD militia forces. It was the first time in Tunisian history that the PSD admitted to recruiting and deploying a militia. PSD director and former information minister Mohamed Sayah—who was also accused by activists of creating student militias to spy on Tunisians in France in the 1960s and of ordering the torture of students in 1972—publicly acknowledged the existence of the militia forces in March 1978.[61] He claimed to have recruited about 500 members to provide support to police, though unofficial sources put the figure at over 2,500.[62] According to *Afrique-Asie*, the Black Thursday clashes resulted in 250 dead, 1,000 injured, and 2,000 arrested or brought in for interrogation at a detention camp in Oued Ellil near Tunis. Authorities also apprehended 500–600 union members, many of whom cited the use of torture during their captivity.[63] The regime declared a nationwide state of emergency that was not lifted until 25 February, and imposed a curfew in Tunis through national independence day on 20 March. A number of labor leaders were brought before the Special Court that was created in 1968 to prosecute student protesters for crimes against the state.

Reminiscent of the harsh sentences meted out to Mohamed Ben Jennet and Ahmed Ben Othmani over a decade earlier, in October 1978 Achour and Ghorbal were sentenced to ten years of forced labor with thirteen other labor leaders arriving at a similar fate. The court charged thirty union members with article 72 of the Tunisian Penal Code, for which the death penalty could be applied. Charges included "aggression aimed at changing the government; inciting citizens to kill each other; inciting disorder, murder, and pillaging; distribution of arms and groups seeking to destroy the property of others."[64] At least ninety-two UGTT members were imprisoned for crimes related to the Black Thursday events. The majority of those charged would be released by the summer of 1979 thanks to the efforts of human rights watch groups.[65] Though tensions were often high among various factions of the opposition movement throughout the postindependence era, many found common ground in seeking political rights for Tunisian citizens and more humane prison conditions.

While the 1960s' iterations of Perspectives were entrenched in theory and focused on intellectual critique of the regime, massive imprisonments gave way in the 1970s to a new group dedicated to direct and confrontational protest that had salient resonance with a larger and more diverse following. By 1973, Perspectives had been paralyzed by prison sentences of its intellectual core and splintered when a new generation on the left created the populist group Amel Tounsi (the Tunisian Worker). Original Perspectives members like Ahmed Othmani and Gilbert Naccache criticized Amel Tounsi for its naive and perfunctory support of Third World communism, in which it favored uncompromising positions and superficial political identification with popular movements while sacrificing the intellectual origins of Perspectives. Othmani explained the political and generational split within the Left. While the younger group blindly supported communist parties around the world, "We—the old guard—had finished with all that long ago. . . . The first generation of *Perspectives* was thus intellectually ready to join the human rights movement from the mid-1970s on. This evolution illustrates the capacity of the various components of the Tunisian opposition to come together again, no longer around a political programme, but in the wider defence of human rights. The Tunisian Human Rights League was founded in 1977 as a front uniting the political strands, no longer through partisan interest, but around the common denominator of the rights of the individual."[66] Perspectives and Amel Tounsi officially split in 1973, with Othmani and Naccache's "old guard" group opting to seek advancements in human rights issues among a plurality of political positions. Despite rifts with Amel Tounsi, even before the Black Thursday clashes and subsequent repression, the networks and infrastructure created during previous movements were in place. The last piece of ideological common ground solidified with the creation of a home-grown, legally recognized Tunisian Human Rights League that had support systems and groups located abroad to disseminate information. Their joint efforts led to the comparatively swift release of UGTT activists in 1979, the same year long-term political prisoners like Othmani and Naccache were set free.

Paris again proved to be a center of activist coordination with Tunis when human rights groups took action after the atrocities of 26 January 1978. As they had done since 1968, activists across the Mediterranean responded to state-sponsored violence and mobilized to liberate political prisoners. Paris was home to advocates in organizations like the Tunisian Collective of 26 January and the CTIDVR, while the newly formed Tunisian Human Rights League led efforts in Tunisia to liberate Black Thursday activists. The PSD media outlets sought to frame the events as a traitorous plot by a UGTT minority to overthrow the regime, whereas human rights organizations focused on state repression and published alternative news reports. Many of their activities were devoted to information production and dissemination to communities in Tunisia and France. For its part, the PSD engaged in its own media campaign and narrative construction with the aid of a national radio station (Radio Tunis) and the regime-friendly daily *L'Action*, as well as yet another *livre blanc* on the January events.

The Paris-based Tunisian Collective of 26 January was created to "undertake the largest possible information and solidarity campaign with all those who wish to come to the aid of the working class and of the UGTT to actively and effectively express solidarity and to sensitize international opinion on the bloody repression in Tunisia."[67] The organization released newsletters and "Information Flashes" that acted as correctives to official Tunisian sources. On 10 February, Lellouche Othmani wrote to the collective expressing concerns of the spread of government misinformation, resulting in "confusion [that] persists" and emanating from "official Tunisian communiqués" that contradicted facts known by human rights organizations.[68] The collective thus acted similarly to a public forum in which members and community activists could issue revisionist accounts (in the literal sense) and negotiate the publication of facts. Given the lack of faith in state-controlled sources of information, the major impact of the collective was to act as a check on the state's discursive power. In addition, human rights groups like the collective and the International Association of Democratic Jurists and Amnesty International sent legal observers to report back to Paris on prison conditions. An Amnesty International report released on 20 March 1979, the twenty-third anniversary of Tunisian independence, denounced human rights violations in Tunisia regarding the use of torture on prisoners including cigarette burns on the skin and brutal clubbings, which resulted in the poor health of prisoners such as Achour.[69] The collective's reporting aided in obtaining the support of French political organizations like the French Socialist and Communist Parties, as well as the French labor unions CFDT and the CGT.

The Tunisian Human Rights League launched an investigation into the death of activist and UGTT member Houcine el Kouki, whom many believed to have been literally tortured to death.[70] The collective also published personal accounts of prison conditions and torture. In a letter signed by thirty-two UGTT members detained at the Sousse civil prison, one prisoner described his experience:

In effect we were encircled by members of the BOP security services, the firefighters corps, the army and the Destourian militia, which ordered us to lift our arms and began to beat us, slap and kick us, along with blows on all parts of the body. . . .

Other trade union members were thrown on the ground, against walls and windows, then stomped. To the point that one comrade suffered a broken vein and has problems with his arm today. . . . The most odious was inflicted upon 10 women who were arrested with us. Their female dignity was besmirched with a rare cruelty. They were insulted, ridiculed, knocked down, and humiliated with degrading gestures and savagely beaten. This lasted until the morning in an atmosphere of terror and fear, in front of agents armed to the hilt and led by A . . . A and M . . . H.[71]

These descriptions used only the first letter of the first and last names of the violent perpetrators, who remained unidentified in the report for fear of retribution. Prisoners received only one piece of harissa-dipped bread per day and had access only to contaminated water twice per day. Thanks in large part to the efforts of the Tunisian Human Rights League, the CTIDVR, and the Collective of 26 January, Achour and several others received presidential pardons on 3 August 1979, well before their ten-year sentences had been served.[72]

Tunisian students at home and abroad joined in denunciations of the regime's use of violence. In Paris, CAL-UGET published a series of tracts detailing its own version of events and called for government reform. Students made historical connections between the Korba Congress of 1971, in which PSD loyalists hijacked the executive office of UGET, and a similar plot executed by Bourguibists in the UGTT, who assailed Achour and the 26 January protests while naming new leadership during a Special Congress in February 1978.[73] In Tunisia, students called for unlimited strikes at universities in Sfax, Tunis, and Monastir when sessions resumed from vacation on 6 February, and regional high schools joined the strikes a few days later. Demonstrators employed tactics similar to those of the French and Senegalese workers of 1968, who used the momentum of the student movement to promote their own initiatives before the government and their employers. This time, however, students fueled the flames of protest already ignited by workers. While calling for the liberation of detained protesters, they also rejected a new policy laid out by Hédi Nouira that refused recognition of degrees granted to Tunisians from politically contentious campuses at Paris 8 in Vincennes and the University of Nanterre.

Yet their support of the UGTT was measured. They were aware of its historical links with the Western-friendly International Confederation of Free Trade Unions, as well as Achour's multiple rebukes of student movements dating to 1968. Tunisian university students in Paris pondered the following, "Must we choose between Sayah and Achour? No, we will not choose between the plague and cholera. We leave this choice to those who stay in the tow of the bourgeoisie."[74] In spite of these critiques of PSD and UGTT leadership, students demanded the immediate liberation of imprisoned labor leaders and identified with "the struggle led by the working class for an autonomous, democratic and combative UGTT [that] is the same as our goals for an autonomous UGET."[75]

The PSD responded with its own propaganda pamphlet, *Contract Politics and the Events of January 1978*, penned by party director Mohamed Sayah.[76] This took a slightly different tone from *The Truth about the Subversion at the University of Tunis* (1968). This time, Sayah devoted an entire section of the pamphlet to data demonstrating Tunisia's economic growth and detailing the terms of the 1977 Social Pact that he claimed were carefully negotiated among the government, the employers, and the union. Through statistical evidence of gradual wage increases, job creation, and increased consumption, the pamphlet cast Achour and the UGTT strikers as traitorous plotters who reneged on a contract with the state and employers. Without citing inflation rates, the pamphlet notes the increases in minimum wages thanks to the Social Pact.[77] Sayah further accused the writers of *Ech-Chaâb*, the mouthpiece of UGTT, of defamation, of psychological preparation for a coup, and of attempting to overthrow the regime. In addition to the new method of leaning on statistics, the PSD deployed battle-tested tactics from the aftermaths of March '68 and February 1972. *L'Action* recycled charges it had leveled against the student movements when it labeled the UGTT as a "union infiltrated by Marxists and Ba'athists," and blamed January 1978 events on "communists, Ba'athists, and agitators linked to Libya."[78]

Contract Politics sought to prove the foreign influence of the French and Libyan national labor unions, again extracting any Tunisian national character from the events. The pamphlet accused UGTT leadership of first inviting France's CGT, "a *foreign* organization to meddle in our internal affairs," and second of commiserating with Libyan labor leaders friendly to the Zionist movement.[79] Just as it had done with Tunisian student agitators a decade earlier, the regime suggested that Achour was acting on behalf of foreign interests, this time in France and Libya. The PSD had experienced the shock and tumult of the end of Ben Salah's collectivization and a new economic liberalization with asymmetrical social impact. It had also sacked former foreign affairs minister Muhammad Masmoudi, who was living in exile in Libya to organize Tunisian immigrant workers abroad and working on a failed attempt at unification with Libya. Another former interior minister, Ahmed Mestiri, broke ties with the PSD in 1973 and, in the wake of Black Thursday, formed the splinter group the Democratic Socialist Movement (Mouvement des Démocrates Socialistes [MDS]). Meanwhile, after being shunned by Bourguiba's administration and blamed for the country's economic problems, Ben Salah headed the Popular Unity Movement (Mouvement d'Unité Populaire

[MUP]) after escaping prison in 1973 and fleeing to Algeria.[80] The PSD clearly faced a new set of challenges from shunned members of its own ranks, and the pamphlet provided an opportunity to marginalize the currents of dissent.

Beyond claiming that protesters terrorized women and children, attacked banks, and pillaged public and private property, the PSD pamphlet also noted a new form of protest. During Ramadan in August 1977, a group of devout UGTT members from Sfax allegedly attacked café and restaurant customers who failed to respect religious fasting during daylight hours. "On this day and the next, for the first time in Tunisia, a wind of fanaticism blew through the city. The vandals were led by the General Secretary of the regional workers' union in Sfax [Abderrazak Ghorbal]."[81] The PSD further pondered, "Has the UGTT become a religious party?"[82] Not only did the regime fear PSD's splinter groups in the likes of Mestiri's MDS and Ben Salah's MUP, but it now faced religious opponents organized through the sole legal labor organization.

The group in Sfax was not merely upset over the regime's economic policies but clearly targeted infidels whose indifference to religious practices had been enabled under Bourguiba's secular reforms. Of course, the framing of these events in the PSD pamphlet should be approached with caution and the direct connections between the assailants and the UGTT called into question. Just as many of the protesters' actions were blamed on foreign influences, the regime also sought to label actions against the state as fanatical. However, with the ascendancy of the Islamist movement in Tunisia in the late 1970s and the creation of the Movement of the Islamic Tendency in 1981, it seems quite likely that some UGTT members may have espoused religious conservatism. Marguerite Rollinde concluded of oppositional Tunisian social movements that "far from weakening the state with their actions, they contributed initially to its reinforcement, through its capacity of repression and recuperation."[83] Given the divisions on the left and the persistence of PSD political power beyond 1978, this perspective is not without merit. Yet the evidence set forth here suggests a slightly more nuanced position. The contestations of March '68, February 1972, and January 1978 led to concerted and consolidated human rights efforts that continued beyond the Bourguiba regime to the present. When the PSD extended repressive measures beyond students to the masses of organized workers in January 1978, the vast network of activists from Tunis to Paris engaged in a successful campaign to release labor leaders and mobilize international public opinion in support of human rights in Tunisia. Resistance also ushered in a new campaign of repression against a rising Islamist movement.

Ultimately, the Tunisian movements of 1968 and 1972 laid the foundation for sustained resistance to the Bourguiba regime that extended far beyond student activism. The honeymoon period between Bourguiba's PSD and Achour's UGTT during the early days of decolonization came to a screeching halt in 1978, when the state faced a more generalized challenge to its authority. Thanks to students' earlier efforts, not only were organizations in place to defend the rights of striking union members, but "intellectual workers" such as teachers and professors had been marked by the university upheaval and educated in the language of resistance. Teachers and university professors organized under the UGTT, and many had participated in either March '68 or February 1972 as students. When Achour finally severed ties with the regime, this intellectual corps of the labor movement supported both labor and student strikes. The rather local causes of the worker strikes—demands to act independently of one-party state rule—set in motion transnational networks of support to secure the rights of political prisoners.

Though the student movement did not directly catalyze the mass worker strikes of January 1978, students were instrumental in providing oppositional discourse and infrastructure to defend human rights. Many of the calls for trade union autonomy and democratic freedoms mirrored the type of decolonization that students had been calling for since 1968. The transnational activism between Paris and Tunis that began in March '68 was revived a decade later, as seen through exile groups like the Tunisian Collective of 26 January and the CTIDVR, and the alternative student groups like CAL-UGET in Paris, which experienced greater success in liberating political prisoners than in the past. Once the labor leadership sought to free itself of the PSD, Tunisia's large nationalized industries in textiles and mining exposed the regime to the collective action of organized workers, as the CGT and CFDT had done in France, and the UNTS in Senegal in 1968.

CHAPTER 6

Immigrant Activism and Activism for Immigrants in France

> *I am convinced that Mai 68 is only the beginning of a much more significant movement.*
>
> —Pierre A. Vidal-Naquet, ex-établi, "Une sombre experience"

The 1970s in France were marked by the increased presence of postcolonial laborers, racist violence, and French antiracism. A ballooning immigrant population, French leftist identification with anti-imperialism and immigrant workers' causes, and a resurgence of right-wing racist extremism converged in the aftermath of 1968. At the heart of this social tension was France's colonial past, which was selectively remembered and re-presented by interest groups on the left and right sides of the political theater. Similar to the intellectual migration patterns that informed the nature of 1968 protests across France and its former empire, labor migration to France shifted the landscape of workers' movements in the 1970s. The increase in immigrant worker protests of the post-1968 era was part and parcel of what Daniel Gordon refers to as the "rise of anti-racism in France," linking the events of France's May '68 to antiracist movements in the 1970s and early 1980s.[1] Taking Gordon's important insights one step further—breaking down foreign workers to focus attention on a subset from France's former colonies—demonstrates how this group had specific postcolonial experiences with labor and protest that marked the activism of the 1970s. Many immigrant workers transformed into activists themselves, at times collaborating with leftist sympathizers against racist attacks. But they also occupied more abstract spaces in the minds of the radical Right and Left, who imagined them, respectively, as either cancerous threats to national unity or legitimate allies in the international revolution.

Indeed, 1968 inspired new French leftist groups to identify with "the working condition," including immigrant causes and new postcolonial projects. They actively sought to organize immigrant workers, with varying degrees of success. Even when immigrant activists resented French support as intrusive, this animus often led immigrant workers to form their own associations and heighten activism. While French organizers may or may not have had particular affinities for immigrants from former colonies over those from Spain or Italy, Spanish and Italian immigrants were not the immediate targets of racist violence by France's radical Right. In a decolonizing world, immigrant workers from North and West Africa faced acute forms of racism that were practiced unevenly by governments, employers, and society writ large. The 1970s in France marked a new era of increased immigrant worker protest and government policies geared specifically toward subsets of postcolonial immigrants.

In more radical cases, anticolonial sensibilities and a desire for concrete experiences led revolutionary Régis Debray, another Louis Althusser student, to engage in armed resistance for Third World liberation in Latin America. Like their French counterparts, North and West African students in France displayed a strong interest in, and identification with, Third World and immigrant worker causes that only increased after 1968. Chérif Ferjani, a Tunisian studying in Lyon in the early 1970s, went on a rather naive and short-lived adventure to the Middle East to train with guerrilla fighters in the Dhofar rebellion; he promptly returned to France after being turned away in Iraq and Syria for lack of a visa.[2] Their actions reflect a common desire for authentic revolution that would be achieved through advocacy and protection of the most repressed communities, against either foreign imperialist threats or domestic racist attacks in France.

Le Monde journalist Jean Lacouture published a recurring column in the spring of 1970 raising the issue of French racism historically and in contemporary French culture. "Les Français sont-ils racistes?" (Are the French racists?) appeared from 20 March through 20 April and probed France's history of anti-Semitism and anti-Arabism from the Dreyfus affair through the Algerian War.[3] The timing of Lacouture's submissions coincided with a surge of violence against immigrants, especially workers, which dates back to France's first wave of colonial immigration during World War I. Recruitment of foreign labor to replace Frenchmen who had left for the front not only precipitated France's first experience with large numbers of ethnic minorities but also led to a marked increase in attacks targeting these immigrants. A second wave of violence took place during the Algerian War, when Paris operated as an active battleground for the Algerian resistance, ushering in an era of French policing that specifically targeted North Africans over other immigrants.[4] Similar turbulence resurfaced in the early 1970s to counter the rise of the New Left and the events of 1968 with the arrival of neofascist groups like New Order (Ordre Nouveau), which wreaked havoc on leftists and North African populations throughout France.

Right-wing groups were emboldened by the massive Gaullist counter-demonstrations on 30 May 1968, with what appeared to be the government's courting of the Right. Presumably to hedge against the leftist threat, Gaullist operatives eased penalties it had imposed on dangerous Far Right leadership of the OAS, a pro-French Algeria group notorious for carrying out terrorist activity during the Algerian War. In June 1968, the de Gaulle government allowed the exiled Georges Bidault to return to France and liberated disgraced generals Raoul Salan and Edmond Jouhaud, despite some of them being convicted of war crimes.[5] At the same time, French interior minister Raymond Marcellin dissolved multiple leftist groups, including Cohn-Bendit's March 22 movement and Alain Krivine's JCR. Occident clashed with left-wing groups like the Anti-fascist University Front and the UJC(ml) at demonstrations. The right-wing Occident was finally banned in October 1968 after a series of escalating violent acts. Not to be deterred, former Occident members launched the Ordre Nouveau (New Order) in 1969, which continued to antagonize leftist and immigrant groups. While historians have long characterized 1930s' right-wing politics as an antidote to perceived Marxist and Jewish threats, Todd Shepard suggests that the postwar era reflected a diversion of anti-Semitic energy toward "a ballooning anti-Arab obsession."[6] This postcolonial shift was reflected in right-wing publications like *Combat* and *Minute*, which blamed youth drug use, sexual deviance, and prostitution at Nanterre on "Algerian inhabitants of the surrounding *bidonville* (ghetto) and Algerian students."[7] Fears of "an Arab invasion" that could only be confronted with white male virility to protect France's vulnerable were in fact expressions of the Right's own version of postcolonial nationalism. Anxious over losing their white supremacy, the Right increased its attacks on the immigrant population in the early 1970s, prompting leftists to engage in antiracist activism and, in some cases, to strengthen bonds with postcolonial immigrant communities forged out of the events of 1968.

Organizations such as the Communist League, an offshoot of the defunct JCR, joined immigrant workers in confronting Far Right attacks and rejecting new anti-leftist and anti-immigration policies of Georges Pompidou's government.[8] With Communist League leader Alain Krivine's support of foreign workers, France's colonial past was brought to the fore of post-1968 struggles, which were bound up in racism, immigration, and the memory of Algeria.

The government's crackdowns on leftist militant groups laid bare its position toward both past and present activism. Even incarceration of activist leaders did not prevent certain Trotskyists from engaging in a hunger strike to rebuke the French judicial system and take up the cause of working-class immigrants. In a pamphlet published by François Maspero, *Ce que veut la Ligue communiste* (What the Communist League wants), Krivine called for solidarity with foreign and immigrant workers and proposed a plan of *alphabétisation* whereby French communists would implement strategies to eradicate illiteracy among foreign workers.[9] He also used the Communist League's active participation against a New Order rally in 1971 and its outreach to immigrant workers to illustrate the authenticity of the league compared with the impotence of the more moderate PCF.[10] In addition to Krivine's support, a group of activists were arrested for circulating copies of the Proletarian Left's *La cause du peuple*—the group's journal created in May 1968 by Roland Castro—and later published a series of prison writings.

One prisoner noted that the majority of inmates were "young rebels, immigrant workers, and people hit with bourgeois repression."[11] Activists such as Jean-Noël Darde and Serge Minoc declared solidarity with immigrants who were forced into abominable living conditions, hazardous workplaces, and terrible pay. One issue of *La cause du peuple*, in which Darde and Minoc accused prominent industrialists like Henri de Wendel of assassinating workers by knowingly placing them in hostile work environments, resulted in the arrest of the two activists. What outraged them almost as much as de Wendel consciously exposing workers to toxic chemicals was the stacked legal system that had liberated OAS war criminals while cracking down on leftist free speech. While de Wendel faced no legal consequences for his failure to protect employees, "we have a false tribunal created specially for fascists of the OAS, where people who are regularly accused of espionage are going to judge me for having distributed a journal stating that M. de Wendel assassinated people in his factories and that he should be judged."[12] Darde, along with Maoists Gilles Sussong and Jean Stefanaggi, circulated tracts denouncing the municipality of Argenteuil for restricting the housing of Muslim workers in favor of card-carrying members of the PCF and whites who paid bribes under the table.[13] Another inmate, Nicolas Canu, drew direct historical connections between the Nazi collaboration under the Vichy regime and the authorities' response in the aftermath of 1968. According to Canu, "France has not seen since the repression of German Nazis and French police collaborators against the resistance, or since the repression of the French army and police against the FLN."[14] The accusations of detained militants like Canu and Darde thus mobilized the colonial memory of the Algerian War to link right-wing extremism with

French policing. Given the release of OAS members and the lack of charges brought against derelict employers like de Wendel, the state's position was clear to Canu and Darde: tacit approval of crimes against North Africans and concerted efforts to suppress both immigrants and their advocates on the left.

As they had done in 1968, activists continued to revisit the experiences of 17 October 1961 and Charonne to denounce the repetition of racist violence that the war had brought home to the streets of Paris. Before heading the teachers' union and becoming a member of the Proletarian Left in 1968, Alain Geismar was active in anti-imperialist organizations as a student in the early 1960s, which clashed regularly with the Right over Algerian independence during the war. For Geismar, the police violence of 1968 and beyond recalled earlier iterations from his antiwar activism. "All of that reminded me of what happened at the end of the Algerian War, at the time of the major FLN demonstrations when Algerians were thrown in the Seine, the era when Papon was police commissioner. For us there was a sort of continuity in police actions there."[15] Charonne in particular continued to operate as a political space for rejecting police violence well after the conclusion of the Algerian War. On 28 February 1972, Geismar participated in a cortege commemorating Maoist Pierre Overney, who was killed a few days earlier by plant security during a protest at the Renault-Billancourt auto factory. Geismar and other mourners consciously selected the site of Charonne to protest brutality against activists and drew comparisons between the unjust violence of the OAS and the CRS police forces.[16]

Overney, the inspiration for the Charonne protest, had been a member of the Proletarian Left and one of the établis hard-liners who clandestinely entered the workforce for the purpose of revolutionizing workers. Both Overney and fellow établi Robert Linhart lied about their education in order to take manual labor jobs, with Linhart landing a position at the Citroën-Choisy plant.[17] Despite his lack of experience and job skills, Linhart earned higher wages than the majority of immigrant workers owing to his skin color and French citizenship. Linhart effectively organized majority immigrant laborers to stage a strike in February 1969 against prolonged work hours without remuneration.[18] While the strike succeeded in briefly slowing operations, Linhart and his followers were unable to secure the shorter work day, and Citroën employed such strikebreaking strategies as physical violence, firing, threat of deportation, and the eviction of immigrants from company-owned housing.[19] Despite their limited success, back-to-the-factory organizers like Linhart and Overney reveal the importance of immigrants for the 1968 generation, as both direct actors and victims of gross oppression whose rights as humans and workers had been violated. Even établis who may not have intended specifically to reach immigrants often found themselves in immigrant-heavy industries where they established new opportunities to collaborate.[20] When protesting the violent repression of activists—whether the antiwar Algerians and French communists of the early 1960s or Maoists like Overney in 1972—politically charged sites like Charonne remained important spaces of postcolonial struggle.

French leftists were not alone in reactivating metonyms surrounding immigrant oppression. On 17 October 1968, exactly seven years after the 1961 atrocities in which French police murdered North African protesters, Algerian head of government Houari Boumedienne declared that 17 October would henceforth be commemorated as National Emigration Day. In addition, Boumedienne responded to French anti-immigrant violence and racist immigration restrictions by temporarily suspending all immigration to France on 19 September 1973.[21] Messoudi Zitoumi, spokesman for the Algerian provisional government's information minister, issued a warning that Algeria would order the return of Algerians to their home country "unless French authorities took measures to allow 'the Algerian colony to live in conditions other than anxiety and terror.'"[22] The massacre of 17 October and the police violence of Charonne thus resonated in the political consciousness of actors in France and Algeria, whether they were leftist students, racist neofascists, or North African officials. Events taking place within France at the local level rippled across national borders to Algeria and dictated the transnational state policies of both nations. Not only did various groups deploy similar symbols for their own purposes, but they also revived France's and Algeria's collective colonial pasts to make claims about their postcolonial presents.

One of the most egregious acts of unatoned racism of this era occurred when a fifteen-year-old Algerian boy was killed on 27 October 1971 in the Parisian immigrant neighborhood of the Goutte d'Or. Djellali Ben Ali was shot in the back by his apartment concierge's husband, Daniel Pigot, in what became known as the Djellali affair. Community members confirmed Pigot's penchant for spewing racist vitriol directed toward Arabs, yet authorities failed to initially launch an investigation into Ben Ali's death. The Palestine Committees (Comités Palestine [CP])—a group of pan-Arab nationalists and French Maoists—recalled Charonne when reaching out to immigrant communities who were dealing with this act of violent racism.[23] Though the event was tragic, it mobilized several elements of a fractured French Left, who joined immigrant activists in denouncing racism. Among the many significant factors surrounding the Djellali affair was that it brought together Jean-Paul Sartre and Michel Foucault, both of whom had previously engaged in public media mudslinging. Sartre had accused Foucault of abdicating his responsibilities to promote social change, whereas Foucault criticized Sartre's simplistic positions on Marxism and structuralism.[24] Had he not experienced the horrors of Tunisia's 1968, which Foucault proclaimed had "forced [him] to enter the political debate," he might have been more reticent to join Sartre for immigrant causes in Paris.[25] The outcry against this racist injustice unified formerly opposed intellectuals, radical French and North African youth, and North African immigrant workers. At the same time, it marked a shift in the sites of resistance beyond the student milieu of the Latin Quarter to the heart of the North African working-class community in Paris: the streets of Barbès and the Goutte d'Or.

A committee for Djellali organized two large demonstrations in late November and early December 1971. The committee's efforts at justice for Djellali expanded into larger community-building projects like the *alphabétisation* of illiterate immigrants and legal assistance for filling out employment- and immigrant-related paperwork. These had limited success, and the early engagement with Goutte d'Or residents on the part of superstar intellectuals did not endure. There were also a number of tensions among activists whose relationships to the Djellali affair differed significantly. For some pan-Arabists within the CP, the Goutte d'Or provided a potential breeding ground for recruitment to the Palestinian cause. Foucault, on the other hand, deplored racism and inhumane living conditions, yet was sympathetic to the plight of Israelis. He also decried the prison system, finding it extremely difficult to take a strong position in the case where many were calling for Pigot's head or life in a jail cell.[26] Djellali's murderer was not brought to justice until 1977, when he received a sentence of five years in prison. Yet the significance of the affair spread far beyond the streets of the Goutte d'Or. The Franco-Tunisian Committee for the Protection of Human Rights in Tunisia also linked the affair to the long-term imprisonment of Foucault's former student Ahmed Ben Othmani.[27] Activists from Tunis to Paris accused state officials of repressing Maghrebi youth, and Tunisians in Paris tracked and reported repression and mobilized in the defense of victims abroad.

The Paris-based CP issued a pro-Palestinian platform as early as February 1969 and grew in numbers in September 1970 (Black September) after King Hussein's army forces killed thousands of Palestinians in an effort to expel the Palestinian Liberation Organization from Jordan. The CP sent money and supplies to the Red Crescent to show political support for the Palestinian cause. The group consisted of newly arrived students in Paris who were not necessarily engaged in politics in their home countries, workers who had been politicized by the Palestinian struggle, and the French radical Left.[28] Though they formed around the singular political issue of Palestinian liberation, their participation in the antiracist protest of Djellali's death demonstrated a new engagement with social issues within the larger diasporic Arab community, and not just Palestinian politics. Rabah Aissaoui has argued that out of a fear that "their movement might run out of steam," the CP transformed into the MTA in June 1972 in order to fight French racism and to better address immigrant workers' causes.[29] In addition to these motivations, the MTA was also created out of competition with other French activist groups on the left, such as the Cahiers de mai and the Proletarian Left, which had been reaching out to Arab workers since 1968.

Immigrant Activism in Post-'68 France: The Cahiers de mai, Penarroya, and the MTA

On 9 February 1972, workers at factories in Lyon and Saint-Denis (on the outskirts of Paris) put down their tools to protest depressed wages, unsafe equipment, and deplorable housing conditions. Among their many complaints were a lack of masks to combat lead inhalation and the death of a colleague on site that was covered up by employers. These were the first coordinated efforts in France of immigrant workers across factories, and they were soon joined by workers at the Penarroya factory in Escaudoeuvres near the Belgian border in northern France. Though each factory strike experienced its own trajectory, the over one hundred North African workers at the Lyon Penarroya site worked most intimately with the French Left, held out the longest during negotiations with employers, and achieved the most gains of any factory site. After a little over five weeks of coordinated action, they obtained 18 percent wage increases, relocation to better housing offsite, the release of their medical records, and a full-time on-site nurse.[30]

Founded in the 1880s by the Rothschild family to mine and manufacture nickel, the Penarroya Trust employed over four thousand workers in France and over twelve thousand total in twenty-eight countries by 1972. The industrial powerhouse was the second-highest revenue generator in France, ranked fourth Europe-wide, and could claim then French president Georges Pompidou as a member of its board of trustees.[31] The trust had been mining in Tunisia since at least the 1930s and also had operations in Morocco, Burkina Faso, Mauritania, Ivory Coast, Namibia, Gabon, and Madagascar, as well as throughout Latin America.[32] Several Penarroya metal refineries were located in France, and the factories recruited the bulk of the labor force directly from former French colonies during the decolonization period from the 1950s through the 1970s, or from neighboring European nations.[33]

At the Penarroya-Gerland factory in Lyon, North Africans lived in housing units adjacent to the factory. Two workers shared one bed, with one working a night shift and the other working the day shift so that they alternated usage of the living quarters. They were not allowed to wash up for meals, which resulted in the ingestion of lead from their hands. Workers inhaled fumes throughout the workday and in the evenings since the factories operated around the clock and their living quarters were on company property. While the factory conducted physical exams of its employees, workers did not have access to their own medical records. Independent doctors brought in by French activists to examine workers diagnosed several of them with saturnism (lead poisoning). The Penarroya Trust knew about problems with saturnism in its factories as early as 1936, when workers at a Tunisian plant were prescribed one liter of milk per day and a weekly shower as antidotes to lead poisoning.[34]

The 1972 Penarroya strikes provide a critical example of the direction of social movements in the post-1968 era, as well as the type of collaboration necessary for the realization of a movement's goals. Whether through direct contact or through the media, it is also highly probable that the Tunisian workers at the Penarroya factory in Lyon helped spark a concurrent strike in March 1972 at a Penarroya site in Megrine, Tunisia, in the environs of Tunis. The leader of the Megrine strike, Belgacem Kharchi, was later arrested by Tunisian authorities for his participation in the January 1978 general workers' strike following Black Thursday.[35] The simultaneity of the strikes at the Megrine and Lyon factories suggests that North African workers in Tunisia and France were in touch with each other, or at least aware of each other's actions. The French and Tunisian state responses were similar in each case, where strikers in Lyon and Tunis were evacuated from factory buildings by armed police officers.

If immigrant worker activism was somewhat limited in 1968, this was certainly not the case by the early 1970s. Kristin Ross found that "far-left groups in May and June acted as a catalyst for distinctly new forms of expression, representation, and mobilization of immigrant workers; by 1970, rent strikes, hunger strikes, squatting, and other collective struggles unseen before May '68 began to bring immigrants into direct confrontation with the state apparatus."[36] Rather than merely following suit, the Penarroya workers indeed shaped the nature of their claims. However, evidence also suggests that collaboration with French activist organizations was absolutely crucial to the success of the strikes, which would likely not have been as extensive without the influence and memory of 1968. One activist group, the Cahiers de mai, which emerged in May 1968 and became an advocate for immigrants in France, took a particularly strong interest in organizing at Penarroya factories in the 1970s.

The Cahiers de mai assisted workers in drafting their claims and coordinated efforts with French and immigrant workers at other Penarroya factories in Saint-Denis and Escaudoeuvres.[37] Members also located and funded translators to attend general assembly meetings and transcribe hearings to distribute to the other factories. Cahiers de mai attracted public attention to the workers' plight, created a committee of support, and raised funds that were critical for striking workers to survive. These funds also paid for train tickets that ensured the circulation of workers between factories to attend general assemblies, to produce a film documenting working and living conditions, and to organize galas where celebrities raised funds for the cause.[38] In this regard, the Cahiers de mai can be seen as facilitators and messengers for the immigrant cause (see figures 4A and 4B). They provided an infrastructure and organization that helped workers articulate their goals in such a way that the Penarroya workers were able to win over public opinion and sustain their struggle until their demands were met.

Even after new safety measures were put in place across France, Penarroya metallurgy factories remained dangerous. Cahiers de mai activist Michel Leclercq, who helped connect workers with doctors in the 1970s, continued his advocacy at Moroccan Penarroya factories after learning that more than thirty children of workers had died in 1981, allegedly from lead poisoning.[39]

Without the coordinating efforts of the Cahiers de mai, it is doubtful that Penarroya immigrant workers would have come into contact with workers at its other factories facing similar problems, or that they would have been able to overcome the financial burden of a long-term strike. And yet, collaboration between workers and the French Left was not without tension. After the work-related death of blacksmith Georges Ravier at a Vénissieux Berliet factory on the outskirts of Lyon, a group of blacksmiths expressed annoyance at a tract distributed by "a Maoist enquête group" at the factory. Drawing on Linhart's method, the new strategy developed by French Maoists and employed by the Cahiers de mai, enquête was designed to eliminate the vertical communication of union leadership in favor of "liaison between factories so frequently disparaged."[40] Instead, enquête would place "the project under the direction and control of workers . . . [resembling] any number of experiments in collective authorship 'from below' that proliferated in those years."[41] Though the enquête methods had the opposite of the desired effect among skeptical blacksmiths, in the case of Penarroya-Gerland in Lyon, the Cahiers de mai successfully facilitated communication between workers from different factories, and workers themselves controlled funds to cover the daily needs of those on strike.

Yet the Penarroya–Saint-Denis strike, which was led and negotiated by the CGT in the sort of "vertical" relationship described above (as opposed to the more autonomous negotiations of the Lyon group), lasted only one day after CGT negotiators were offered 3 percent wage increases and promises to discuss other demands further once the 550 workers returned to their posts.[42]

**n° 3
3 frs**

mars 74

bulletin

du comité de soutien

aux revendications

des travailleurs

de penarroya

Pour toute correspondance :
- Section syndicale CFDT de Penarroya-Lyon

Driss FARHANE
Ramadane SAADOUNI
Laïd AGGOUN

Foyer-hôtel SONACOTRA
148 avenue Félix Faure
69003 LYON

- Comité de soutien aux revendications des travailleurs de Penarroya
Docteur Gérard BENDRIHEM   35 rue Bichat   69002 LYON

FIGURE 4A. "Bulletin du comité de soutien aux revendications des travailleurs de Penarroya" (Bulletin of the Committee of Support of the Demands of the Penarroya Workers), no. 3 (March 1974). Reproduced with permission from La contemporaine, in Fonds Othmani, Collection La contemporaine/cote FDR_578_70.

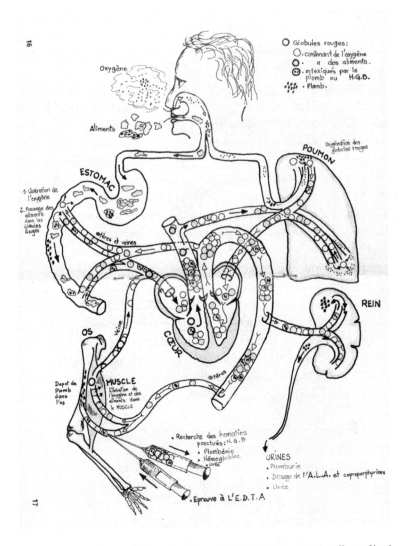

Figure 4B. Diagram from the Cahiers de mai pamphlet detailing the negative effects of lead inhalation on workers at the Penarroya factory. "Bulletin du comité de soutien aux revendications des travailleurs de Penarroya" (Bulletin of the Committee of Support of the Demands of the Penarroya Workers), no. 3 (March 1974). Reproduced with permission from La contemporaine, in Fonds Othmani, Collection La contemporaine/cote FDR_578_70.

For the blacksmiths at Vénissieux, Maoist opportunists had manufactured the details of their colleague's death. In a hostile message to an *enquête* group, union members warned that "the unified blacksmiths have no lessons to learn from these individuals who are controlled by remote and who try to turn attention to management. Mao, go practice workerism in the salons from where you came, but not in front of our factories, and definitely not by using our deaths to serve yourself."[43] The acceptance of external activism by workers was thus uneven, and workers and organizers faced challenges coordinating united fronts across factories and industries.

The eventual success of the Penarroya strike in Lyon informed social movement strategies for groups that were not directly involved. For example, the CP, initially formed in support of Palestinian liberation, evolved into the more worker-conscious MTA after Penarroya. What began in 1970 as a collaborative political movement between members of the primarily French Proletarian Left and various Arab leftists shifted significantly toward a more autonomous movement focused on the daily needs of Arabs living in France. The MTA was formed out of the first national Arab workers conference held in June 1972 in Paris, gathering Arab workers and activists from over ten industrial regions throughout France to discuss their postcolonial situation. Indeed, the combination of post–World War II reconstruction efforts and the economic boom of the Thirty Glorious Years (1945–1975) in France led to rapid increases in North African immigrant populations.[44] In the aftermath of the bloody Algerian War, these groups faced the challenges of racial profiling, emotional and economic abuse by employers, and dangerous living conditions often linked to their employment. The conference's chronological proximity to the Penarroya strikes no doubt prompted participants to evaluate lessons learned for Arab workers moving forward, and to interrogate the utility of coordinating with other French groups.

Activists weighed the merits of creating an autonomous, Arab-led group versus continued collaboration with French Maoists. As a result, they vowed to better organize Arabs in France, merging the struggle for Palestinian liberation with the daily struggles of exploited Arab workers. While conference delegates from the northeastern town Douai portrayed the French Maoists as friends who were "leading the same struggle as us against imperialism and colonialism," representatives from Genevilliers, a northern suburb of Paris, pushed for "a truly autonomous organization" because "when we're Arab and we want to lead a struggle, we shouldn't have to seek out a French organization. We must organize ourselves to decide on and lead our own struggles."[45] Others resented French labor unions like the CFDT, which made decisions on behalf of workers without holding the more democratic general assemblies.

In voicing frustration over the lack of support of the Penarroya strikes by the Arab activist community, one meeting attendee lamented that "the CFDT organizes Arabs across factories, and it's the CFDT which speaks in the name of the Arab struggle! So why can't Arabs organize themselves!"[46] The success at mobilizing immigrant workers witnessed by the French Left, and even more mainstream unions like the CFDT and CGT, propelled the MTA to compete with French organizations over constituents and influence over Arab communities. In spite of their turn toward autonomy and the specific needs of Arab immigrants in France, the MTA continued to work with French groups like the Proletarian Left. Many MTA members also broke ties with North African Amicale organizations from their home countries because of suspicions that they were linked to both the French state and state agencies back home.[47] Just as 1968 led to increased attention to foreign workers on the part of French activists, it had a similar impact on groups like the MTA, which gradually shifted toward *sans-papiers* (without papers) causes.

The MTA's increased activity coincided with a spike in violence against immigrants, primarily targeting North Africans. At least twelve Algerian workers were murdered across France in just over one month in the summer of 1973, but lackluster investigations did not lead to any convictions.[48] Anti-Arab public sentiment enabled French legislation like the 1972 Marcellin-Fontanet decrees, aimed at restricting immigration to "desirable groups" who were thought to be more "assimilable" (i.e., white Europeans). With the oil crisis of 1973, France's period of rapid industrialization, as well as its desire for immigrant labor, had attenuated. In what Catherine Wihtol de Wenden has called a critical moment in the politicization of immigration, the Marcellin-Fontanet decrees limited residence to workers with full-time employment and encouraged repatriation.[49] Under the new plan, workers would have to obtain a one-year work contract with a specific employer before being eligible for a residency permit (*carte de séjour*), which subjected laid-off or seasonal workers to the status of "illegal alien" and ineligible for unemployment benefits. One of the MTA founders, Tunisian activist Saïd Bouziri, responded to the decrees with a series of hunger strikes and the creation of the Committee in Support of Life and the Rights of Immigrant Workers (Comité de Défense de la Vie et des Droits des Travailleurs Immigrés).[50]

Bouziri's actions began in Paris but set off hunger strikes in Valence in December 1972 when eighteen Tunisian immigrant workers were threatened with deportation related to the decrees. One of the Tunisians facing deportation, Rabah Saïdani, had joined Bouziri in his first Parisian hunger strike and brought this tactic to Valence.[51] The relationship among the workers, their employers, the state, and the law was laden with postcolonial dimensions. North Africans in the community were targeted by corrupt police and faced regular threats of deportation. Workers had left the economically depressed Maghreb in search of employment in the territory of their former colonial oppressor. Many employers withheld official pay stubs from specifically North African worker populations to avoid paying unemployment insurance. Journalist

Michel Duyrat, a writer for the Proletarian Left publication *La cause du peuple*, interviewed a number of the hunger-striking Tunisians who described their various predicaments. Even those who had proper papers and a valid French social security number faced the threat of a corrupt police commissioner known as "Tebessi," who notoriously extorted monthly fees from the Moroccan and Algerian café owners in exchange for allowing them to operate.[52]

Tebessi was an Algerian police chief of French nationality who allegedly targeted Tunisians since he viewed them as racially inferior. He was reported to have arranged the deportation of an Algerian café owner who refused to pay the monthly bribe. In 1962, Tebessi survived an assassination attempt by three FLN operatives in Valence who were later captured and mutilated by Tebessi in the local police station. Once Saïdani's 1972 hunger strike began, Tebessi visited all of the North African cafés to warn against the strikes, claiming he could sort out the paperwork but would ensure strikers' deportation in cases of noncompliance. Yet many employers refused to give immigrant workers pay stubs, which were necessary to obtain a social security number. Other employers lied to hospital staff who were treating work-related injuries, claiming that they had never employed the immigrants. Even those whose papers were in order were brought to the station by Tebessi, stripped of their clothing, and forced to sit in isolation for several hours before being released.[53]

One strike supporter made direct correlations between the harsh conditions for immigrant workers and the postcolonial political situation in Tunisia.

> No politics; we want to live in our own country where we were born and where we left our families. The Bourguiba regime controls the radio and the press to abuse and blind the Tunisian people. THE SUPREME COMBATANT IS THE PEOPLE.
>
> The students' struggle is our struggle and the people's struggle. The Bourguibist regime equals bourgeois exploitation of the people. We want to know where all the money is going?! Fifteen years of independence. Nothing has changed. How long will Bourguibist politics leave us to live abroad far from our land and our families? Tortured, naked, exploited, underpaid, and poorly housed. These are Bourguiba's promises? Before leaving the country, we were told that France is paradise. But unfortunately it's hell for us Tunisians.[54]

Rather than targeting French immigration policies like the Marcellin-Fontanet decrees, in this instance the strike supporter outlined how Tunisian workers deemed Bourguiba to be directly responsible for the plight of his countrymen abroad. The author recycled student slogans in an identification with their democratization movement. The hunger strike also sensitized a number of other groups in the Valence community. A local church provided meeting space and engaged French supporters while CFDT delegates marched alongside the strikers at rallies. One regularized Algerian worker joined the movement after police drove him fifty kilometers from Valence in the middle of the night and left him to walk home. "After that, I joined the strike with my Tunisian comrades against these racists. . . . The expulsions today are for Tunisians. That could be us tomorrow."[55] Others referenced the Algerian War by chanting FLN slogans such as "war against racism" and "war against narks."[56] Ultimately, the hunger strikers' mobilization of a cross-section of Valence, coupled with the national media attention the strike received, resulted in Minister of State Edgar Faure's lifting of the expulsion orders and issuing a Christmas Day promise to provide the eighteen Tunisians with residency and work permits.[57]

Indeed, the restrictive immigration practices and anti-Arab violence set off a series of protests by North Africans in the 1970s. Right-wing papers like *Le Meridional* in Marseille supported New Order activity denouncing "Algerian syphilitics, Algerian rapists, Algerian pimps, Algerian lunatics, Algerian killers . . . ," and Marseille groups warned against "the Brown Threat," mirroring earlier anti-Arab racism targeting students and workers from Nanterre in 1968. Yet these expressions of postcolonial white nationalism moved immigrant organizations like the MTA to stage strikes in Marseille, Toulon, Toulouse, and Paris in September 1973.[58] Whether reacting to repression from employers, French government expulsions, or violent, often neofascist thugs, Maghrebi workers overcame fears of a repeat of 17 October 1961 by organizing en masse. In February 1972 they assembled on behalf of a Maghrebi worker who had been killed by equipment that employers knew was faulty, and in the spring of 1973 hundreds of militants at the Renault plant outside Paris demanded equal pay for equal work. This culminated in a strike of nine thousand migrant workers at the Renault factory and sparked rent strikes over dreadful housing conditions in bidonvilles.[59] Despite the threat of arrest and deportation, immigrants participated in increasingly large numbers after the wave of violence in the summer of 1973.

Beyond North Africa: Sub-Saharan African Protest Movements in 1970s France

North Africans were not the only immigrant group in France to actively resist following May '68. Abdoulaye Gueye has addressed an "imbalance in the research literature" on immigrant activism in France by highlighting non-Maghrebi African protest movements.[60] It is worth noting, however, that this imbalance is in part due to the large difference in the number of immigrants across nationalities and regions. For example, officially there were only 20,000 sub-Saharan immigrants in France in 1962 versus nearly 500,000 from North Africa, though some have estimated that, by 1969, the number of sub-Saharan African immigrants was between 200,000 and 250,000.[61] The 50 percent devaluation of Malian currency in 1967 combined with the poor harvest and reduction in market price of Senegalese peanuts (groundnut) in 1968 facilitated the French recruitment of African labor as thousands fled dire straits.[62]

As part of the government crackdown on migration in Interior Minister Marcellin's moment of panic, the African House, the primary residence for African students in Paris, was shut down and its residents were expelled in August 1972. This move coincided with the government's attempt to close down other residence halls of Congolese and Ivoirian students. Again in August 1973, police forcefully evacuated students from the Upper Volta (Burkina Faso) living in a designated apartment building in Paris, which doubled as the seat of their student organization. While at least a dozen of the evacuated students had permission to reside there, as many as thirty others were staying while on vacation, eliciting a police response and an order of expulsion without a proper hearing. Following news of the eviction, FEANF declared solidarity with the students from the Upper Volta in protest of immigrant repression.[63]

In 1970, the Senegalese journalist and intellectual Jean-Pierre N'Diaye dedicated a book on the Black workers of France to the memory of five Black laborers who died of asphyxiation during a fire at an immigrant slum in Aubervilliers. A slumlord had converted an abandoned factory into sleeping quarters and had cut off heat to portions of the building in the middle of winter for lack of payment. Some tenants resorted to starting a fire in a trashcan, causing exposure to toxic levels of carbon monoxide.[64] Maoists from the Proletarian Left framed the incident as a product of capitalist neo-imperialism. Literary celebrities Marguerite Duras and Jean Genet occupied the headquarters of an employers' lobbying group alongside immigrants. French prime minister Jacques Chaban-Delmas then launched an investigation into the three hundred or so immigrant worker slums that had sprouted up in Paris during the Thirty Glorious Years. The investigation produced a plan to eradicate Paris of the inhabitable dwellings, which the prime minister deemed a "symbol of anti-modernity."[65]

Yet without the initial interest in the immigrant workers' cause of the 68er generation, it is unlikely that the Aubervilliers tragedy would have garnered such media attention. As N'Diaye noted, "The 'incident' became an event, feeding the written and spoken press for 15 days."[66] Immigrant deaths caused by poor living conditions were no rarity, yet the Aubervilliers incident drew national media attention and the support of the activist community. It marked the beginning of sustained action on the part of, and on behalf of, the immigrant community that would endure throughout the 1970s. Aubervilliers was also a product of the radical Left's heightened interest in France's most vulnerable after 1968. This increased attention earned intellectual stars like Jean Genet a broken wrist and Pierre Emmanuel Vidal-Naquet a bloodied face when CRS riot police intervened during a demonstration documented by national media. Finally, Aubervilliers swung potential immigrant protesters into action, as Malians from the Ivy shantytown occupied their landlord's office in the aftermath of the tragic incident turned event.[67]

Like their French counterparts, the immigrant worker movement was thus about working conditions and wages. But it was also about overpriced rents, unbearable living quarters, and racism. In 1972, sub-Saharan African immigrants coordinated rent strikes against the plans of the National Company of Housing Construction for Workers (Société Nationale de Construction de Logements pour les Travailleurs [Sonacotra]) to relocate them to new projects. Since employers were integrally involved in the construction and administration of the housing units, they could impose restrictions on the tenants such as curfews and limits on visitation, which they intended to implement in the new units. Abdoulaye Gueye has argued that at the root of the protesters' claims was their resistance to "an attempt to imprison them in the condition of factory workers."[68] While attempts to garner French public support varied in success across regions, Sonacotra housing units faced repeated rent strikes throughout the 1970s from this point forward. Coordinated efforts peaked in 1975 when majority Algerian residents linked up with Senegalese and Malian tenants to denounce 30 percent rent hikes. A Coordination Committee of residents and Maoists advocated and negotiated for residents, though they never achieved official recognition from Sonacotra or the government, and they were not able to obtain a special category of tenants' rights for immigrant residents.[69]

The African immigrant worker movement was in many ways separate from the African student movement. While FEANF members were quick to denounce evictions and expulsions of Ivoirian and Upper Volta students from the African House, support of immigrant workers was less uniform. Challenges with connecting workers and students were brought to light at a meeting in Paris organized by the Office of African Studies and Research (Bureau d'études et des recherches Africaines [BERA]) as early as the mid-1960s. Outside of the racism that immigrant laborers endured from employers and slumlords, they also faced classism from privileged African students who, in some cases, expressed conservative anti-immigrant views.

Following one worker's call for students to assist them with learning to read and navigate a foreign legal system, one student—whose cousin was an ambassadorial adviser—had this to say:

> What you have to consider is this: these African workers, once they've acquired job training and returned to Africa, they want cars and villas. This guy left Africa on 3 March with papers to take a tour of all the states that send workers here and to collect subsidies. I'm aware of the action undertaken by BERA, but I find that it's bad to give clothes, etc., which promote laziness, and we can see the creation of this laziness if they get used to receiving clothing, coats, and other goods. I think that out of the 70,000 A.F. [Central African francs] that they earn each month, it should be possible to sustain 20,000 A.F. to by a coat or something wind-proof.[70]

Another African student insisted that workers explain exactly why they emigrated and what they expected on arrival. Pan-African solidarity was nowhere to be found with the following commentary: "We see them in the metro, in the streets, everywhere they are poorly dressed, they don't speak French. The real problem is that they [should] stay in Africa. Now the worker comrade should tell us with precision why he came here."[71] Not all responses to African immigrants were so hostile. Some participants found it obvious that Africans immigrated to France because there was no work in home countries and they needed to feed their families. Sub-Saharan African workers from largely peasant backgrounds often found themselves on the bottom rung of the labor ladder, behind Portuguese and North African counterparts who either had been in-country long enough to develop skilled trades or had previous exposure to mechanized industry before arrival.

Indeed there were efforts by FEANF members to work with the Senegalese Amicale, though this was an apolitical organization and could not advocate for workers' rights in the same manner as a union. Senegalese activist Sally N'Dongo was instrumental in the creation of the General Union of Senegalese Workers in France (Union Générale des Travailleurs Sénégalais en France [UGTSF]) in 1961. In a reversal of the trajectories of the CP and the MTA, which shifted from political goals to material needs, the UGTSF was originally established to provide services to Senegalese immigrants but transformed in the 1970s to address France's neocolonial economic and political relationship to Senegal.[72] Rather than blaming the poor conditions of African workers on the immigrants themselves, N'Dongo put forward a more systemic view, arguing that French colonialism was in fact the culprit. French colonialism had produced Senegalese single-crop dependency, dissuading agricultural differentiation while reserving mechanized industrial production to France's borders. N'Dongo charged that French employers intentionally recruited *sans-papiers* to avoid paying workmen's compensation benefits and making double profits through overpriced and degraded housing, all at the expense of African immigrants over whom they lorded contacting authorities with the threat of deportation.[73]

Yet while Tunisian students in 1974 called for greater coordination with workers, and organizations like the MTA brought the two groups together, this merger was not so evident in the sub-Saharan African case.[74] When asked about the Senegalese student perception of African immigrants, one Dakar 68er responded, "That was pretty far from our preoccupations. . . . The drought was worse and closer to home. [Emigration] was a solution for these people to leave and find work. It was a strategy to be able to support their families. It's tough. It's true they suffered exploitation, terrible living conditions and hard labor, etc. . . . But, let's just say, it was a choice, just like today. But they thought that arriving in Europe no matter what the conditions, that it would be better than living here. Domestic questions were more at the center of our preoccupations."[75] These comments illustrate that there were certainly limits to the fascination with immigrant workers, even on the left. The statements cited here were more measured than the classist reaction of some African students living in Paris, who directed a sense of disdain and even shame toward illiterate and poorly dressed African laborers. Yet there was still a sentiment that immigrants met their fates abroad by choice. African students' attitudes regarding displaced African labor reflected another form of postcolonial nationalism. Immigrant workers were not met with blanket sympathy since they had, through free will, abandoned their developing nations without seeking job training or skills to bring home. And if sympathy was a finite sentiment to be rationed, sub-Saharan African immigrants would receive far less of it from the African intellectual base than their brothers and sisters in Senegal, who faced drought and dismal harvests, or those in Mali, who had to cope with severe currency devaluations.

Generally speaking, the activism of 1968 produced a desire for putting revolutionary theories into practice through direct engagement with society's most oppressed groups. In France, this created acute attention to immigrant causes by the radical Left, as evidenced in the emergence of both the établis and the Cahiers de mai. In many cases, these groups were able to help immigrant workers achieve real material gains through collective action. These limited successes prompted increased direct action on the part of immigrants. Arabs in France sought autonomous organizations led *by* Arab workers and *for* Arab workers. Once mobilized, the MTA hoped their actions would simultaneously act as a force for both social change (in France) and political change (in the Arab world). While the Left elevated the profile of immigrant workers, the trauma of the Algerian War dovetailed with fears of rising immigrant populations to produce a postcolonial white nationalism on the right. It is impossible to characterize the meaning of immigrants within the larger 1968 moment without taking into account the reverberations of Charonne. A striking symbol of police brutality around which neofascist and antifascist groups clashed, Charonne represented the radical Right-Left rivalries rekindled around postcolonial issues of racism and immigration. However, the heroization of the immigrant worker had limits within the activist community more broadly. In some cases, African students even expressed a disdain for what they perceived as a lowly class with little to contribute to the national cause. From this perspective, unskilled immigrant laborers who required social and material assistance rested at best on the margins of a newly expressed Senegalese postcolonial nationalism.

CHAPTER 7

The Birth of Political Pluralism in Senegal

> *We were protesting against the development construction in our capital in anticipation of what we called "the suzerain Pompidou's tour of his African vassals."*
>
> —Diallo Diop (brother of Omar Blondin Diop),
> interview with Mehdi Ba

Although 1968 remains etched in Senegalese memory, the activism of the 1970s proved no less turbulent. The heavy state repression of 1968 activism in Senegal led to a radicalization of certain elements of the student movement. The return of key student leaders from France in the summer of 1968 rejuvenated activism, and after periods of intermittently hot and cold negotiations with university administration and the government, some members of the radical Left turned to violence in the early 1970s. While the state succeeded in quashing the most radical youth leaders through arrests and incarcerations, and in weakening the adversarial nature of the dominant national labor union, the victory over the activists was not total. Unlike in Tunisia, where student agitation was never able to bring the administration to the negotiation table, in Senegal, students achieved at least temporary recognition of previously clandestine organizations and student participation in university decisions. In spite of its continued splintering, the Left exercised significant power in shaping the nature of state discourse on education, democratization, and development.

By the early 1970s, it was not uncommon for President Senghor to justify his positions publicly in relation to radical leftist discourse. Though political parties of these leanings did not gain a strong foothold in Senegalese government on Senghor's watch, his frequent referencing of leftist ideas marked a significant discursive victory for the Left in shaping the political language of

1970s Senegal. The democratization of student representation in universities was paralleled in labor unions and political parties, which were no longer the sole domain of a one-party regime. The raising of youth and labor voices ultimately brought about the birth of political pluralism in Senegal.

The University of Dakar witnessed a brief period of calm after the September 1968 negotiations among UDES leaders, newly appointed education minister Assane Seck, and government delegates. Senghor had selected Seck in June 1968 to replace Ahmadou-Mahtar M'Bow in hopes of starting afresh with oppositional students.[1] The calm was short-lived, however, as students again called a strike after twenty-five engineering students were expelled for disciplinary issues, provoking the regime to evacuate the university in April 1969. This time, authorities were prepared. When UDES called for a boycott of exams, the regime adopted laws that allowed for declaration of a state of emergency. The standoff ended with students ultimately losing out in an *année blanche* (voided year).[2]

Various sectors of labor also held strikes in May, and a UNTS general strike was announced on 10 June. These culminated in the fracturing of the labor movement with the creation of the UPS-friendly rival organization, the National Confederation of Senegalese Workers, with UNTS defector and party loyalist Doudou N'Gom at the helm. In addition to the blow delivered to the student movement in 1969, former student leader Mamadou Diop Decroix remembered that it was also an extremely difficult year for trade unions. "It was the year that Senghor succeeded in conquering the labor movement. Senghor, who had been shaken by the strongest union in '68, was able to sever it."[3] After the rather lofty successes of both the student and worker movements, the regime prepared effective hardline strategies to dismantle and exclude oppositional forces in 1969. Interorganizational conflict among labor leaders gradually weakened UNTS through a series of government measures, ending in the union's eventual dissolution in April 1971.[4]

Students hoping to avoid another lost year of studies begrudgingly accepted university reforms that included more stringent evaluation processes. But the campus heated up again in February 1970 during the international visit of special guest Turner O'Neal, an African American senior legal counsel from the US embassy in Paris. O'Neal had been invited by Rector Seydou Madani Sy and economics professor Abdoulaye Wade (future president and leader of the Senegalese Democratic Party [PDS]) to speak on civil rights. However, students prevented O'Neal from taking the podium at the University of Dakar. Their anti-Americanism was so heightened that the event degenerated into a skirmish leading to the broken wrists of US cultural attaché Leon Slawecki, and spilled into the university hallways, where graffitied walls read "Messieurs Sy and Wade assimilate to the SS and to the CIA."[5] Never mind that O'Neal would have criticized the Nixon administration's record on civil rights had he been able to speak. But with presumed US involvement in both Lumumba's assassination and Nkrumah's removal from power, as well as the known atrocities in Vietnam, the United States began to challenge France as the new symbol of neo-imperialism in African affairs.[6] The resistance to both US and French forms of neo-imperialism was widespread throughout the Francophone world in the aftermath of 1968. To be sure, Tunisian students similarly protested the diplomatic visit of US secretary of state William Rogers to Tunis that same month.

Yet despite this turn toward anti-Americanism, Senghor's pro-French stances still proved easy fodder for opposition groups. By January 1971, the French embassy in Senegal reported the regime's fears of a resurgent PAI. Hoping to assuage rising opposition, moderate members from within the UPS, along with French foreign diplomats, pressured Senghor to release Mamadou Dia, who had been a political prisoner in Kédougou since his failed coup d'état in 1962.[7] Senghor did not give in to these requests until 1974, when he finally issued a pardon after signs emerged that the political pluralization of Senegalese politics was underway. In the same year, he ordered the release of a number of university professors, many of whom were sympathetic to the PAI and the students, and who themselves had gone on strike in January.[8] Though sources are unclear as to the nature of the professors' grievances, the strike coincided with reforms related to more stringent exam evaluation policies in the university. It is clear, however, that the democratization movement students had set forth in 1968 at the university level—including official recognition of multiple student organizations—had migrated vertically by the mid-1970s to comprise fundamental political change and the end of the one-party state.

1970s Dakar: The Pompidou Visit and the "Group of Incendiaries"

Senghor was again concerned about opposition movements as he prepared for the impending visit of his colleague and fellow head of state French president Georges Pompidou, who was set to tour several African nations in February 1971. While university professors were engaged in a strike of their own in January 1971, a radical group of youth activists—in anticipation of Pompidou's visit—set fire to symbols of French colonial authority: the Department of Public Works, the Department of Motor Vehicles, and the French Cultural Center. On 16 January "the Group of Incendiaries" (a moniker given by the Senegalese government) circulated a tract proclaiming the French Cultural Center to be an "instrument of propaganda and intoxication in the service of French imperialism."[9] The "Incendiaries" further charged the government with wasting public funds to finance a "hypocritical spectacle" and proclaimed that "Pompidou might be a friend of Senghor, but he is certainly an enemy of the people of Senegal and all of revolutionary Africa."[10] Finally, they questioned the legitimacy of the Special Court for Attempts on National Security, which had been created in 1968 to suppress opposition. In the eyes of the militant activists, the notion that Senegal would open its arms to the head of state of its former colonial oppressor was an absolute farce, and one that warranted direct action.

Despite the activists' multiple references to "spectacles" and the significance of the artist and philosopher Guy Debord for Omar Blondin Diop and other Senegalese studying abroad, the Senghor regime initially suspected UNTS trade union leaders of starting the fires. Debord's famous La Société du spectacle (1967) was extremely influential on the 1968 generation and a foundational text for the leftist group Situationist International, in which Blondin Diop and his brothers were active. The Diop brothers, along with another group of Senegalese Maoists and communists, all studied in universities in France before returning to Senegal in the summer expressly to join the movement in Dakar.[11] Rather than targeting young Situationists, the regime arrested ten of the labor union's most prominent members on 22 and 23 January 1971, including General Secretary Abdoulaye Thiaw and Iba Der Thiam, head of the UNTS-affiliated Senegalese Union of Teachers, both of whom were interrogated under the jurisdiction of the Special Court.[12] Undeterred by the lack of evidence linking the labor leaders to the arson, the regime condemned Thiaw and Thiam, along with fellow UNTS member Mbaba Guissé, for distributing tracts harmful to the state. They received three years in prison and large fines by the Special Court in July 1971.[13] Like Bourguiba in Tunisia—who used the February 1972 crackdowns to imprison political foes—Senghor took this opportunity to rid the regime of his own pesky opposition leaders. Following additional acts of aggression, new interrogations ensued as the regime continued to look elsewhere for perpetrators.

Upon hearing the sound of broken glass, authorities caught and brought in three radical activists. They were apprehended carrying a dozen Molotov cocktails intended for Pompidou's cortege on 5 February 1971, as his car proceeded along Dakar's Avenues Lamine Gueye and Faidherbe. Under intense interrogation, the radicals admitted their connection to the January fires.[14] Along with twenty or so others, the young men were implicated as members of the Group of Incendiaries. The group was interchangeably referred to as the blondinistes for their connections to the politically active Blondin family, most notably Omar Blondin Diop and two of his brothers, Mohamed and Diallo. In addition to the arrests of arsonists, authorities charged Jean-Louis Ravel, a French coopérant and psychologist at the Fann hospital, for his role in printing subversive tracts on a Roneo machine from his office.[15] The "trials of the incendiaries" took place 25–27 July and involved sixteen accused of setting fire to the French Cultural Center and two other administrative buildings, distributing tracts with subversive content, and/or possessing Molotov cocktails destined for the Pompidou cortege. The Special Court condemned two of the group's leaders to forced labor in perpetuity, while six other principal actors received sentences ranging from five to twenty years.[16]

The French coopérant Ravel was found guilty of "complicity by aid and assistance and furnishing means of provoking crime or crime by drafting, producing and distributing tracts, conforming to article 250 of the Senegalese penal code," and handed three years of mandatory prison.[17] After significant lobbying on the part of the French embassy, Senghor finally agreed to amnesty Ravel in November 1971, on the condition that he leave Dakar for Paris.[18] Ravel certainly did not earn his amnesty because of remorse, as he declared the following to police: "In my estimation, the French-Senegalese 'cooperation' is a fraud for the benefit of France. . . . I observed and studied the misery and difficulty of the Senegalese peasantry. I know that French imperialism is partly responsible for this misery."[19] Ravel was thirty years old at the time of his arrest and identified with the May-June uprisings. His denunciations of French neo-imperialism in postcolonial Senegal placed him in the global community of anti-imperialists. Like the French établis, who rejected their privileged origins in search of authentic immigrant and worker experiences, Ravel disavowed the so-called French economic and political cooperation that he witnessed firsthand. Just as the Tunisian and Senegalese activists' postcolonial nationalisms articulated alternative visions of independent African nations, his rejection of foreign policy equally qualified as postcolonial French nationalism. Ravel sought to redefine the French nation in a new era that would be devoid of colonial exploitation.

Ravel's position fell more in line with that of Senegalese students than with his French counterparts in Dakar. Senegalese university students boycotted spring exams in 1971 in a "crossing arms strike" while French students enrolled at the same institution held their own separate meeting to discuss their future and to understand "the position of Senegalese students through whom all solutions to conflicts must pass."[20] In spite of the relatively high proportion of French students at the University of Dakar (nearly one-third) and the fact that Senegalese students were not even in the majority, the events of 1968 had established them as the most powerful student voice on campus. Ultimately, against the wishes of most French students, the university was again closed in the spring of 1971 following boycotts. Although the majority of French students in Dakar did not side with the movement, there was a subset of activists, like Ravel, who aided the cause. One Senegalese activist recalled,

> At the time there were French, mostly teachers who helped the movement. They were coopérants, so that had a certain diplomatic status and they helped us. Either they typed up tracts or others in UNESCO, one, a teacher, and even some in the private sector, helped with finances, typing things up, or bought equipment or even printed tracts from their offices.
>
> Mostly it was people from the Left affiliated with the Communist or Socialist Party. There were links but after Pompidou many became fearful. After this time we had a lot of difficulty circulating literature. . . . In France, the PCF always supported us. Not as much with the PS in France because they were close with Senghor.[21]

The involvement of coopérants from a variety of largely left-leaning political backgrounds paralleled the situation in Tunisia, where French sympathizers like Jean-Paul Chabert—coopérant at the Institute of Applied Economic Sciences in North Africa—were politically active abroad while engaged in bilateral cooperation and development projects.[22]

Following independence, French aid continued to pour in to both Tunisia and Senegal in the form of economic, military, and technical assistance. The human aspect of this assistance involved the physical migration of people to former French territories whose experiences shaped their political positions. These individuals' actions often ran counter to the larger French foreign policy mission and to newly independent nations' development projects. While support groups existed in France for social movements taking place in Senegal and Tunisia, transnational actors like Ravel and Chabert embodied the postcolonial activism that crossed borders in either direction, whether from colony to metropole or from metropole to colony. In both of their cases, angered regimes expelled these foreign troublemakers and, somewhat paradoxically, exported political activists to France, where they could influence French public opinion and increase international support for local causes.

Even among Senegalese activists there is no consensus on the importance of the Pompidou attacks to the student cause more generally. A series of interviews with participants revealed conflicting levels of identification with the arsonists. One activist who participated in protests in both France and Senegal, "Mariane," recalled that while she was with a group at the Lycée Van Vo, other groups set the French Cultural Center afire and attempted to attack other sites.[23] Sources from the French diplomatic archives and the Senegalese National Archives document these transgressions and the subsequent arrests. However, Mariane's statements confirmed the coordinated activity at Lycée Van Vo that was nowhere to be found in archival sources. She was not arrested, as the attacks were eventually attributed to the Blondin brothers. Omar was in France during the Pompidou visit, but his brothers were brought to trial and found guilty of crimes against the state.

For historians interested in transnational activism in decolonizing nations with tight state controls on media, oral history proves a vital source that otherwise remains a missing fragment in the history of the global 1960s.[24] Yet interviews with participants and observers produced conflicting responses on the degrees of identification with the anticolonial acts in 1971 Dakar. Mariane stated clearly of the Blondins, "They were with us," and claimed that the attacks were organized jointly. However, "Abdou," who had not studied in France, claimed that the Pompidou affair was "a situationist movement. It was not linked to the Senegalese political movement. It was a completely external movement, and its referent was the Situationist International, with Guy Debord and all that. So Blondin Diop and his group were arrested. We didn't feel solidarity with this movement."[25]

Both Mariane and Abdou were entrenched in the protests at the University of Dakar, and each used terms like "we" and "us" to describe their relationship to the Blondins and the Pompidou affair. Yet they provided two divergent claims about activist identification with the anticolonial arson. Mariane, who had studied in France and was part of a circle of Maoists in the Proletarian Left, was open to, and in contact with, Senegalese Situationists who had received their political education (*formation*) in France. For Abdou, however, the activism in Senegal was entirely about national issues and national politics, and he separated the attacks on French symbols from narrower student issues. In his eyes, the Situationists represented France; their goals and concerns were externally motivated. He preferred to highlight Moscow and Prague—rather than France—as sources of inspiration and influence, however measured. His anti-French sentiment grounded his view of events in which he attempted to extricate from the movement any French characteristics, including activism conducted by Senegalese returnees from abroad.

In the context of situating the *blondinistes* in the broader political landscape, Mariane and Abdou represented the Sino-Soviet split in Senegal. Mariane found Maoism via France, and Abdou, the new communist, was concerned with a return to the fundamental texts of Marx and Lenin as they applied to present-day Senegal.[26] Both described a fracture of the Left in the 1970s that was explicitly tied to debates over Communist Party loyalty and a burgeoning global interest in Mao's Cultural Revolution. While the inclusion of oral history has produced contradictory interpretations of the importance of the Group of Incendiaries, it has also provided a democratization of viewpoints and of versions of the past.[27] Not only do these testimonies provide alternative truths to the state's version of events, but listening to 68ers at once tells a more global story of 1968 in Dakar (Mariane) while unearthing local responses to ubiquitous global forces (Abdou) circulating within postcolonial spheres.

The Battle over the Death of Omar Blondin Diop

The trials of the incendiaries did not resolve the Pompidou affair. In addition to further igniting an already volatile campus that was shut down in the spring of 1971, they also set in motion a series of retaliatory actions by the *blondinistes*. Though Omar Blondin Diop was not even in the country during the attacks, his brothers' involvement led authorities to suspect his complicity. A gifted student, Blondin Diop studied at the École Normale Supérieure of St. Cloud in France. His erudition landed him a special grant from the Senegalese government awarding him three times the funding of a normal stipend. He was active in Daniel Cohn-Bendit's March 22 movement at the University of Nanterre and detained for his participation in May '68 protests in Paris, eventually receiving an order of expulsion by French authorities on 9 October 1969.[28] Upon his return to Dakar, Blondin Diop frequented intellectual circles led by French Marxist Pierre Fougeyrollas, a sociologist and head of the African Institute of Basic Research who assisted Blondin Diop in obtaining a fellowship there.[29] Blondin Diop, however, hoped to return to Paris for his studies, and, somewhat ironically, Senghor helped him by personally writing on his behalf to Pompidou, who agreed to lift the expulsion order.[30] Clearly not feeling compelled to return the favor to Senghor, Blondin Diop left France again in February 1971, this time for Bamako, Mali, following the arrests of his brothers.

Senegalese authorities suspected Blondin Diop of helping to orchestrate—from afar—an attempted prison mutiny at the Dakar civil prison of Rebeuss in April 1971 as part of an escape plot.[31] Campus crackdowns and arrests of the *blondinistes* and labor leaders did not go unnoticed by movement supporters at home or abroad. Renewed university protests in Dakar led Senghor to dissolve the UED and UDES, and on 27 April 1971, one hundred members of FEANF responded by staging their own demonstration in front of the Senegalese embassy in Paris.[32] Students in Paris expressed their solidarity with the prison mutineers and condemned Senghor's dissolution of the student associations in Dakar. Even though a number of Senegalese students had returned to Dakar in the summer of 1968, they left behind a politically active network of African students in France who increasingly participated in AESF and FEANF. Along with the embassy strike, AESF and FEANF jointly stated in May 1971,

> The arrest of the union leaders came about in a wave of general eradi-cation of all undesirables during the French Presidential visit. Several people were picked up by police and brought to camps near Linguère in Ferlo some 280 km from Dakar; notably, 40 students were taken in the night from University residence halls. The campus has since been cut off from the rest of the city by a cordon of machine guns and police inside the campus prevented all student assemblies and meetings. . . .
>
> Under these circumstances, students at the University of Dakar launched a protest movement against repression and the format of finals and examinations, freshly imported from France by Senghor, which chal-lenge the particularities of our university and our own concrete prob-lems and which continues in the name of Francophonie to transplant and impose everything that is done in France in our country.[33]

As the joint statement suggests, African students in France informed on events to international communities in Paris. By rejecting the Frenchness of the Uni-versity of Dakar, they expressed a new postcolonial nationalism that continued to call for African autonomy well after the territorial and political independence of Senegal in 1960. Decolonization was thus far from achieved.

Senghor's use of the Pompidou visit to suppress opposition groups was strikingly similar to Bourguiba's preparation of the visit of Ivoirian president Félix Houphouët-Boigny in March 1968. Bourguiba chastised students for be-ing disruptive, declaring that he would not allow protesting students to em-barrass the nation and that foreigners must be protected. To make certain that students would not be able to organize on campus, he closed the university in anticipation of Houphouët-Boigny's visit.[34] In both cases, Paris acted as a site of postcolonial protest for West and North African students abroad who ex-pressed solidarity with activists back home. As in Tunisia, networks relayed information and broadcast Senghor's repression to diasporic communities in France and to the French public. Senegalese students also resisted the contin-ued adoption of French university reforms that they found even more oppres-sive than had French 68ers. The Senegalese National Education Ministry's implementation of stricter French evaluations of exams—designed to limit ac-cess of students from neighboring African nations—led to a lively response from Paris.[35] The FEANF and AESF members very consciously selected the

Senegalese embassy—an iconic symbol of Franco-Senegalese cooperation—as their site of protest. Before 1968, rather than taking its own direction based on the specific local challenges facing a young African nation, the Senegalese National Education Ministry applied reforms designed for a much larger and more complex university system in industrialized France. Yet by 1970, the Franco-Senegalese commission on higher education was well aware of the need to address Senegal's unique needs in agriculture and engineering. The commission implemented reforms that streamlined these necessities and began to distance itself from French initiatives. By this point, however, students viewed the university restructuring as a form of French neo-imperialism and attached political claims to education issues.

In a special diplomatic visit to Bamako in December 1971, Senghor arranged for Omar Blondin Diop's extradition from Mali, which ultimately took place in February 1972. The Senegalese Special Court sentenced Blondin Diop to three years in prison on Gorée Island in March.[36] The Dakar campus again ignited with agitation in May 1973 when Blondin Diop was mysteriously found dead in his cell. Authorities claimed that he hanged himself on the night of 12–13 May, though several sources, including Pierre Fougeyrollas, suspected the Senghor regime of ordering his assassination. Students in Dakar censured the regime's alleged role in Blondin Diop's death as riots erupted on 14 May in the city center and exploded into widespread protests in the days that followed. His death also elicited condemnation of the regime in the *Nouvel Observateur*. A French colleague of Blondin Diop's, Georges Kleiman, called on the "friends of Senegal, who naively thought that their silence would favor clemency from President Senghor," to denounce "all the regimes who gag the youth whose only weapon is their voice."[37] The torrent of emotion from within Senegal as well as on the international scene surrounding this suspicious death led authorities to publish a white paper on the affair, akin to tactics employed by the PSD in Tunisia in 1968.

Indeed, Blondin Diop's death sparked a transnational debate over the sequence of events leading up to this tragic event. Fougeyrollas alleged that the regime was responsible for Blondin Diop's death in a June 1973 article in the Parisian daily *Combat*, while the state-sponsored Senegalese *Le Soleil* reported it as a suicide, citing a coroner's report. Protesting students in Dakar and the negative press abroad prompted the regime to publish *Livre blanc sur le suicide d'Oumar Blondin Diop* (White paper on the suicide of Omar Blondin Diop) before the end of the year. Fougeyrollas maintained that Blondin Diop was killed by the regime, along with other revolutionary figures, and even publicly stated his belief that "no humanist or pseudo-humanist declaration from Senghor will enable us to forget the heroism and martyrdom of Omar Blondin Diop."[38] These charges were further supported by *Lettre de Dakar*, written anonymously in 1973, supposedly from a Dakar prison, and later published by Champ Libre from the safety of Paris in 1978.[39]

The regime's *Livre blanc* and *Lettre de Dakar* gave opposing accounts of Blondin Diop's death and pitted the rhetorical powers of the state's press squarely against anonymous Blondin Diop supporters (quite possibly led by his brother). The letter's diatribe against the corrupt state was published, perhaps unsurprisingly, by the same press, Champ Libre, that published famed Situationist Guy Debord's complete works.[40] According to the Ministry of Information's *Livre blanc*, Omar Blondin Diop received his political education in France. Attempting to show the dangers of French influence, the ministry further alleged that "he made his mark through his active participation in the March 22 movement as second in command to the rebellious Daniel Cohn-Bendit," and later "took part in the electoral campaign of the Trotskyist Alain Krivine."[41] The ministry's narrative established Blondin Diop as a gifted student who was afforded opportunities by the Senegalese and French governments but who was radicalized by French agitators. Even after Blondin Diop was expelled from France for his role in violent protests in the Latin Quarter in May '68, Senghor personally wrote to Pompidou to facilitate his reinstatement at the École Normale Supérieure of St. Cloud so that he might continue his educational track that was not offered in Dakar. Once back in France in September 1971, Blondin Diop left St. Cloud for Nanterre, known as a center for French university activism and the site from which Cohn-Bendit had launched the March 22 movement. The regime claimed that Blondin Diop left Paris for Bamako to form a network of other Senegalese activists who had been expelled from the country, composed of three groups adhering to the extremist organization known as "the incendiary brothers."[42]

Perhaps what is most interesting about the pamphlet is its use of official documents to prove the regime's innocence. Much of the *Livre blanc* reads like a legal document, with references to the annex, which includes reproductions of the letter written by Senghor to Pompidou advocating for Blondin Diop, as well as the autopsy reporting his death by suicidal hanging. Yet even the inclusion of such "official" documents suggests the regime's desire to regain legitimacy in the eyes of an increasingly skeptical public. Similarly, the annex consisted of a long list of Blondin Diop's personal effects, like cigarettes and several books, to demonstrate he was treated humanely in prison. The last pages of the pamphlet contain such legalese as "such are the presented facts" and "the biases and positions taken following this suicide were, in the end, nothing but attempts to exploit the event for political ends even though all facts have been revealed from the beginning."[43] Merely stating the regime's version of the story was insufficient; the Ministry of Information deemed it necessary to mobilize factual evidence in support of its claims and to reproduce an annex of seven official documents.

To counter the state's framing, the anonymous *Lettre de Dakar* provided an alternative version beginning with quotes from Friedrich Engels and Debord. The authors maintained that the regime lied about Blondin Diop's death. They cited torture by police during interrogation of the Group of Incendiaries, during which police chiefs sought to connect the group to foreigners.[44] They also called out the "idiotic editors" of *Le Soleil*, who claimed that the actors were "driven by this sad fellow Iba Der Thiam (would this be because he's a fat and happy trade union leader!), whom they knew to be incapable of such acts."[45] The letter thus served as a corrective to state claims that the activists were led either by traitorous UNTS labor leaders or by French or Chinese communists. This battle over the retelling of events played out similarly in Tunisia. Bourguiba's political party issued *The Truth about the Subversion at the University of Tunis* regarding events in March 1968, while Perspectives activists responded with *Liberty for the Convicted of Tunis: The Truth about Repression in Tunisia*, published by François Maspero in 1969.[46] As in the Senegalese case, the activists' response pamphlet was printed from the relative safety of Paris, likely intended to influence French public opinion at least as much as to provide information back home.

Yet the *Lettre de Dakar* was quite divisive. It slammed both the Senghor regime and various opposition groups as insufficiently radical. It even criticized the outcomes of the 1971 opposition: "The only real victory of the 'Group of Incendiaries' was, simply, to have existed."[47] No group escaped the ire of the pamphleteers. They called out members of the PAI and the various organizations it influenced (UNTS, UDES, UED) as "sharks without teeth" who stopped short of carrying out complete revolution in favor of collaboration with "feudal-marabout forces" and "Muscovite infiltration of the state apparatus and national unions."[48] But the pamphlet shared notions of *indépendance inachevée* with the protesting students of May-June 1968 and January 1971. The authors noted a substitution of French colonial officials with Senegalese elites who were "created in the image of their former masters, these elites, who had no means of social promotion other than the colonial state . . . have only jumped on the nationalist bandwagon and, once in power, demonstrate the fallacious character of victories with cringe-worthy collusion with their former masters."[49] Their indictment of the regime and state administrators in many ways mirrored what student protesters began to express in 1968. It was a classic case of substituting one evil for another, of exchanging French civil servants for Senegalese ones whose goal was simply to replace their predecessors, not to dismantle the system under which they operated.

What students called for in 1968 was not simply the removal of French professors in favor of Africans; it was also about ridding the university of French course content. In 1968, the Democratic Rally of Senegalese Students demanded that history and geography give primacy to "the study of Senegal and the principal countries of Africa" and "the study of the Third World (notably problems with underdevelopment)."[50] During the second large wave of activity in 1971, another student group proposed a "patriotic ideal for youth schooling" by setting a cultural agenda to include "theater, literary competitions around themes imprinted with African life and expressed in our national languages."[51] The regime finally passed a 1968 initiative to officially recognize six African languages with the *loi d'orientation* of 1971.[52] In addition, rapid Africanization of teaching corps was implemented to appease protesting students and with the approval of the Franco-Senegalese commission. By 1979, the total number of African professors at the university had increased from 91 in 1970 to 236, or from 47 percent to 60 percent of the total faculty. The student population experienced an even more acute Africanization: the French student population plummeted from 27 percent in 1967 to just 3 percent by 1979, while that of Senegalese students climbed from 32 percent to 75 percent in the same period.[53] If Senghor was able to repress many of the more radical elements of the Senegalese student movement, it is quite evident that they were enormously successful in pushing through Africanization agendas.

Perhaps the most lasting collective impact of Dakar's May-June '68, the Pompidou affair, and the death of Omar Blondin Diop was a discursive victory on the left that pushed Senghor to use their vocabulary. By the early 1970s, Senghor had begun to publicly couch his policies using the language of Marxism, Leninism, and Maoism. Even while promoting opposing political ideas, he felt compelled to speak directly to his adversaries quite literally on their terms. Landing Savané's radical Marxist group Reenu-Rew (Roots of the Nation) clandestinely published the journal *Xarébi* (Struggle) in the mid-1970s to challenge state narratives. While many radical groups like Savané's and the Blondin Diop brothers' were disrupted and truncated with arrests throughout the 1970s, they did succeed in influencing national conversations and in forcing Senghor to include outside political voices. This paved the way for political opposition that would challenge him in future elections. With intense pressure from both student and labor groups after 1968, Senghor gradually began the process of political decentralization. Through a constitutional reform, Senghor began to share power, at least nominally, when he named Abdou Diouf as his prime minister in February 1970. While some have argued that this was no more than a ploy to offer up a scapegoat to his detractors—since wielding sole power in government also meant receiving sole blame—the new constitution nonetheless opened pathways for a plurality of voices in governance.[54]

Student protests starting in the late 1960s guided Senghor along the path of first acknowledging, then officially recognizing, political opposition. For a leader who openly criticized communism, Senghor spent significant political energy addressing Marxism-Leninism and Maoism, attempting to integrate them into his theories on Negritude. In a December 1971 public address at the University of Abidjan, he historicized the dominant oppositional ideologies. "Mao Zedong transformed Marxism-Leninism, Sinicizing it to adapt to Chinese realities. This is how he placed emphasis on peasants as much as workers, on the artisanal classes and small enterprises as much as on heavy industry, on the education of the national bourgeoisie and not on its physical liquidation. . . . To recap: Lenin refused the German model in order to create a Russian model; Mao refused the Russian model in order to create a Chinese one. And us, will we be the only ones to imitate instead of invent? You see, this question brings us to Negritude."[55]

By this logic, Senghor was arguing that Negritude was a form of African Socialism with roots in Marxism. Just as leaders like Lenin and Mao had adapted Marx's teachings to their specific national economic and social contexts, Senghor was attempting to do the same for Senegal with Negritude. Yet with his hostile remarks on foreign subversion in the form of alleged Chinese propagandists who were expelled from Senegal, as well as Maoist nodes that had returned to Dakar from France, it would seem that Marxist-leaning activists had in some ways dictated the terms of discussion. Senghor began to justify his own practices and ideologies using Marxist language, history, and rationale. It was not that his version of Negritude was somehow in opposition to Marxism, Leninism, or Maoism; rather, Senghor was in fact applying their concepts in an African setting. If he succeeded in stamping out the most radical activists by the mid-1970s, their gains could be witnessed in the opening of the political process to moderate opposition groups and in the inseparability of leftist ideologies from national political conversations at the highest levels.

The Senegalese student movement was perhaps the least transnational in terms of wide reach beyond Senegal when compared with international organizations that emerged for human rights in Tunisia, or with the vast networks of immigrant workers and intellectual activists who were politicized in France in the 1970s. Somewhat paradoxically, it was also perhaps the most successful in terms of altering its own national political and education systems. Students were instrumental in the decentralization of political power and in bringing about the end of the one-party state in Senegal. Likewise, their efforts expedited the Africanization of the University of Dakar in terms of student population, professoriate, and curricula. The movement's transnational dimensions were not insignificant, however. French figures like Jean-Louis Ravel and Georges Kleiman supported youth causes in Senegal and pointed to France's continued neocolonial presence there. Paris acted as a site of Third World activism when Senegalese students again protested outside their nation's embassy in Paris after convictions were levied against the Group of Incendiaries. The former metropole was also the site from which antistate protest pamphlets like the *Lettre de Dakar* were published against the regime.

If Omar Blondin Diop became a paradoxical martyr for the movement, it was more because of his mythical status as a French-educated film star and French May '68 activist than any actions he carried out in his home country. In fact, he was not even present during the events in May and June 1968 in Dakar and had not actually engaged in the violence directed at the French Cultural Center or at Pompidou's cortege. It was rather ironic, then, that the movement so keen on extracting itself from any French characteristics for fear of being labeled imitators found as its martyr a French *mai 68* agitator. But Blondin Diop's death laid bare and affirmed the state corruption many activists had been excoriating since before 1968. And if Senghor displayed a willingness, at least initially, to give Blondin Diop a second chance and personally request his readmission into France to complete his studies, it was because the gifted Blondin Diop represented Senegal's future.

African students in Dakar helped bring about a new era of democratization with increased student representation in universities. Beginning with autonomy of affiliation first demanded and won by students, labor unions and political parties followed suit in the 1970s when Senghor capitulated. Democratization of student and labor unions thus spilled over into state politics and prompted the one-party state to loosen its grip on competing political rivals. In the aftermath of the Blondin Diop suicide scandal, the regime recognized future president Abdoulaye Wade's PDS. By March 1975, less than a year after the creation of the PDS, Wade had already gained nearly fifty thousand adherents.[56] An amended constitution of 9 July 1975 enabled the entrance of three strands of political ideology to replace one-party rule. Even the despised PAI was recognized in 1976 after its 1960 dissolution.[57] Wade, the head of the PDS that emerged in 1975 to challenge Senghor's Socialist Party, ran for the presidency in the 1978 elections and, after four attempts, finally gained the nation's highest office in 2000. The gradual democratization in politics in the 1970s coincided with increased national debt in that decade. As part of the decolonization process, France pulled

Conclusion

Toward a Decolonial Order of Things

> *Part of the importance of the fragmentary point of view lies in this: that it resists the drive for a shallow homogenization and struggles for other, potentially richer definitions of the nation and the future political community.*
>
> —Gyanendra Pandey, *Routine Violence: Nations, Fragments, Histories*

Moving between and across events and activist networks in Tunis, Paris, and Dakar, this book has narrated a postcolonial version of 1968. Yet while leaning on postcolonial studies and events to decolonize and, hence, deconstruct the historiographic and cultural hegemony of France's May '68, this has very much been a project of constructing a road map of tangled transnational webs of activists that tell a more global story of 1968, even as Paris still features prominently. From Michel Foucault's support of Tunisian detainees and Daniel Cohn-Bendit's resistance to authoritarianism in Senegal, to Simone Lellouche Othmani's and Omar Blondin Diop's participation in May '68 in Paris, activist networks within the former empire clearly overlapped and legitimated each other's causes. Methodologically, the former French empire provided a useful model for concretizing the transnational and the global. Once key anchors of empire, the three cities I have zeroed in on were connected by their shared colonial pasts. The scars of colonialism—etched in postcolonial memories of the French defeat at Dien Bien Phu or the police violence against North Africans in Paris in October 1961—weighed heavily on the density of events in 1968. Moreover, postcolonial wounds colored the ways local actors perceived, responded to, and strategically appropriated the same global references and flashpoints (e.g., Charonne, the Six-Day War, the Tet Offensive in Vietnam, and Mao's Cultural Revolution). Perhaps unsurprisingly, then, even after imperial collapse, Paris continued to act as an important nexus for Third World protest, if not the only one (others include Cohn-Bendit's anti-Senghor rally in Frankfurt or protests against Hubert Humphrey's presence in Tunis).

Within the former empire, the book's methodological approach also moves between the comparative and the transnational. Evaluating together the experiences of activists in Tunis, Paris, and Dakar highlights the geographic, cultural, and political differences produced through social action. At the same time, shared activist goals could flatten these geographic barriers, while old colonial networks and new postcolonial cooperation provided the infrastructure to carry out transnational protest. The preceding chapters contribute to the scholarship of the "global 1968" by entering two important understudied areas of the Francophone Third World into the conversation on the global 1960s (Tunis and Dakar) and resituating them in a global and postcolonial context alongside related happenings in Paris. After empire, these three regions remained connected through activists' experiences in the French education system. New representative student groups emerged, drawing on French models and established on French soil. Intellectual migration during the colonial period was pivotal in the production of an international network of student and activist organizations. And student migration back to university campuses in Dakar and Tunis was a key feature of decolonization, as rapidly increasing university populations concentrated educated and discontented youth on campuses.

Historiographically, *Decolonizing 1968* has endeavored to place decolonization into the history of the global 1960s, and the history of the global 1960s into studies on decolonization. This required a practice of seeking out Third World voices and putting them in conversation with the often more visible First World ones. Inspired in part by Gyanendra Pandey's work on the fragmentary voices of India that often do not make it into narratives of national identity, *Decolonizing 1968* has made a conscious effort to highlight the extra-state voices of activists who articulated alternative visions of postcolonial nationalism. To highlight the stories of non-European activists, I mined both public and private archives for underground pamphlet literature, anticolonial political tracts, and event posters; I also relied on the activists' individual memories, which required historical listening. Often alongside more well-known intellectuals, the protagonists of this postcolonial story resisted the continued French presence in Tunisian and Senegalese economic, political, and cultural institutions. They rejected the notion that national unity would be achieved through singular political parties, student organizations, or labor unions, and they demanded the right to include multiple political currents in their nations' key institutions. In France, the immigrant activism of the 1970s kick-started new debates about inclusion in the French nation that are still present in contemporary society. Through this decolonial practice in the archives, I hope to not only contribute to the globalization of 1960s studies but also bring attention to the experiences of everyday intellectuals and activists who were nothing short of extraordinary.

With postcolonial networks in place in 1968, social and political action in one corner of the former empire reverberated, often via the metropole, to other critical centers of the old empire. Though organizations often transformed after independence—as seen with the emergence of leftist groups like Perspectives—transnational activism was made possible through the development of strong footholds in both the former metropole and in newly independent state capitals undergoing decolonization. An international community of activists responded to events in Tunis and Dakar with declarations of support from Paris, regular information sessions, and underground pamphlet circulation. Likewise, foreign students witnessing events in Paris, while following news of student strikes in their home countries, viewed these movements collectively as part of the broader winds of global change. Moreover, though universities proved a breeding ground for protest in 1968, activism in Paris and Dakar spread beyond the student milieu to a vast circuit of well-organized labor unions, which ultimately exceeded what students had set in motion.

In Senegal, efforts to decolonize university decision-making processes and Africanize teaching corps were transmitted to other sectors of political life. Organized labor helped usher in the official recognition of multiple political currents in government in the following decade. While the university campus strikes in 1968 were often based on very local conditions, transnational networks of activists were particularly important in the aftermath of protests when responding to state repression. Ultimately, youth activism led to the increased democratization of Senegalese and Tunisian unions by the end of the 1970s and helped inspire important antiracism and autonomous immigrant workers' movements in France. But perhaps the most important feature of the activist networks was their role in counteracting state-controlled media with alternative, activist-centered versions of events. Underground lines of communication were activated in the face of authoritarianism, most notably in the case of Tunisia, to advocate for the freedoms of speech and assembly and for prisoners' rights.

For students and heads of state in Tunisia and Senegal alike, one measure of the success of decolonization was to assess the degrees of progress of their young universities. Modeled heavily on the French system, these institutions were at once sites of contestation and important symbols of modernity and national pride for leaders like Léopold Sédar Senghor and Habib Bourguiba, who themselves had excelled in French institutions. The 1968 university protests in both Dakar and Tunis can thus be viewed, in part, as conflicts between a relatively privileged sector of society and the state over unfulfilled expectations for their decolonizing nations. With universities as putative harbingers of modernity and progress, leaders like Senghor and Bourguiba insisted on the importance of education, and students held an elevated status in these societies as future nation-builders. After investing so many resources in their nations' youth, it is no surprise that university activism was so troubling to Third World leaders in the midst of initiating modernization projects.

Yet the movements across the former French empire were certainly not uniform in all respects. In Dakar, as in Paris, the 1968 student strikes quickly received broad support from labor unions that were able to achieve their own sets of goals; however, similar collaboration in Tunis did not generalize to a large segment of the population until much later. Instead, violent suppression of dissident Tunisian intellectuals led to demands for human rights, while in Senegal protesters faced the incompatibility of seeking to cut French ties yet maintain generous scholarships once subsidized by France. The circumscribed movement in Tunisia and subsequent overreaction by the repressive Bourguiba regime inspired the creation of new, Paris-based human rights organizations like the CISDHT. When Tunisia finally experienced a general strike in 1978, the same activist networks that advocated for students again mobilized on behalf of the workers' union that had spurned earlier student agitation. Furthermore, though Tunisian students witnessed little success collaborating with labor, they developed a language of resistance that Tunisian labor leaders drew on when ultimately challenging the regime a decade later. As in the aftermath of Omar Blondin Diop's death in 1973, Paris continued to act as a political space from which dissident opinions could be articulated with relative freedom. In each case, the historical relationship to France was a determining factor in the articulation of postcolonial resistance to authoritarian leadership in decolonizing societies.

In Dakar, where repression of activists in 1968 was less harsh than in Tunis, demands for political openness generally trumped cries for penal reform. While Senghor actually negotiated with student protesters in 1968, albeit after a number of arrests and brief internment in military camps, Tunisian activist leaders faced repeated torture and some even spent nearly all of the 1970s in prison. Workers and students alike made significant gains in Senegal, with wage increases for union members and recognition of student groups outside of single-party organization. The initial victory in the summer of 1968 helped force Senghor's hand, in the mid-1970s, when he released former prime minister Mamadou Dia from prison. Shortly thereafter, Senghor officially acknowledged oppositional political parties such as the PAI and future president Abdoulaye Wade's PDS. Through their 1968 grievances against unfulfilled independence, students in Dakar paved the way for the integration of multiple political parties in Senegal while Tunisian 68ers laid the foundations for transnational human rights activism in support of detainees. In both cases, student and worker activists converted anticolonial themes of national independence movements, once directed at French colonial oppressors, and pivoted them toward heads of state Bourguiba and Senghor. The outcome was the expression of a new postcolonial nationalism outside of the cultural synthesis discourses of their one-party state leaders.

Back in the former metropole, students' demands were slightly different. For obvious reasons, students in France were less concerned with the ethnic and cultural backgrounds of their professors. They did, however, share serious concerns about the content of their education. The 1966 essay presumably authored by Mustapha Khayati expressed what many students felt: that they were living in "a society of *commodities* and *spectacles*" in which student life is "a rehearsal for his ultimate role as a conservative element in the functioning of the commodity system."[1] His conceptualization of the student as an intellectual laborer exploited by the capitalist system allowed for a direct identification with other laboring classes, including large numbers of immigrant workers recruited as cheap labor for reconstruction and the industrial boom of the Thirty Glorious Years. The mass demonstrations of 1968 brought back the old clashes of the Algerian War between the Left and the Right, where 68ers met racist violence and hate speech with a new antiracist movement. By the 1970s, the Left had created its own network of pro-immigrant activists who worked in concert with new autonomous immigrant workers' groups, albeit with varying degrees of success. After failing to overturn the government and witnessing the splintering of the Left over the course of May '68, groups like the Cahiers de mai and the établis sought concrete action in factories, direct contact with workers, and tangible material gains. From Tunis to Paris, and from Paris to Dakar, activists refused to be defined by the legacies of colonial authority, instead demanding a more just decolonial order of things.

Notes

Prologue

1. Sofia Christensen, "Senegal Races to Reform University Sector," *VOA News*, 29 March 2018, https://www.voanews.com/a/senegals-largest-university/4321996.html.

2. "Senegal: manifestations pacifiques des étudiants pour réclamer 'justice,'" *Jeune Afrique*, 24 May 2018, http://www.jeuneafrique.com/562094/societe/senegal-manifestations-pacifiques-des-etudiants-pour-reclamer-justice/.

3. For example, students blocked classroom entrances at the University of Toulouse–Jean-Jaurès for much of the 2017–2018 academic year, and *une année blanche* was only avoided through an emergency implementation of online exams. See David Saint-Sernin, "Université Toulouse Jean-Jaurès: 86% des examens se feront sur internet, des étudiants dans le flou," *Actu Toulouse*, 10 June 2018, https://actu.fr/occitanie/toulouse_31555/universite-toulouse-jean-jaures-86-examens-se-feront-sur-internet-etudiants-dans-flou_17201455.html.

4. "Nicolas Sarkozy veut 'liquider' l'héritage de mai 68,'" *L'Obs Politique*, 30 April 2007, https://www.nouvelobs.com/politique/elections-2007/20070430.OBS4781/nicolas-sarkozy-veut-liquider-l-heritage-de-mai-68.html.

5. Alain Badiou, *The Rebirth of History: Times of Riots and Uprisings*, trans. Gregory Elliott (New York: Verso, 2012), 5, 113–114.

Introduction

1. See, for example, Timothy S. Brown, "'1968' East and West: Divided Germany as a Case Study in Transnational History," *American Historical Review* 114, no. 1 (2009): 69–96; and Anna von der Goltz, "Making Sense of East Germany's 1968: Multiple Trajectories and Contrasting Memories," *Memory Studies* 6, no. 1 (2013): 53–69.

2. On the Mexican student movement, see Jaime M. Pensado, *Student Unrest and Authoritarian Political Culture during the Long Sixties* (Stanford, CA: Stanford University Press, 2013).

3. Although the terms "First World" and "Third World" have been replaced by "global North" and "global South" since the fall of the Soviet Union, I employ the former to refer to the historical context in which they were created. Indeed, from the 1950s to the 1970s, leaders of anticolonial nationalist movements, and the European leftists who identified with them, were referred to and self-identified as "Third Worldists." See also Christoph Kalter, *The Discovery of the Third World: Decolonization and the Rise of the New Left in France, c. 1950–1976* (Cambridge: Cambridge University Press, 2016).

4. See Samantha Christiansen and Zachary A. Scarlett, *The Third World in the Global 1960s* (New York: Berghahn Books, 2013).

5. Ann Laura Stoler has evoked terms such as "imperial debris" to describe the degenerative relationships between institutions established during the colonial period and the imperial ruins they leave behind. Rather than focusing on "ruined landscapes," *Decolonizing 1968* suggests certain empowering possibilities for formerly colonial societies, particularly on African university campuses that were the partial remains of the empire. Ann Laura Stoler, "Introduction. 'The Rot Remains': From Ruins to Ruination," in *Imperial Debris: On Ruins and Ruination*, ed. Ann Laura Stoler (Durham, NC: Duke University Press, 2013), 1–35.

6. By "political geography" I mean the political relationships of different regions around the protest issues of the day.

7. For a similar reading regarding Great Britain, see Paul Gilroy, *Against Race: Imagining Political Culture beyond the Color Line* (Cambridge, MA: Harvard University Press, 2000).

8. Antoinette Burton challenges this binary in *After the Imperial Turn: Thinking with and through the Nation* (Durham, NC: Duke University Press, 2003), 12.

9. The bulk of scholarship taking France as a national unit through which to examine 1968 is too vast to cite here. But even studies on France's May '68 that are interested in its global dimensions, such as David Caute's, have hardly considered its specific relationship to activism in the ex-colonies (though he does discuss the Vietnam War at length). See Caute, *The Year of the Barricades: A Journey through 1968* (New York: Harper & Row, 1988).

10. Arjun Appadurai, "Putting Hierarchy in Its Place," *Cultural Anthropology* 3, no. 1 (1988): 36–40, cited in Akhil Gupta and James Ferguson, "Beyond 'Culture': Space, Identity, and the Politics of Difference," *Cultural Anthropology* 7, no. 1 (1992): 14.

11. For a groundbreaking work seeking to dewesternize 1968, see Christiansen and Scarlett, *The Third World in the Global 1960s*.

12. There is a newer body of scholarship linking First and Third Worlds with action rooted in Europe. See Quinn Slobodian, *Foreign Front: Third World Politics in Sixties West Germany* (Durham, NC: Duke University Press, 2012); and Timothy S. Brown, *West Germany and the Global Sixties: The Antiauthoritarian Revolt, 1962–1978* (New York: Cambridge University Press, 2013).

13. I am unaware of any monographs specifically focusing on the merging of these fields, though one exception would be Françoise Blum's excellent article "Années 68 postcoloniales? 'Mai' de France et d'Afrique," *French Historical Studies* 41, no. 2 (2018): 193–218.

14. Here I apply Dipesh Chakrabarty's notion of "provincializing Europe" to the shorthand "May '68." Chakrabarty seeks to "decenter [an] imaginary figure that remains deeply embedded in *clichéd and shorthand forms* in some everyday habits of thought." Chakrabarty, *Provincializing Europe: Postcolonial Thought and Historical Difference* (Princeton: Princeton University Press, 2000), 4.

15. Catherine Walsh identifies the renaming of the Americas as "Abya Yala" as a reclamation of Indigenous identity by the Kuna-Tule peoples of Panama and Colombia, and as a salient example of decolonial praxis. See Catherine E. Walsh and Walter D. Mignolo, *On Decoloniality: Concepts, Analytics, Praxis* (Durham, NC: Duke University Press, 2018), 17, 21–24.

16. Walsh and Mignolo, *On Decoloniality*, 146. I explore the application of decolonial studies in Francophone spaces in "Periphery and Intimacy in Anti-imperial Culture and Politics: From French Others to Othering Frenchness," *French Politics, Culture & Society* 38, no. 2 (2020): 105–125.

17. Ilham Khuri-Makdisi, *Contextualizing Radicalism in the Eastern Mediterranean: Globalization and Change, 1860–1914* (Berkeley: University of California Press, 2010), 2.

18. My readings on the production of difference across interconnected space and time draw inspiration from Gupta and Ferguson, "Beyond 'Culture,'" 14; and Gary Wilder, *Freedom Time: Negritude, Decolonization, and the Future of the World* (Durham, NC: Duke University Press, 2015), 9–12.

19. Georges Balandier was perhaps the first to push for studying metropole and colony together in "La Situation Coloniale: Approche Theorique," *Cahiers internationaux de sociologie* 11 (1951): 44–79. Balandier has stressed that globalization has led to a questioning of identity in which "we are all, in different forms, in a *post*-colonial situation." See his preface in Marie-Claude Smouts, ed., *La situation postcoloniale: Les postcolonial studies dans le débat français* (Paris: Fondation nationale des sciences politiques , 2007), 24.

20. Wilder, *Freedom Time*, 10. For a critique of the limits of "deterritorialization" in global studies, see Frederick Cooper, *Colonialism in Question: Theory, Knowledge, History* (Berkeley: University of California Press, 2005), 92–93.

21. Here my thinking is influenced by Geoff Eley's interesting discussion of how German nationhood, and Nazism in particular, was imagined in relation to empire. See Geoff Eley, *Nazism as Fascism: Violence, Ideology, and the Ground of Consent in Germany, 1930–1945* (London: Routledge, 2013), 134–136. Thanks to Katharine White of George Washington University for alerting me to this literature for the Cold War context in Germany.

22. I would like to thank "Reader 1" for making this important connection.

23. On desire and consumption in the Arcades, see Walter Benjamin, *The Arcades Project*, trans. Howard Eiland and Kevin McLaughlin (Cambridge, MA: Belknap Press of Harvard University Press, 1999), 60–61, 417.

24. Henri Lefebvre, *The Explosion: Marxism and the French Revolution*, trans. Alfred Ehrenfeld (New York: Monthly Review Press, 1969), 104.

25. Arif Dirlik, "The End of Colonialism? The Colonial Modern in the Making of Global Modernity," *Boundary 2* 32, no. 1 (2005): 8n7. This is a departure from other formulations such as Todd Shepard's preferred "post-decolonization" to refer to France and Algeria after the conclusion of the Algerian War (1954–1962). See Shepard, "'Something Notably Erotic': Politics, 'Arab Men,' and Sexual Revolution in Post-decolonization France, 1962–1974," *Journal of Modern History* 84, no. 1 (2012): 80–115.

26. Zancarini-Fournel's research group, the Institut d'histoire du temps présent, organized a series of lectures from 1994 to 1998, "Les années 68. Événements, cultures politiques et modes de vie." See also Arthur Marwick, *The Sixties: The Cultural Revolution in Britain, Italy, France, and the United States, c. 1958–1974* (Oxford: Oxford University Press, 1998).

27. I thank Julian Bourg for pointing to similar imagery of a palimpsest in chronological terms after hearing his excellent presentation, "The Times and Spaces of 1968," at the Columbia University Maison Française, 27 April 2018.

28. Statistics gathered from the United Nations Statistics Division, "Population by age, sex, and urban/rural residence—UNdata," last updated August 26, 2021, available online at http://data.un.org/Data.aspx?d=POP&f=tableCode%3A22; and Mamadou Fall, "Jeunesse et entreprise au Sénégal: De la mystique de l'alternative au credo 'managerial,'" in *Les Jeunes en Afrique: La Politique et la ville*, Tome 1, ed. Hélène d'Almeida-Topor, Catherine Coquery-Vidrovitch, Odile Goerg, and Françoise Guitart (Paris: L'Harmattan, 1992), 502.

29. Fall, "Jeunesse et entreprise au Sénégal," 504–505.

1. Colonialism, Intellectual Migration, and the New African University

1. Alice L. Conklin, *A Mission to Civilize: The Republican Idea of Empire in France and West Africa, 1895–1930* (Stanford, CA: Stanford University Press, 1997), 23.

2. This coincided with Victor Schoelcher's efforts to abolish slavery at the onset of the Second Republic in early 1848. For debates on citizenship in the AOF before the 1946 French Union, see Conklin, *A Mission to Civilize*, 151–172; and Gary Wilder, *The French Imperial Nation-State: Negritude and Colonial Humanism between the Two World Wars* (Chicago: University of Chicago Press, 2005), 129–139.

3. Patrick Manning, *Francophone Sub-Saharan Africa, 1880–1995* (Cambridge: Cambridge University Press, 2004), 79.

4. Wilder, *The French Imperial Nation-State*, 129–130.

5. See Eric T. Jennings, *Vichy in the Tropics: Pétain's National Revolution in Madagascar, Guadeloupe, and Indochina, 1940–1944* (Stanford, CA: Stanford University Press, 2004), 2.

6. Manning, *Francophone Sub-Saharan Africa*, 138.

7. On *coopération* in the AOF, see Rachel Kantrowitz, "Triangulating between Church, State, and Postcolony: *Coopérants* in Independent West Africa," *Cahiers d'Études africaines* 1/2, no. 221 (2016): 219–242. On the Franco-African Community, see Anton Andereggen's *France's Relationship with Subsaharan Africa* (Westport, CT: Praeger, 1994), 49–61. Early member states included the Central African Republic, Chad, Congo, Dahomey, Gabon, Ivory Coast, Malagasy Republic, Mauritania, Niger, Senegal, Sudanese Republic, and Upper Volta, many having changed names upon entry.

8. See Moshik Temkin, "Europe and Travel Control in an Era of Global Politics: The Case of France in the Long 1960s," in *Peoples and Borders: Seventy Years of Migration in Europe, from Europe, to Europe [1945–2015]*, ed. Elena Calandri, Simone Paoli, and Antonio Varsori (Baden-Baden, Germany: Nomos, 2017), esp. 118–126.

9. Robert Aldrich and John Connell, *France's Overseas Frontier: Départements et Territoires D'outre-mer* (Cambridge: Cambridge University Press, 1992), 35.

10. See Fatma Ben Slimane, "Entre deux empires: L'élaboration de la nationalité tunisienne," in *De la colonie à l'État-nation: Constructions identitaires au Maghreb*, ed. Pierre-Noël Denieuil et al. (Paris: L'Harmattan, 2013), 107–117.

11. Kenneth J. Perkins, *A History of Modern Tunisia* (New York: Cambridge University Press, 2004), 40.

12. Mustapha Kraïem, *Nationalisme et syndicalisme en Tunisie, 1918–1929* (Tunis: Union Générale Tunisienne du Travail, 1976), 249; and Perkins, *A History of Modern Tunisia*, 144.

13. See Julia A. Clancy-Smith, *Mediterraneans: North Africa and Europe in an Age of Migration, c. 1800–1900* (Berkeley: University of California Press, 2011), especially chapter 1.

14. See Boubaker Letaief Azaiez, *Tels syndicalistes, tels syndicats ou Les péripéties du mouvement syndical tunisien*, 1ère partie (Tunis; Carthage: Éditions Imprimerie S.T.E.A.G., 1980), 13.

15. See Mustapha Kraïem, *Le parti communiste tunisien pendant la période coloniale* (Tunis: Institut supérieur d'histoire du mouvement national, Université de Tunis 1, 1997), 6–20.

16. Perkins, *A History of Modern Tunisia*, 62. "Collège" is the equivalent of junior high school in the United States.

17. See Yoshiko Sugiyama, "Sur le même banc d'école: Louis Macheul et la rencontre franco-arabe en Tunisie lors du Protectorat français (1883–1908)" (PhD diss., Université Aix Marseille, 2007). Samuel D. Anderson similarly compares the role of Franco-Muslim *médersa* schools in the Algerian and Senegalese contexts in "Domesticating the Médersa: Franco-Muslim Education and Colonial Rule in Northwest Africa, 1850–1960" (PhD diss., University of California Los Angeles, 2019).

18. See Janet Horne, "'To Spread the French Language Is to Extend the Patrie': The Colonial Mission of the Alliance Française," *French Historical Studies* 40, no. 1 (2017): 95–127. Horne notes the desire of the Alliance Française's founding members to spread French culture not only to the bey's subjects but also to sizable non-French.

19. Habib Belaïd, "Bourguiba et la vie associative pendant la période coloniale et après l'indépendance," in *Habib Bourguiba: La trace et l'héritage*, ed. Michel Camau and Vincent Geisser (Paris: Karthala, 2004), 330.

20. Secrétariat d'Etat à l'Education Nationale, *Une récente réalisation du gouvernement Bourguiba: Nouvelle conception de l'enseignement en Tunisie* (Tunis: La Presse, 1959), 10–11.

21. See Mohamed Sayah, interview, in Camau and Geisser, *Habib Bourguiba*, 611; and François Siino, *Science et pouvoir dans la Tunisie contemporaine* (Paris: Karthala, 2005), 91–112.

22. Peggy R. Sabatier, "'Elite' Education in French West Africa: The Era of Limits, 1903–1945," *International Journal of African Historical Studies* 11, no. 2 (1978): 247–249; and Sabatier, "Educating a Colonial Elite: The William Ponty School and Its Graduates" (PhD diss., University of Chicago, 1977).

23. See Wilder, *The French Imperial Nation-State*, 119; and Conklin, *A Mission to Civilize*, 198–208.

24. Cited in Fabienne Guimont, *Les étudiants africains en France (1950–1965)* (Paris: Harmattan, 1997), 28.

25. A. Adu Boahen, *The Role of African Student Movements in the Political and Social Evolution of Africa from 1900 to 1975* (Paris: UNESCO, 1994), 14.

26. See table 18, "Effectifs (élèves) de l'enseignement primaire (secteur public)," in Abdeljabbar Bsais and Christian Morrisson, *Les coûts de l'éducation en Tunisie* (Tunis: Université de Tunis, Centre d'études et de recherches économiques et sociales, 1970), 76.

27. Kamel Chenoufi and Gilles Gallo, *La Tunisie en décolonisation (1957–1972): Genèse des structures de développement et des structures de la République* (Le Pradet, France: Editions LAU, 2003), 201.

28. Letter from French ambassador to Senegal, Jean de Lagarde, to Minister of Foreign Affairs, Maurice Couve de Murville, 4 January 1967, in Archives Diplomatiques du Ministère des Affaires Étrangères (ADMAE), Afrique: Sénégal (1959–1972), carton 49, Politique intérieure, , La Courneuve. See also Pierre Fougeyrollas, "L'Africanisation

de l'Université de Dakar," in *Problèmes et perspectives de l'éducation dans un État du Tiers monde: Le cas du Sénégal*, ed. Jean Louis Balans, Christian Coulon, and Alain Ricard (Bordeaux: Centre d'étude d'Afrique noire, 1972), 35.

29. See telegram no. 438/45 of 28 May 1968 of Jean de Lagarde, in , *Mai 68 vu de l'étranger: Les Événements dans les archives diplomatiques françaises*, ed. Maurice Vaïsse (Paris: CNRS Éditions, 2008), 94.

30. Driss Abbassi, *Quand la Tunisie s'invente: Entre Orient et Occident, des imaginaires politiques* (Paris: Autrement, 2009), 11.

31. Driss Abbassi, *Entre Bourguiba et Hannibal: Identité tunisienne et histoire depuis l'indépendance* (Paris: Karthala, 2005), 66.

32. See James McDougall, "Dream of Exile, Promise of Home: Language, Education, and Arabism in Algeria," *International Journal of Middle East Studies* 43, no. 2 (2011): 251–270.

33. Emily Marker, "France between Europe and Africa: Youth, Race, and Envisioning the Postwar World 1940–1960" (PhD diss., University of Chicago, 2016), 10.

34. Student exchanges between France and Africa proliferated in the 1950s as part of the construction of new postwar "European" identities emerging in the backdrop of the French Union and the European Coal and Steel Community. See Marker, "France between Europe and Africa," 5–10.

35. Fiche no. DAM/1, "Activité des associations d'étudiants africains," undated, ADMAE, Afrique: DAM (1959–1979), carton 393, Situation des Associations Africaines, La Courneuve.

36. See Ruth Schachter Morgenthau, "Old Cleavages among New West African States: The Heritage of French Rule," *Africa Today* 18, no. 2 (1971): 12–13.

37. See table 20, "Effectifs de l'enseignement supérieur," in Bsais and Morrisson, *Les Coûts de l'éducation en Tunisie*, 83.

38. Catherine Coquery-Vidrovitch, "Colonisation, coopération, partenariat: Les différentes étapes (1950–2000)," in *Étudiants africains en France (1951–2001): Cinquante ans de relations France-Afrique, quel avenir? Études et témoignages*, ed. Michel Sot (Paris: Karthala, 2002), 34.

39. Chérif Ferjani, interview by the author, Lyon, 10 February, 2010.

40. Guimont, *Les étudiants africains en France*, 7. This figure excludes students from former protectorates such as Morocco and Tunisia.

41. See Fougeyrollas, "L'Africanisation de l'Université de Dakar," 42; and Fiche no. 354 DAM, 17 July 1968, ADMAE, Afrique: Sénégal (1959–1972), carton 49, Politique intérieure, La Courneuve. Abdoulaye Bathily cites figures compiled in 1980 from the University of Dakar that show a slightly higher percentage of total French students. I have cited figures from the Direction des affaires africaines et malgâches since they list a higher total number of students and thus likely include a larger pool of university students in Senegal. See table 1 in Bathily, *Mai 1968 à Dakar: Ou la révolte universitaire et la démocratie* (Paris: Éditions Chaka, 1992), 44.

42. Hélène d'Almeida-Topor, "Le nombre d'étudiants africains en France (1951–2000)," in Sot, *Étudiants africains en France*, 109–115.

43. Michael Goebel, *Anti-imperial Metropolis: Interwar Paris and the Seeds of Third World Nationalism* (Cambridge: Cambridge University Press, 2015).

44. Michael Goebel notes that AEMNA all but copied word for word the founding documents of the Association Générale des Étudiants Indochinois, while a founding member of the General Union of Tunisian Students (Union Générale des étudiants de Tunisie [UGET]) claimed he borrowed heavily from UNEF. See Sayah, interview; and Goebel, *Anti-imperial Metropolis*, 145.

45. Goebel, *Anti-imperial Metropolis*, 59–62, 106–107.

46. See Todd Shepard, *Sex, France & Arab Men, 1962–1979* (Chicago: University of Chicago Press, 2017), 20–21; and Benjamin Stora, *Le transfert d'une mémoire: De l'Algérie française au racism anti-arabe* (Paris: La Découverte, 1999). Shepard suggests a longer history of anti-Arabism that heightened after 1962.

47. See Andrew Daily, "Race, Citizenship, and Antillean Student Activism in Postwar France, 1946–1968," *French Historical Studies* 37, no. 2 (2014): 340–344.

48. Mohamed Dhifallah, "Bourguiba et les étudiants: Stratégie en mutation (1956–1971)," in Camau and Geisser, *Habib Bourguiba*, 316.

49. UNEF has a complex history of vacillating between positions on both the Algerian revolution and Palestinian liberation. In 1960 it finally called for peace in Algeria, for which it was lauded by UGET. See telegram from UGET in Tunis to UNEF, 27 October 1960, in Archives d'Association: UNEF, AN-19870110, Article 130, Archives Nationales, Fontainebleau.

50. See Jennifer Boittin, *Colonial Metropolis: The Urban Grounds of Anti-imperialism and Feminism in Interwar Paris* (Lincoln: University of Nebraska Press, 2010), 45, 82–86; and Philippe Dewitte, *Les mouvements nègres en France, 1919–1939* (Paris: L'Harmattan, 1985).

51. The UGEAO was created when the Association générale des étudiants de Dakar broke from UNEF because UNEF refused to recognize its autonomy. Ibrahima Thioub, "Le mouvement étudiant de Dakar et la vie politique sénégalaise: La Marche vers la crise de mai-juin 1968," in Almeida-Topor et al., *Les Jeunes en Afrique*, 267–281.

52. France created agencies such as the Office of Overseas Students (Office des étudiants d'outre mer) in 1955, which later became the Office of University Cooperation and Orientation (Office de coopération et d'accueil), ostensibly to welcome foreign students but also to engage in surveillance and control of students from overseas territories. See Guimont, *Les étudiants africains en France*, 119–121.

53. See Nicole Grimaud, "La Crise de Bizerte: Bourguiba et de Gaulle," in Camau and Geisser, *Habib Bourguiba*, 483–491.

54. Christopher Alexander, *Tunisia: Stability and Reform in the Modern Maghreb* (Milton Park, Abingdon, Oxon, England: Routledge, 2010), 97.

55. Momar-Coumba Diop, *Gouverner le Sénégal: Entre ajustement structurel et développement durable* (Paris: Éditions Karthala, 2004), 12.

56. Dhifallah, "Bourguiba et les étudiants," 320.

57. Clement Henry Moore, *Politics in North Africa: Algeria, Morocco, and Tunisia* (Boston: Little, Brown, 1970), 171.

58. Salah Ben Youssef, who represented a more isolationist approach to governance and advocated a sharper rift with France, was Bourguiba's rival within the Neo-Destour. He was condemned to death for treason because of his open opposition to Bourguiba and was assassinated in exile in 1961 at a hotel in Frankfurt; his supporters continued to identify as Youssefists after his death.

59. About 30 percent of Tunisian students, or three thousand in total, were card-carrying members of UGET. Perspectives was much more loosely organized and did not keep official records, though some members estimate that there were between two hundred and five hundred members internationally. See Moore, *Politics in North Africa*, 170; and "Jamil," interview by the author, Tunis, 19 April, 2011.

60. On student cooperation, see "Motion UNEF-UGEMA du IVe Congrès à Tunis," July 1960, in Archives d'Association: UNEF, AN-19870110, Article 128, Archives Nationales, Fontainebleau.

61. Abdoulaye Bathily, Mamadou Diouf, and Mohamed Mbodj, "Le mouvement étudiant sénégalais, des origines à 1989," in Almeida-Topor et al., *Les Jeunes en Afrique*, 282–310.

62. For certain economic sectors with particularly high levels of foreign influence, like transportation, see Y. Hazemann, "Routes et routiers du Sénégal au XXe siècle: Les sources de l'histoire des transports," in *Les Transports en Afrique: XIXe et XXe siècles*, ed. Hélène d'Almeida-Topor, Chantal Chanson-Jabeur, and Monique Lakroum (Paris: Harmattan, 1992), 210–221.

63. See also Kantrowitz, "Triangulating between Church, State, and Postcolony," 221–223; and Robert Cornevin, "La France et l'Afrique Noire," *Études internationales* 1, no. 4 (1970): 92.

64. See André Bailleul, "L'Université de Dakar, institution et fonctionnement (1950–1984)" (PhD diss., Université de Dakar, 1984), 204–220. Figures vary slightly in Fougeyrollas, "L'Africanisation de l'Université de Dakar," 44.

65. Bathily, *Mai 1968 à Dakar*, 44.

66. Sabatier, "'Elite' Education in French West Africa," 252.

67. See Jean-Paul Chabert, interview by Michaël Béchir Ayari, Bourgoin Jailleux, 2005, in *Parcours et discours après l'indépendance*, ed. Michaël Béchir Ayari and Sami Bargaoui (Tunis: Éditions DIRASET, 2011); and Dépêche of H. Argod, 28 July 1971, "Procès des 'indendiaires,'" ADMAE, Afrique: Sénégal (1959–1972), carton 51, Politique intérieure, La Courneuve.

68. "Toast du Président de la République au diner offert en l'honneur de M. le Sec. de'Etat aux Affaires Etrangères chargé de la coopération et de Mme. Yvon Bourgès," 2 April 1968, in Dossier Léopold Sédar Senghor: 1968, Archives Nationales de Sénégal (ANS), Dakar.

69. Dhifallah, "Bourguiba et les étudiants," 315. "Zaytunians" refers to students of the Zaytuna theology school in Tunis who sought to increase the role of Islam in state government and maintained close contact with theology students in Damascus.

70. Clement H. Moore and Arlie R. Hochschild, "Student Unions in North African Politics," *Daedalus* 97 (1968): 32.

71. Habiba Bourguiba, speech of 21 April 1965, cited in Dhifallah, "Bourguiba et les étudiants," 320.

72. John P. Entelis, "Ideological Change and an Emerging Counter-culture in Tunisian Politics," *Journal of Modern African Studies* 12 (December 1974): 543–568.

73. Entelis, "Ideological Change," 550–551.

74. See Dhifallah, "Bourguiba et les étudiants," 318.

75. Hassan El Nouty, "Pour une démythication des problèmes de l'éducation du Sénégal," in Balans, Coulon, and Ricard, *Problèmes et perspectives de l'éducation*, 90–92.

2. Tunis

Portions of this chapter were drawn from Burleigh Hendrickson, "March 1968: Practicing Transnational Activism from Tunis to Paris," *International Journal of Middle East Studies* 44, no. 4 (2012): 755–774, ©, published by Cambridge University Press, reproduced with permission.

1. See also Burleigh Hendrickson, "Finding Tunisia in the Global 1960s," *Monde(s): Histoire, espaces, relations* 11 (2017): 61–78.

2. See Gershon Safir, *A Half Century of Occupation: Israel, Palestine, and the World's Most Intractable Conflict* (Berkeley: University of California Press, 2017), 1–3.

3. Many Perspectives participants in the events claimed that police officers, under instruction of the PSD, in fact sanctioned the violence against the Jewish community. Simone Lellouche Othmani, interview by the author, Paris, 22 September 2010; and "Jamil," interview by the author, Tunis, 19 April 2011. Tunisian scholar Imen Amiri has also presented research on Perspectives on the panel, "1968 in 2018: Geographies and Temporalities of *Mai 68*" at the Columbia University Maison Française, 27 April, 2018.

4. *L'Action*, June 8, 1967.

5. The *brochure jaune* was originally published as "La question palestinienne dans ses rapports avec le développement de la lutte révolutionnaire en Tunisie," *Perspectives Tunisiennes*, brochure no. 2 (février 1968).

6. The notion of "webs of empire" is borrowed from Tony Ballantyne's discussion of transcolonial information exchange in the British empire, *Orientalism and Race: Aryanism in the British Empire* (New York: Palgrave, 2002).

7. "Mémoires de militants," *Perspectives Tunisiennes*, brochure no. 3 (December 1968). For a slightly different take on periodization that emphasizes early 1960s Tunisian student activism and downplays June 1967 and March 1968, see Idriss Jebari, "'Illegitimate Children': The Tunisian New Left and the Student Question, 1963–1975," *International Journal of Middle East Studies* (2022): 1–24.

8. A former member of the Neo-Destourian Party, Slimane became an anti-Bourguibist and cofounded the PCT's journal *Tribune du Progrès*, which was banned along with the PCT under Bourguiba in 1963, following Slimane's increasingly scathing critiques of the government.

9. "Lettre rédigée signée par les membres du Comité de Solidarité avec le peuple vietnamien et remise à l'ambassade des U.S.A. pour le vice-président Humphrey," 7 January 1968, in Fonds Simone Lellouche et Ahmed Othmani (Fonds Othmani), SOL 28 bis, Bibliothèque de Documentation Internationale Contemporaine (BDIC), Nanterre.

10. From 1964 to 1969, Ben Salah implemented a socialist plan to nationalize agricultural land into a series of collectives. The plan was largely unpopular with peasants, many of whom battled government corruption and lost their private holdings of small plots.

11. See "La lutte des étudiants en Tunisie . . . et dans le monde," *Tribune Progressiste* 1 (February 1968); and "Appel du Comité pour la libération de Ben Jennet et des autres militants anti-impérialistes," undated, in Fonds Othmani, SOL 28, BDIC, Nanterre.

12. Timothy S. Brown, "'1968' East and West: Divided Germany as a Case Study in Transnational History," *American Historical Review* 114, no. 1 (2009): 69–96.

13. Brown, "'1968' East and West," 75.

14. Perspectives members in Paris solicited the help of French activists in protesting Bourguiba's diplomatic visit with French president Georges Pompidou. See "Un seul combattant: Le peuple!," 24 June 1972, in Fonds Othmani, SOL 2; and "Tunisie: La curé néo-colonialiste," *Politique Hebdo* 35, nouvelle série (29 June 1972).

15. "Tunisie: Le divorce étudiant," *Jeune Afrique* 377, 25–31 March 1968; and "Communiqué de Presse," dated 25 March 1968 and signed La Comité pour la libération de Ben Jennet et des autres militants anti-impérialistes, Paris, in Fonds Othmani, SOL 28, BDIC, Nanterre.

16. "Sur les journées de solidarité avec Mohamed Ben Jennet," *Perspectives Tunisiennes*, review, numéro spécial, no. 18 (18 June 1968): 3. Razgallah accused UGET of representing the PSD's desires regarding student demands.

17. Mohamed Dhifallah, "Bourguiba et les étudiants: Stratégie en mutation (1956–1971)," in Camau and Geisser, *Habib Bourguiba*, 321.

18. See Ahmed Othmani, with Sophie Bessis, *Beyond Prison: The Fight to Reform Prison Systems around the World* (New York: Berghahn Books, 2008), 11; *Tribune Progréssiste* 3 (April 1968): 1; *Jeunesse Démocratique* (June 1976): 25–26; and Gilbert Naccache, *Qu'as-tu fait de ta jeunesse? Itinéraire d'un opposant au régime de Bourguiba, 1954–1979: Suivi de récits de prison* (Paris: Cerf, 2009), 136, 160. According to Naccache, women activists such as Aysha Ben Abed were not spared from torture; her breasts were scarred from cigarette burns while she was detained.

19. See "À la lumière du procès G.E.A.S.T.: Les acquis et les perspectives de la lutte révolutionnaire en Tunisie," *Perspectives Tunisiennes*, brochure no. 4 (June 1969); and Naccache, *Qu'as-tu fait de ta jeunesse?*, 101.

20. "Mémoires de militants," *Perspectives Tunisiennes*, brochure no. 3 (December 1968): 9. The law protecting the images of heads of state dates back to the colonial period, when it was applied to protect powerful beylical families from public criticism.

21. Gilbert Naccache notes that the May '68 events in France made a deep impression on Bourguiba while he was visiting Spain, and that his advisers confirmed that Tunisian opposition leaders had been influenced by French "subversives." Naccache, *Qu'as-tu fait de ta jeunesse?*, 99.

22. *L'Étudiant Tunisien* (February–March 1968).

23. Driss Abbassi found that the 1970s witnessed a massive program of Arabization in which school textbooks and manuals were translated into Arabic, though much of the content initially maintained its French cultural referents. Abbassi, *Quand la Tunisie s'invente*, 67, 76; and Abbassi, *Entre Bourguiba et Hannibal*, 109–111.

24. *L'Étudiant Tunisien* (February–March 1968).

25. See Bathily, *Mai 1968 à Dakar*; and Gobille, *Mai 68*.

26. In an effort to reach working-class Tunisians in the early 1970s, activists in Paris published the bilingual journal *El Amel Tounsi* (*Le Travailleur tunisien*). It primarily targeted Tunisian immigrants in France and had minor clandestine distribution in Tunis, but did not make significant inroads into these communities. More successful were groups jointly founded by intellectuals and immigrant workers such as the Arab Workers' Movement (Mouvement des Travailleurs Arabes), which emerged in the early 1970s and included a number of North Africans residing in France.

27. *Perspectives Tunisiennes* 16 (December 1967). For examples of correspondence between Perspectives and UGET sections in Paris and Tunis, see Fonds de la Fédéra-

tion des Tunisiens pour une citoyenneté des deux rives, carton G2/2 (1), UGET Paris, Génériques, Paris.

28. "Sur les journées de solidarité avec Mohamed Ben Jennet," 12.

29. "Solidarité des étudiants tunisiens avec leurs camarades français: Vive la lutte juste des étudiants français et tunisiens," 14 May 1968, in Fonds Mai 68, carton 8: dossier 14, Centre d'Histoire Sociale du XXe Siècle (CHS), Paris.

30. See *Tribune Progressiste* 5 (December 1968): 30–35.

31. Letter from UNEF to the Comité National Bulgare pour le festival, 30 June 1968, in Archives d'Association: UNEF, AN-19870110, Article 107, Archives Nationales, Fontainebleau.

32. "Intervention de la section étudiante de Paris du GEAST au Congrès de l'UNEF de Marseille," undated, in Fonds Mai 68, carton 8: dossier 14, CHS, Paris.

33. The majority of Tunisian students in Paris resided at the Maison de Tunisie, which became a site for political meetings. *Tribune Progressiste* 5 (December 1968): 25.

34. Othmani, with Sophie Bessis, *Beyond Prison*, 17. Geismar confirmed this in email correspondence, January 2011.

35. Raymond Beltran, interview by the author, Carcassonne, 7 December 2010. In 1968, Beltran was a representative of FEN in Tunis, of which SNESup was an affiliate.

36. Othmani, with Sophie Bessis, *Beyond Prison*, 8.

37. See Foucault, interview by D. Trombadori, Paris, 1978, published in "Le rôle politique et culturel de Perspectives et des Perspectivistes dans la Tunisie indépendante," *Mouvements nationaux tunisiens et maghrébins*, series 3, 17 (September 2008): 50.

38. See petition of the CISDHT regarding a 4 December 1972 hunger strike signed by Foucault and letter from Professor Paul Kraugi to Simone Othmani, undated, in Fonds Othmani, SOL 28 bis, BDIC, Nanterre. Foucault joined intellectuals such as Gilles Deleuze and Jean-Paul Sartre, as well as French and Arab students from Comités Palestine, to protest the racist killing of an Algerian adolescent in a Parisian immigrant neighborhood, the Goutte d'Or, in October 1971. See Abdellali Hajjat, "Alliances inattendues à la Goutte d'Or," in *68: Une histoire collective, 1962–1981*, ed. Philippe Artières and Michelle Zancarini-Fournel (Paris: La Découverte, 2008, 521–527. CISDHT also linked the Djellali affair, discussed in further detail in chapter 6, to the long-term imprisonment of Foucault's former student Ahmed Othmani. See "On réprime ici [Paris], on réprime là-bas [Tunis]," undated, in Fonds Othmani, SOL 28 bis, BDIC, Nanterre.

39. In April 1968, Bourguiba purportedly assured Marangé that he would investigate the torture accusations and liberate any detainee who had been wrongly imprisoned. *Le Monde*, 16 August 1968; Beltran, interview. Many Tunisian activists believe that Bourguiba may not have been aware of the full extent to which authorities employed torture methods.

40. On the day of Tunisia's commemoration of armed resistance, Bourguiba announced that it was time "to turn the page" by releasing many of the condemned students. *Presse de la Tunisie*, 17 January 1970.

41. "Sur les journées de solidarité avec Mohamed Ben Jennet," 12.

42. From *Discours: Général Charles de Gaulle*, transcription by the Centre Virtuel de la Connaissance sur l'Europe (Paris: CLT, 1968).

43. Gobille, *Mai 68*, 88.

44. Maurice Vaïsse, ed., *Mai 68 vu de l'étranger* (Paris: CNRS Éditions, 2008), 93.

45. See *Tribune Progressiste* 5 (December 1968): 24.

46. Letter of support from Jean-Maurice Verdier to Mohamed Charfi, undated, in *Tribune Progressiste* 5 (December 1968): 24.

47. "Lettre ouverte de la Fédération Internationale des Drois de l'Homme au Président Bourguiba," signed and dated by General Secretary Suzanne Collette-Kahn, 13 September 1968, Paris, published in *Tribune Progressiste* 5 (December 1968).

48. See Chabert, interview by Ayari, in Ayari and Bargaoui, *Parcours et discours.*

49. *The Observer*, 22 June 1969; and *CISDHT*, Bulletin no. 1, undated, in Fonds Othmani, SOL 28 bis, BDIC, Nanterre.

50. Gattégno wrote a series of letters to *Le Monde* from April to September 1968. *Le Monde*'s editorial staff responded by noting the censorship of *Le Monde* in Tunisia. See Fonds Othmani, SOL 28, BDIC, Nanterre.

51. Parti Socialiste Destourien, *La vérité sur la subversion à l'université de Tunis* (Tunis: Parti Socialiste Destourien, 1968); *L'Action*, 4 August 1968.

52. "Tunisie: Le divorce étudiant."

53. *L'Action*, 21 March 1968.

54. *L'Action*, 27 and 28 March 1968.

55. *Liberté pour les condamnés de Tunis: La vérité sur la répression en Tunisie* (Paris: Maspero, 1969). Maspero also published a series of Perspectives brochures from 1967 to 1972.

56. *Liberté pour les condamnés de Tunis*, 3–4.

57. *L'Action*, 6 April 1968.

58. *L'Action*, 6 April 1968.

59. Parti Socialiste Destourien, *La vérité sur la subversion*, 36–40.

60. Parti Socialiste Destourien, *La vérité sur la subversion.*

61. Parti Socialiste Destourien, *La vérité sur la subversion*, 43.

62. "Mémoires de militants," *Perspectives Tunisiennes*, brochure no. 3 (December 1968): 14.

63. *Le Monde*, 16 August 1968.

64. For further discussion on the question of ruptures between historical periods, see Julia A. Clancy-Smith, "Ruptures? Governance in Husaynid-Colonial Tunisia, c. 1870–1914," in *Colonial and Post-colonial Governance of Islam: Continuities and Ruptures*, ed. Marcel Maussen, Veit Bader, and Annelies Moors (Amsterdam: Amsterdam University Press, 2011), 65–88.

65. Balandier in Smouts, *La situation postcoloniale*, 24.

66. Gerd-Rainer Horn, *The Spirit of '68: Rebellion in Western Europe and North America, 1956–1976* (Oxford: Oxford University Press, 2007).

67. Samuel Moyn, *The Last Utopia: Human Rights in History* (Cambridge, MA: Belknap Press of Harvard University Press, 2010), 3. In contrast, Salar Mohandesi has written on the shift from anti-imperialism to human rights beginning in the 1960s in the context of the international anti–Vietnam War movement in "Bringing Vietnam Home: The Vietnam War, Internationalism, and May '68," *French Historical Studies* 41, no. 2 (2018): 219–251.

3. Paris

1. Geneviève Dreyfus-Armand, "D'un mouvement étudiant l'autre: La Sorbonne à la veille du 3 mai 1968," in *Mai 68: Les mouvements étudiants en France et dans le monde*,

ed. Geneviève Dreyfus-Armand and Laurent Gervereau (Paris: Editions La Découverte, 1988), 139.

2. See Todd Shepard, "Algerian Reveries on the Far Right: Thinking about Algeria to Change France in 1968," in *May 68: Rethinking France's Last Revolution*, ed. Julian Jackson, Anna-Louise Milne, and James S. Williams (New York: Palgrave Macmillan, 2011), 78.

3. The Frankfurt protest is explored in detail in chapter 4.

4. For excellent discussions of the importance of the memory of Algeria in 1968, see Kristin Ross, *May '68 and Its Afterlives* (Chicago: University of Chicago Press, 2002), 34–64; and Shepard, "Algerian Reveries," 76–91.

5. Quoted by Jean-Louis Hurst, "Ils y étaient, ils se souviennent . . . ," *Libération*, 17–18 October 1981.

6. Thanks to the anonymous reviewer for pointing out that the seventh *wilaya* was the separately structured FLN division based in Paris. Kader's experiences support the notion of the Fédération de France as a seventh *wilaya*, division, or battle zone for FLN resisters, the other six being located in Algeria proper. See Ali Haroun, *La 7e Wilaya: La guerre du FLN en France, 1954–1962* (Paris: Seuil, 1986); and Joshua Cole, "Remembering the Battle of Paris: 17 October 1961 in French and Algerian Memory," *French Politics, Culture & Society* 21, no. 3 (2003): 33.

7. Todd Shepard, *The Invention of Decolonization: The Algerian War and the Remaking of France* (Ithaca, NY: Cornell University Press, 2006), 85–86. The OAS primarily targeted innocents, though it also occasionally collaborated with a commando wing of a French counterespionage unit. See Jim House and Neil MacMaster, *Paris 1961: Algerians, State Terror, and Memory* (Oxford: Oxford University Press, 2006), 175–176.

8. House and MacMaster, *Paris 1961*, 256.

9. Joshua Cole, "Massacres and Their Historians: Recent Histories of State Violence in France and Algeria in the Twentieth Century," *French Politics, Culture & Society* 28, no. 1 (2010): 109. Ross cites graffiti and slogans from 1968 in Paris such as "Nouveau Charonne à Paris" and "CRS: Assassin de Charonne." Ross, *May '68 and Its Afterlives*, 47–48. For a minority viewpoint decoupling "Charonne" from the colonial context from the son of a Charonne victim, see Alain Dewerpe, *Charonne 8 février 1962: Anthropologie historique d'un massacre d'État* (Paris: Éditions Gallimard, 2006).

10. The Djamila Boupacha case was one highly publicized example taken up by Simone de Beauvoir, who was appalled by Boupacha's story. During questioning as an FLN militant in 1960, Boupacha was sexually assaulted and tortured for more than one month of captivity. Using Boupacha's case, de Beauvoir garnered public opinion to denounce the gruesome French war practices and end conflict in Algeria. Prominent Tunisian attorney Gisèle Halimi took on several similar cases of Algerian women. See Simone de Beauvoir and Gisèle Halimi , *Djamila Boupacha* (Paris: Gallimard, 1962).

11. Daniel Cohn-Bendit and Gabriel Cohn-Bendit, *Obsolete Communism: The Left-Wing Alternative*, trans. Arnold Pomerans (London: AK Press, 2000), 42, 129.

12. From "War Gas!," distributed by the 3 May Action Committees on 13 May 1968, found in *The French Student Uprising, November 1967-June 1968; an Analytical Record*, ed. Alain Schnapp and Pierre Vidal-Naquet (Boston: Beacon Press, 1971), 183.

13. "Mabrouk," interview by the author, Tunis, 15 June 2011.

14. Shepard, *The Invention of Decolonization*, 85–86; and Ross, *May '68 and Its Afterlives*, 42.

15. Telegram from UGET in Tunis to UNEF, 27 October 1960, in Archives d'Association: UNEF, AN-19870110, Article 130, Archives Nationales (AN), Fontainebleau.

16. "Rapport présenté par Jean-Louis Peninou, délégué de l'UNEF, sur la XIIe C.I.E., Nairobi, August 17–27, 1966," in Archives d'Association: UNEF, AN-19870110, Article 110, AN, Fontainebleau.

17. "Le Problème palistinien: Rapport de la Commission Internationale," 9 June 1967, in Archives d'Association: UNEF, AN-19870110, Article 92, AN, Fontainebleau. This report directly references the Vichy era and links France's World War II past with anti-Semitism.

18. "Le Problème palistinien: Rapport de la Commission Internationale."

19. Daniel Gordon, *Immigrants & Intellectuals: May '68 and the Rise of Anti-racism in France* (Pontypool, Wales: Merlin Press, 2012), 24.

20. Direction Centrale des Reinseignements Généraux, "Les activités du bureau de la Ligue Arabe à Paris," June 1972, in Intérieur, Direction des Libertés Publiques et des Affaires Juridiques, sous-direction étrangers, AN-19990260, Article 23, AN, Fontainebleau.

21. See Alain Geismar, Serge July, and Erlyne Morane, *Vers la guerre civile* (Paris: Éditions et publications premières, 1969), 339–342; and, more generally, Ethan Katz, *The Burdens of Brotherhood: Jews and Muslims from North Africa to France* (Cambridge, MA: Harvard University Press, 2015), 242–278.

22. Ross, *May '68 and Its Afterlives*, 90–91.

23. See Poster: "Grand meeting anti-impérialiste au grande salle de la mutualité à Paris, avec le montage théatral 'Vietnam Vaincra,'" sponsored by the General Association of Guadeloupean Students and FEANF, 24 May 1968, in Tracts et documents de propagande / FEANF, Bibliothèque Nationale de France, Paris.

24. Romain Bertrand, "Mai 68 et l'anticolonialisme," in *Mai-Juin 68*, ed. Dominique Damamme, Boris Gobille, Frédérique Matoni, and Bernard Pudal (Ivry-sur-Seine, Paris: Éditions de l'Atelier, 2008), 96–97.

25. Parti Communiste Français, Comité Central, Commission de travail de la main-d'oeuvre immigrée du Maghreb, *L'Immigration algérienne en France, quelques aspects* (1975), quoted in Laure Pitti, "Quand une experience commune de mobilization fait réseau. L'impact de la guerre d'Algérie dans les reconfigurations militantes en terrain ouvrier, 1956–1975," Journée d'études *Tout est-il réseau?* CRESC, 13–14 March 2007, Université Paris 13.

26. Michelle Zancarini-Fournel, "Sud-Aviation, Nantes: La première occupation de mai," in Artières and Zancarini-Fournel, *68: Une histoire collective*, 326–331.

27. Gobille, *Mai 68*, 8.

28. Gobille, *Mai 68*, 8.

29. In his denunciation of French colonialism in Algeria, Frantz Fanon famously located the revolutionary potential of oppressed classes in the Third World. Fanon, *The Wretched of the Earth*, trans. Constance Farrington (New York: Grove Press, 1982 [1963]).

30. See Dirlik, "The End of Colonialism," 8n7.

31. Daniel Singer notes that these figures were for registered students and estimates that, by 1968, there were more like six hundred thousand total students including those who were unregistered. Singer, *Prelude to Revolution: France in May 1968* (Cambridge, MA: South End Press, 2002), 45.

32. Maxim Silverman, *Deconstructing the Nation: Immigration, Racism and Citizenship in Modern France* (London: Routledge, 1992), 41–42.

33. Lefebvre, *The Explosion*, 104–105. On the importance of the sociology department for the movement in Nanterre, see Cohn-Bendit and Cohn-Bendit, *Obsolete Communism*, 28, 33–39.

34. Ross, *May '68 and Its Afterlives*, 95.

35. "Nous, la pègre du Comité 'bidonvilles,'" 27 May 1968, in Fonds Mai 68 en région parisienne, F delta 1061 (11)/2, Bibliothèque de Documentation Internationale Contemporaine (BDIC), Nanterre.

36. Many thanks to the anonymous reader who emphasized this point.

37. Alfred Sauvy, "Trois mondes, une planète," *L'Observateur*, 14 August 1952. For an excellent genealogy and analysis of Third Worldism in France, see Kalter, *The Discovery of the Third World*.

38. Mohandesi, "Bringing Vietnam Home," 238.

39. See Xavier Vigna and Michelle Zancarini-Fournel, "Les rencontres improbables dans 'les années 68,'" *Vingtième Siècle. Revue d'histoire* 101, no. 1 (2009): 163–177.

40. Bethany S. Keenan, "Vietnam Is Fighting for Us: French Identities and the U.S.-Vietnam War, 1965–1973" (PhD diss., University of North Carolina, 2009).

41. See Donald Reid, "*Établissement*: Working in the Factory to Make Revolution in France," *Radical History Review* 88 (2004): 85; and Julian Bourg, "The Red Guards of Paris: French Student Maoism of the 1960s," *History of European Ideas* 31, no. 4 (2005): 472–490. On the influence of Maoism on the French Left more generally, see Richard Wolin, *The Wind from the East: French Intellectuals, the Cultural Revolution, and the Legacy of the 1960s* (Princeton, NJ: Princeton University Press, 2010).

42. Donald Reid made this connection to Mao's speech in "*Établissement*," 86.

43. Pierre Alban Delannoy, "Nos usines ont été des vallées," in *Ouvriers volontaires: les années 68: l'"Établissement" en usine*, ed. Juliette Simont, Jean-Pierre Martin, and Jean-Pierre Le Dantec (Paris: Les Temps Modernes, 2015), 228–236.

44. Louis Althusser, "Ideology and State Apparatuses: Notes towards an Investigation," in *Lenin and Philosophy, and Other Essays* (London: New Left Books, 1971), 153.

45. Marnix Dressen, *De l'amphi à l'établi: Les étudiants maoïstes à l'usine (1967–1989)* (Paris: Berlin, 2000).

46. Donald Reid, "Daniel Anselme: On Leave with the Unknown Famous," *South Central Review* 32, no. 2 (2015): 113, 122.

47. My translation from passages cited in Daniel Gordon, "'À Nanterre, ça bouge': Immigrés et gauchistes en banlieue, 1968 à 1971," *Historiens et Géographes* 385 (2004): 77; from Roland Castro, *1989* (Paris: Bernard Barrault, 1984).

48. Gordon, "'À Nanterre, ça bouge,'" 77.

49. Juliette Campagne, "Roubaix: Du petit livre rouge aux livres d'images," in Simont, Martin, and Le Dantec, *Ouvriers volontaires*, 255.

50. Pierre A. Vidal-Naquet, "Une sombre expérience," in Simont, Martin, and Le Dantec, *Ouvriers volontaires*, 238. Vidal-Naquet expressed some difficulty in speaking publicly about his time as an établi based in part on his horror at the violence perpetrated by the Soviet Union and China in the name of the intellectual currents that had initially inspired his activism.

51. Yvan Gastaut, "Le rôle des immigrés pendant les journées de mai-juin 1968," *International Migration* 23, no. 4 (1993): 29; and Xavier Vigna, "Une émancipation des invisibles? Les ouvriers immigrés dans les grèves de mai-juin 68," in *Histoire politique des immigrations post(coloniales): France 1920–2008*, ed. Ahmed Boubeker and Abdellali Hajjat (Paris: Éditions Amsterdam, 2008), 94.

52. Michael Seidman, *The Imaginary Revolution: Parisian Students and Workers in 1968* (New York: Berghan Books, 2004), 174. By contrast, Daniel Gordon's excellent scholarship points to an overlooked role for immigrants. See Gordon, *Immigrants & Intellectuals*.

53. "Direction générale de la Police nationale, renseignements généraux," 28 June 1968, AN 820599/41. Xavier Vigna found this same police report in the Bulletin quotidien de la DCRG, ministère de l'Intérieur, Centre des archives contemporaines (CAC), 19820599/41, which he dated 26 June 1968.

54. See Vigna, "Les ouvriers immigrés dans les grèves de mai-juin 68," in Boubeker and Hajjat, *Histoire politique des immigrations post(coloniales)*, 92; and Lilian Mathieu, "Décalages et alignements des dynamiques contestataires: Mai-juin 1968 à Lyon," présenté at the colloque "La conflictualité sociale et politique en mai-juin 1968" at the Université de Dijon.

55. *Le Monde*, 15 June 1968; and Léon Gani, *Syndicats et travailleurs immigrés* (Paris: Éditions Sociales, 1972), 147.

56. See Gordon, *Immigrants & Intellectuals*, 79–80. Gordon notes the relatively small sample size (accounting for under three thousand arrests in what appear to be urban centers). It is difficult to discern from these figures whether this indicated heavy targeting in arrests by police or whether foreigners were drawn to protests in greater proportion to their population size than French nationals.

57. See Ivan Bruneau, "Quand des paysans deviennent 'soixante-huitards,'" in Damamme et al., *Mai-Juin 68*, 344–356.

58. *Discours: Général Charles de Gaulle*, transcription by the Centre Virtuel de la Connaissance sur l'Europe (Paris: CLT, 30 May 1968).

59. *En Bref Lyon* 167 (1 June 1968), from Information Cercle Toqueville, in Fonds Mai 68, Centre d'Histoire Sociale, Paris.

60. Gerd-Rainer Horn, "The Changing Nature of the European Working Class: The Rise and Fall of the 'New Working Class' (France, Italy, Spain, Czechoslovakia)," in *1968: The World Transformed*, ed. Carole Fink, Philip Gassert, and Detlef Junker (Washington, DC: German Historical Institute, 1998), 354.

61. "On the Poverty of Student Life" and "Address to Revolutionaries of Algeria and of All Countries," in *Situationist International Anthology*, ed. and trans. Ken Knabb (2006 [1981]), 410 and 189–194, respectively.

62. "On the Poverty of Student Life," 409–410.

63. See "Adresse aux prolétaires et aux jeunes révolutionnaires arabes et israéliens contre la guerre et pour la révolution prolétarienne," in *Khamsin* (Paris: François Maspero, 1976).

64. Cohn-Bendit and Cohn-Bendit, *Obsolete Communism*, 26.

65. "Monde: La France en Révolution," *Jeune Afrique*, 386–387 (27 May–6 June 1968).

66. "Une Tunisienne citoyenne des deux rives: Simone Lellouche-Othmani," *Mémoire & Horizon*, numéro spécial, published by Citoyenne des Deux Rives (April 2007), 42–43.

67. "Une Tunisienne citoyenne," 43.

68. Gastaut, "Le rôle des immigrés," 11–13.

69. Sénégal: Évenements Généraux 1966–1968, Liasse Dossiers Généraux1968, ANS, Dakar.

70. Michael Wlassikoff, Marc Riboud, Jean-Claude Gautrand, and Philippe Vermès, *Mai 68, l'affiche en héritage* (Paris: Éditions Alternatives, 2008), 29; and "Monde: La France en Révolution," *Jeune Afrique*, 386–387 (27 May–6 June 1968).

71. Communiqué signed by the Executive Committee of FEANF, 11 May 1968, in Tracts et documents de propagande / FEANF, Bibliothèque Nationale de France, Paris.

72. For a critique of Western "pilgrims" who sought salvation through cultural revolution and interaction with the East, see Gita Mehta, *Karma Cola: Marketing the Mystic East* (New York: Fawcett Columbine, 1991).

73. Lefebvre, *The Explosion*, 109.

4. Dakar

1. For rich accounts of these events from decidedly Senegalese perspectives, see Bathily, *Mai 1968 à Dakar*; and Omar Guèye, *Mai 1968 au Sénégal: Senghor face aux étudiants et au mouvement syndical* (Paris: Karthala, 2017). Guèye suggests, however, that Senghor, more so than Senegalese students, drew on French practices and experiences, albeit to suppress students. Guèye, *Mai 1968 au Sénégal*, 215–218.

2. Pierre Fougeyrollas, "L'Africanisation de l'Université de Dakar," in Balans, Coulon, and Ricard, *Problèmes et perspectives de l'éducation*, 44.

3. Bathily, *Mai 1968 à Dakar*, 44. Figures vary slightly but are similar to results in Fiche no. 354 DAM, 17 July 1968, ADMAE, Afrique: Sénégal (1959–1972), carton 49, Politique intérieure, La Courneuve.

4. See "Mémorandum sur les événements de l'Université de Dakar," UDES, 26 May 1968, in Sénégal: Événements 1966–68, Liasse Crise Mai 1968, ANS, Dakar.

5. For a detailed narrative of events, see Bathily, *Mai 1968 à Dakar*; and Françoise Blum, "Sénégal 1968: Révolte étudiante et grève Générale," *Revue d'Histoire Moderne et Contemporaine* 59, no. 2 (2012): 142–175.

6. "Mémorandum sur les événements de l'Université de Dakar."

7. "Mémorandum sur les événements de l'Université de Dakar."

8. "Abdou," interview by the author, Dakar, 1 December 2011.

9. Mamadou Diop Decroix, *La Cause du Peuple: Entretien avec El Hadj Kassé* (Dakar: Panafrika, 2007), 15–16.

10. Diop Decroix, *La Cause du Peuple*, 21.

11. Mamadou Diop Decroix, interview by the author, Dakar, 22 November 2010.

12. See also telegram of Jean de Lagarde to the Minister of Foreign Affairs, 28 May 1968, ADMAE, Afrique: Sénégal (1959–1972), carton 49, Politique intérieure, Liasse: Crise de mai 1968, La Courneuve.

13. Blum, "Sénégal 1968," 161.

14. "Mémorandum sur les événements de l'Université de Dakar."

15. Letter from Jean de Lagarde to the Minister of Foreign Affairs, 2 June 1968, ADMAE, Afrique: Sénégal (1959–1972), carton 49, Politique intérieure, Liasse: Crise de mai 1968, La Courneuve.

16. See Hendrickson, "March 1968," 772n56.

17. Letter from Jean de Lagarde to the Minister of Foreign Affairs, 2 June 1968, ADMAE, Afrique: Sénégal (1959–1972), carton 49, Politique intérieure, Liasse: Crise de mai 1968, La Courneuve. Dakar has maintained a sizable merchant class of Syro-Lebanese, many of whom immigrated to Senegal in the late nineteenth century and continued to do so clandestinely in spite of French efforts to control migration during the Mandate period in the Levant. See Andrew Kerim Arsan, "Failing to Stem the Tide: Lebanese Migration to French West Africa and the Competing Prerogatives of the French Imperial State," *Comparative Studies in Society and History* 53, no. 3 (2011): 450–478.

18. Diop Decroix, interview. Ferlo is a semiarid region in northeastern Senegal.

19. Diop Decroix, interview.

20. Letter from Jean de Lagarde to the Minister of Foreign Affairs, 2 June 1968, ADMAE, Afrique: Sénégal (1959–1972), carton 49, Politique intérieure, Liasse: Crise de mai 1968, La Courneuve.

21. Senghor's 28 February 1971 decree is cited in Kalidou Diallo's "Libérté académiques, franchises universitaires et luttes syndicales, le cas du Sénégal, 1957–2003," published in Dakar as part of the 4ième Conference Internationale sur l'enseignement supérieur et la recherche, 30 octobre à 1 novembre, 2003, 4.

22. Leo Zeilig, *Revolt and Protest: Student Politics and Activism in Sub-Saharan Africa* (London: Tauris Academic Studies, 2007), 190.

23. "Mariane," interview by the author, Dakar, 30 November 2011; and "Abdou," interview.

24. See Magatte Lô, *Sénégal: Syndicalisme et participation reponsable* (Paris: L'Harmattan, 1987); and Dispatch of Jean de Lagarde to the Minister of Foreign Affairs (no. 350/DAM/S2), 8 May 1968, ADMAE, Afrique: Sénégal (1959–1972), carton 31, Synthèse de l'ambassade de France au Sénégal: Comptes rendus et dépêches hebdomadaires (mai-septembre 1968), La Courneuve. *Petits blancs* is a pejorative term used to describe either poor whites (often within France) or white colonial settlers of limited financial means and social status.

25. Bathily, *Mai 1968 à Dakar*, 27–28. See also Adama Mawa Ndiaye, "Sous le Sceau de l'histoire: L'itinéraire syndical (1946–1974) de feu" (Confédération Nationale des Travailleurs du Sénégal, 1986), in Dossier: Syndicalisme-Syndicats, ANS, Dakar.

26. Blum, "Senegal 1968," 156.

27. UNTS cited in 1968 that French capital dominated 70 percent of commerce, 80 percent of industry, and 56 percent of banking in Senegal. See Blum, "Senegal 1968," 156. This was also reflected at the University of Dakar, where non-Africans counted for nearly two-thirds of the teaching corps in 1967–1968.

28. See unidentified press clipping dated 4 June 1968 in Sénégal: Évenements Généraux 1966–1968, Liasse Dossiers Généraux1968, ANS, Dakar; and Guèye, *Mai 1968 au Sénégal*, 82–84.

29. Senghor even mulled plans to expel some of the particularly unruly Dominican priests. Thanks to Liz Foster for pointing out this dynamic. See correspondence to the French diplomatic post of the Holy See, cote 576PO/1 1449, Centre des Archives diplomatiques de Nantes, France; and Guèye, *Mai 1968 au Sénégal*, 223–242.

30. "Sanctions consecutives aux faits de grève," 19 June 1968; telegram of Ibrahima Faye, Governor of Siné-Saloum Kaolack, to President-Intersen Dakar Info, 5 June 1968;

and telegram of Aly Diouf, Governor of St. Louis, 5 June 1968, in Dossier 149: Mai-juin 1968, Archives École de Police, Dakar; and Guèye, *Mai 1968 au Sénégal*, 52.

31. Bathily, *Mai 1968 à Dakar*, 97.

32. Letter of Jean de Lagarde to Michel Debré, 7 June 1968, ADMAE, Afrique: Sénégal (1959–1972), carton 290, Questions syndicales, sociales et sanitaires (1959–1975), La Courneuve.

33. "Declaration du Bureau National de l'UNTS sur: 1) Les Questions d'organisations; 2) le problème de l'Université," 17 August 1968, in Sénégal: Évenements Généraux 1966–1968, Liasse Dossiers Généraux1968, ANS, Dakar.

34. Jakob Vogel, "Senghor et l'ouverture culturelle de la RFA en 68. Pour une histoire transnationale l'Allemagne—France—Afrique," *Vingtième Siècle* 2, no. 94 (2007): 145.

35. See Momar-Coumba Diop, "Le syndicalisme étudiant: Pluralisme et revendications," in *Sénégal: Trajectoires d'un Etat* (Dakar: Codesria, 1992), 440. Diop cites directly from UDES pamphlets from 1968 that call for "all democratic organizations and all patriotic forces to create a united front to rid Senegal of its neo-colonial servants."

36. Hassan El Nouty, "Pour une démythication des problèmes de l'éducation du Sénégal," in Balans, Coulon, and Ricard, *Problèmes et perspectives de l'éducation*, 90, 92–93.

37. Entelis, "Ideological Change," 543–568.

38. Telegram of Jean de Lagarde to the Minister of Foreign Affairs, 28 May 1968, ADMAE, Afrique: Sénégal (1959–1972), carton 49, Politique intérieure, Liasse: Crise de mai 1968, La Courneuve.

39. Details of the agreement can be found in "Communiqué final de la rencontre entre le gouvernement de l'Union Démocratique des Étudiants Sénégalais," signed 13 September 1968 by Emile Badiane, Minister of Technical Education and Professional Training, and Mbaye Diack, President of UDES, ADMAE, Afrique: Sénégal (1959–1972), carton 49, Politique intérieure, La Courneuve. Article no. 6 of the accord states, "The Senegalese government guarantees the participation of all students of Dakar in the elaboration of University reform." See Blum, "Senegal 1968," 171.

40. Table 2, "Africanisation du corps enseignant de 1970 à 1979," in Bathily, *Mai 1968 à Dakar*, 45.

41. "La touche sénégalaise," *Nouvel Horizon*, no. 236, 25 August 2000, 12–13. The article cites the recollections of former UDES president Mbaye Diack.

42. Four hundred and fifty foreign African students left for their countries of origin in spring 1966 in the government crackdown. See Communiqué of French Ambassador to Senegal, Jean de Lagarde, to Minister of Foreign Affairs, Maurice Couve de Murville, "Problèmes de l'Université de Dakar," 24 May 1966, in Education Nationale: Service universitaire des relations avec l'étranger et l'outre mer, AN-19771275, Article 10, Archives Nationales, Fontainebleau.

43. Letter of Jean de Lagarde to the Minister of Foreign Affairs, 11 January 1967, ADMAE, Afrique: Sénégal (1959–1972), carton 49, Politique intérieure, Liasse: Université de Dakar, 1967, La Courneuve.

44. Letter of Jean de Lagarde to the Minister of Foreign Affairs, 4 June 1967, ADMAE, Afrique: Sénégal (1959–1972), carton 48, Politique intérieure, Liasse: Situation Politique, La Courneuve.

45. "Mouvements étudiants africains," Note of the Direction des Affaires Africaines et Malgaches, 18 January 1967, ADMAE, Afrique: Généralités (1959–1979), carton 282, Syndicats d'étudiants africains et mouvements subversifs, La Courneuve.

46. Note from the Ambassador of France in Niamey to the Minister of Foreign Affairs, 6 January 1967, ADMAE, Afrique: Généralités (1959–1979), carton 282, Syndicats d'étudiants africains et mouvements subversifs, La Courneuve. See also Amady Aly Dieng, Mémoires d'un étudiant africain: De l'Université de Paris à mon retour au Sénégal (Dakar: Codesria, 2011), 2:85.

47. "La FEANF soutient l'Union des étudiants de Dakar et exige sa reconnaissance," 7 January 1967, in Tracts et documents de propagande / FEANF, Bibliothèque Nationale de France, Paris.

48. "La FEANF soutient l'Union des étudiants de Dakar et exige sa reconnaissance."

49. Niasse is still active in Senegalese politics and ran for president in 2012 against incumbent Abdoulaye Wade, losing to eventual president Macky Sall in a primary of the opposition coalition Benno Siggil Senegaal. He has been president of the National Assembly since 2012.

50. Letter from Jean de Lagarde to the Minister of Foreign Affairs, 11 January 1967, ADMAE, Afrique: Sénégal (1959–1972), carton 49, Politique intérieure, Liasse: Crise de mai 1968, La Courneuve.

51. Letter from Jean de Lagarde to the Minister of Foreign Affairs, 11 January 1967, ADMAE, Afrique: Sénégal (1959–1972), carton 49, Politique intérieure, Liasse: Crise de mai 1968, La Courneuve.

52. See "Projet de résolution sur les devoirs des étudiants relatifs à la paix," presented at the 9th Congress of UIE in Mongolia by delegates from Japan and Iraq, and passed unanimously, in Fonds AGEL-UNEF: AG UN 7/14, 56e Congrès de Lyon, July 1967, Bibliothèque Municipale (BM), Lyon Part-Dieu; and "Résolutions du 9e Congrès de l'UIE," in Fonds AGEL-UNEF: AG UN 16/1, Correspondances et Communications de l'UIE, BM, Lyon Part-Dieu. The Vietnam struggle received continued support in Dakar in early 1968 following the Tet Offensive. See "Journée de solidarité et de lutte des étudiants africains," UED, 28 February 1968, in Sénégal: Évenements Généraux 1966–1968, Liasse Dossiers Généraux 1968, ANS, Dakar.

53. "Abdou," interview. "Abdou" spoke adamantly about the strong influence of the PAI in spite of what he estimated as only about thirty or so underground student members at the university in 1968.

54. See Blum, "Senegal 1968," 149; and Ibrahima Thioub, "Le mouvement étudiant de Dakar et la vie politique sénégalaise: La Marche vers la crise de mai-juin 1968," in Almeida-Topor et al., Les Jeunes en Afrique, 275.

55. See Bathily, Mai 1968 à Dakar, 18; and letter from Jean de Lagarde to the Minister of Foreign Affairs, 2 June 1968, ADMAE, Afrique: Sénégal (1959–1972), carton 49, Liasse Crise Mai 68, Politique intérieure, La Courneuve.

56. Ousmane Camara, Mémoires d'un juge africain: Itinéraire d'un homme libre (Paris: Éditions Karthala, 2010), 159.

57. Bathily, Mai 1968 à Dakar, 16; and Dakar-matin, 1 June 1968.

58. See Balandier's preface in Smouts, La situation postcoloniale.

59. Bathily, Mai 1968 à Dakar, 155.

60. "Déclaration sur les récents événements," signed FEANF: Association des Étudiants Sénégalais en France, 8 August 1968.

61. "Mariane," interview.

62. Baro Diène, "Il y a eu un Mai 68 à Dakar parce qu'il y a eu un Mai 68 en France," in Special Edition of *Sud Quotidien*, "Que reste-il de Mai 68?" 30 May 2008.

63. See Jean-Pierre Filiu, *Mai 68 à l'ORTF: Une radio-télévision en résistance* (Paris: Nouveau Monde, 2008).

64. *Dakar-matin*, 1 June 1968. Critiques of the student protests included a sharp warning to workers to ignore UNTS orders to strike.

65. "Les troubles de Dakar," *Combat*, 1 June 1968.

66. Bathily, *Mai 1968 à Dakar*; Thioub, "Le mouvement étudiant de Dakar."

67. "La touche sénégalaise," *Nouvel Horizon*, no. 236, 25 August 2000, 12–13.

68. See Homi Bhabha, "Of Mimicry and Man: The Ambivalence of Colonial Discourse," in *The Location of Culture* (London: Routledge, 1994), 85–92.

69. Bathily, *Mai 1968 à Dakar*, 155–156.

70. "Mariane," interview.

71. "Mariane," interview.

72. Guèye, *Mai 1968 au Sénégal*, 214.

73. "Mariane," interview.

74. See telegram of Jean de Lagarde to the Minister of Foreign Affairs, 14 June 1968, ADMAE, Afrique: Sénégal (1959–1972), carton 49, Politique intérieure, Liasse: Crise de mai 1968, La Courneuve.

75. Momar-Coumba Diop, "La population expulsé du Sénégal de 1948 à 1978" (Dakar: unpublished, October 1979), available in ANS, Dakar.

76. Thioub, "Le mouvement étudiant de Dakar," 278–279.

77. Dieng, *Mémoires d'un étudiant*, 7–10.

78. Richard Ivan Jobs, "Youth Movements, Travel, Protest, and Europe in 1968," *American Historical Review* 114, no. 2 (2009): 385–389.

79. See "Il y a 40 ans, l'activiste Omar Blondin Diop mourait en détention à Gorée," *Agence de Presse Sénégalaises*, 10 May 2013, http://www.aps.sn/articles.php?id_article=112868.

80. *Le Monde*, 15 June 1968.

81. Quoted in Vogel, "Senghor et l'ouverture culturelle de la RFA en '68," 145.

82. *Le Monde*, 24 September 1968; and "Halting Movements towards University Reform," *Minerva* 7, no. 3 (1969): 527–533.

83. Reuters sent a reporter to the book fair solely for the purpose of covering Cohn-Bendit. See Peter Weidhaas, *Life before Letters*, trans. Lawrence Schofer (New York: Locus Publishing, 2010). The demonstration received little attention in English. For examples in French and German, see Vogel, "Senghor et l'ouverture culturelle de la RFA en '68"; and Wolfgang Kraushaar, *Frankfurter Schule und Studentenbewegung: Von der Flaschenpost zum Molotowcocktail, 1946–1995*, vol. 1 (Frankfurt am Main: Rogner & Bernhard bei Zweitausendeins, 1998), 468, cited in Martin Klimke, *The Other Alliance: Student Protest in West Germany and the United States in the Global Sixties* (Princeton, NJ: Princeton University Press), 119.

84. Vogel, "Senghor et l'ouverture culturelle de la RFA en '68," 7–12.

85. Senghor studied, among other things, German philosophy and literature in Paris in the 1930s. See Janos Riesz , "Senghor and the Germans," (trans. Aija Bjornson) *Research in African Literatures* 33, no. 4 (2002): 25–37.

86. Open letter to the President, signed by the Comité Exécutif de l'Union Démocratiques des Etudiants Sénégalais (UDES), 28 September 1968.

87. Open letter to the President, signed by the Comité Exécutif de l'Union Démocratiques des Etudiants Sénégalais (UDES), 28 September 1968. Vogel also notes that the SDS students, in true anarchist fashion, created an alternative peace prize, in which they nominated the assassinated Congolese leader Patrice Lumumba and the Maoist guerilla Hamilcar Cabral of Guinea-Bissau. Vogel, "Senghor et l'ouverture culturelle de la RFA en '68," 146.

88. Open letter to the President, signed by the Comité Exécutif de l'Union Démocratiques des Etudiants Sénégalais (UDES), 28 September 1968.

89. Omar Guèye points out that Negritude was thoroughly rejected by students opposed to Senghor. Guèye, *Mai 1968 au Sénégal*, 160–162. See also Burleigh Hendrickson, "The Politics of Colonial History: Bourguiba, Senghor, and the Student Movements of the Global 1960s," in *The Global 1960s: Convention, Contest, and Counterculture*, ed. Tamara Chaplin and Jadwiga E. Pieper Mooney (London: Routledge, 2018), 23–27.

90. Vieux Savané, "Un élan d'audace," in Special Edition of *Sud Quotidien*, "Que reste-il de Mai 68?" 30 May 2008.

91. On the concept of a "double-consciousness," building on W. E. B. Du Bois in the Anglophone context, see Paul Gilroy, *The Black Atlantic: Modernity and Double Consciousness* (Cambridge, MA: Harvard University Press, 1993).

92. Quoted in Stanislas Spero K. Adotevi, *Négritude et Négrologues* (Paris: Éditions Le Castor Astral, 1998), 102.

93. Quoted in Janet G. Vaillant, *Vie de Léopold Sédar Senghor: Noir, Français et Africain*, trans. Roger Meunier (Paris: Karthala, 2006), 426. The tensions in Senghor's cultural identification are also explored in Nassurdine Ali Mhoumadi, *Un métis nommé Senghor* (Paris: Harmattan, 2010).

94. "Être francisé ne représente pas que des avantages," *L'Unité Africaine*, no. 315, 1 August 1968.

95. "Toast du Président de la République au diner offert en l'honneur de M. le Sec. de'Etat aux Affaires Etrangères chargé de la coopération et de Mme. Yvon Bourgès," 2 April 1968, in Dossier Léopold Sédar Senghor: 1968, ANS, Dakar.

96. Quoted in Jaques Louis Hymans, *Léopold Sédar Senghor: An Intellectual Biography* (Edinburgh: Edinburgh University Press, 1971), 71. In addition to Frobenius, Senghor also noted the strong influence of Goethe.

97. "Présentation des Lettres de créance de S.E. M. Hubert Argod, Ambassadeur de France," 26 March 1969, in Dossier: Léopold Sédar Senghor, 1969, ANS, Dakar.

98. See generally Dossiers: Léopold Sédar Senghor, 1969–1971, ANS, Dakar.

99. See "Message à la Nation," 3 April 1970, in Dossier: Léopold Sédar Senghor, 1970, ANS, Dakar; and "Toast du Prés. de la République du Sénégal: Déjeuner en L'honneur de M. et Mme Georges Pompidou," 6 February 1971, in Dossier: Léopold Sédar Senghor, 1971, ANS, Dakar.

100. "Doléances des habitants du Sénégal," Saint-Louis du Sénégal, 15 April 1789, in *Doléances des peuples coloniaux à l'assemblée nationale constituante, 1789–1790* (Paris: Ar-

chives Nationales, 1989), 99. France briefly lost Senegal to the British during the Seven Years' War (1756–1763).

101. For example, Fanon downplayed the efficacy of dwelling on the past: "I concede that whatever proof there is of a wonderful Songhai civilization does not change the fact that Songhais today are undernourished, illiterate, abandoned to the skies and water, with a blank mind and glazed eyes." Fanon, *The Wretched of the Earth*, 148.

102. Fanon, *The Wretched of the Earth*, 151, 154.

103. El Nouty, "Pour une démythication," 98.

104. "Université Lavanium (Kinshasa) de la Négritude par Léopold Sédar Senghor," January 1969, in Dossier: Léopold Sédar Senghor, 1969, ANS, Dakar. On Rousseau's much-debated "noble savage," see his *Discourse on the Origins of Inequality (second discourse)*, ed. Roger D. Masters and Christopher Kelly, trans. Judith R. Bush (Hanover, NH: Dartmouth College, 1992).

105. One of Gary Wilder's ambitious political projects in *Freedom Time* is to "challenge a commonplace attempt to . . . dismiss Senghor as essentialist or comprador." Wilder, *Freedom Time*, 276n18.

106. Léopold Sédar Senghor, *Rapport de politique générale: Politique, nation et développement modern*, 5–7 January 1968 (Rufisque: Imprimerie Nationale, 1968).

107. Senghor's views on modernity were constructed during a period of nation-building and development that coincided with the "modernization theory" articulated by social scientists of the time. For a fascinating discussion of modernity and modernization theory in African historiography, see Lynn M. Thomas, "Modernity's Failings, Political Claims, and Intermediate Concepts," *American Historical Review* 116, no. 3 (June 2011): 727–740; and Cooper, *Colonialism in Question*, chapter 5.

108. "Rapport sur le développement des enseignements supérieurs en Afrique Francophone et à Madagascar: Document Programme," Ministère de L'Éducation Nationale, 1 December 1970, in Éducation Nationale: Service universitaire des relations avec l'Étranger et l'Outre-mer, AN-19770475, Article 01, Archives Nationales, Fontainebleau.

109. Quoted in letter of Hubert Argod to Maurice Schumann, 10 January 1970, in ADMAE, Afrique: Sénégal (1959–1972), carton 51, Politique intérieure, La Courneuve.

110. "Des libertés démocratiques au Sénégal à la veille de la mascarade électorale du 25 février 1968," signed UDES, 24 February 1968, in Sénégal: Événements 1966–68, Liasse: Dossier généraux 1968, ANS, Dakar.

111. Dispatch of Hubert Argod to the Ministry of Foreign Affairs, 10 January 1970, ADMAE, Afrique: Sénégal (1959–1972), carton 56, Politique Extérieure: Relation avec divers pays de l'Afrique noire (octobre 1961—novembre 1972), La Courneuve.

112. "Message à la nation," 10 November 1970, in Dossier: Léopold Sédar Senghor, 1971, Archives Nationales du Sénégal, Dakar.

113. Jean-Pierre N'Diaye, "Francophonie et négritude," *Jeune Afrique* 86 (November 1991).

114. Jean-Pierre N'Diaye, "Les universités en Afrique," *Jeune Afrique* 568 (27 November 1971): 20.

115. Bathily, *Mai 1968 à Dakar*. For a similar reading, see also Pascal Bianchini, *Ecole et politique en Afrique noire: Sociologie des crises et des réformes du système d'enseignement au Sénégal et au Burkina Faso (1960–2000)* (Paris: Karthala, 2004), 99–101.

116. André Bailleul, "L'Université de Dakar, institution et fonctionnement (1950–1984)," (PhD diss., Université de Dakar, 1984), 55. For Senghor's version of African socialism as applied to the University of Dakar, see Léopold Sédar Senghor, *On African Socialism*, trans. Mercer Cook (New York: Praeger, 1964), 60–65.

117. Though the French movement is commonly referred to as mai 68, scholars have highlighted the continued activism after de Gaulle's famous 30 May speech, which coincided with the height of action in Dakar. See Damamme et al., *Mai-Juin 68*.

5. From Student to Worker Protest in Tunisia

1. "Une Tunisienne citoyenne des deux rives: Simone Lellouche-Othmani," *Mémoire & Horizon*, numéro spécial, published by Citoyenne des Deux Rives (April 2007), 43.

2. Lellouche wrote to the ambassador of France describing her consternation upon hearing through the press the news of her prison sentence of five and a half years, after being expelled by the Tunisian police in April 1968. Letter from Simone Lellouche to the Ambassador of France in Tunisia, undated, in Fonds Othmani, SOL 28, BDIC, Nanterre.

3. Letter from Simone Lellouche Othmani to M. Claude Jullien of *Monde Diplomatique*, 3 December 1977, Paris, in Fonds Othmani, SOL 29, BDIC, Nanterre.

4. For a comparison of Tunisia's February 1972 with France's May 1968, see "Une Tunisienne citoyenne des deux rives," 47. The Tunisian minister of national education, Mohamed Mzali, announced closures of the universities of Tunis until September 1972 through the press. *L'Action*, 8 February 1972.

5. Some editions of *El Amel Tounsi* were also published in French as *Le Travailleur tunisien*. Amel Tounsi later became the name of a Perspectives splinter group also known as the Organisation du travailleur tunisien in 1973, which created a new series of *El Amel Tounsi* and gave birth to the current Parti ouvrier des communistes de Tunisie (Tunisian Communist Workers' Party), headed by former Perspectives member Hamma Hammami.

6. See "Tunisie: Une université en grève et . . . un ministre raciste," *Politique-Hebdo* 15 (10 February 1972).

7. See the tract "L'Unité et la cohésion des étudiants sont necéssaires pour faire echec aux forces réactionnaires et aux diviseurs," in Fonds Othmani, SOL 3, BDIC, Nanterre.

8. Simone Lellouche Othmani, interview by the author, Tunis, 16 June 2011.

9. Lellouche Othmani, interview. See also "Une Tunisienne citoyenne des deux rives," 6.

10. Bourguiba gave himself the moniker "the Supreme Combatant," which resulted in a plethora of puns from protesters. "Mouvement de février 1972 en Tunisie: Un nouveau bond dans le combat de la jeunesse intellectuelle," *Perspectives Tunisiennes*, brochure no. 8 (1972), 6, 9.

11. See "Abdel," interview by the author, Tunis, 14 April 2011.

12. Mohamed Dhifallah, "Bourguiba et les étudiants: Stratégie en mutation (1956–1971)," in Camau and Geisser, *Habib Bourguiba*, 321, 323.

13. For an account of the failings of Ben Salah's agricultural experiment and his subsequent charge of treason, see Perkins, *A History of Modern Tunisia*, 150–152.

14. "Abdel," interview.

15. "Bilan du Comité d'Action et de Lutte, 1972," in Fonds de la Fédération des Tunisiens pour une citoyenneté des deux rives (FTCR), carton G2/2 (1), Génériques, Paris.

16. Entelis, "Ideological Change," 554–555.

17. See *Tribune Progressiste*, no. 13 (February–March 1972); "Mouvement de février 1972"; and "Bulletin d'Information du 27 mars 1972," Groupe d'Information pour les Luttes en Tunisie (GILT), in Fonds Simone Lellouche et Ahmed Othmani (Fonds Othmani), SOL 3, BDIC, Nanterre.

18. See US State Department, *Report on Human Rights* (1998), cited in Olivia Ball, *"Every Morning, Just Like Coffee." Torture in Cameroon* (London: Medical Foundation for the Care of Victims of Torture, 2002).

19. "Jamel," interview by the author, Tunis, 19 April 2011. Jamel met with a lawyer for the first time after six months of intermittent isolation and torture. He was released without trial.

20. See letter from Simone Lellouche Othmani to the Tunisian Human Rights League in Tunis, 28 October 1977, in Fonds Othmani, SOL 26, BDIC, Nanterre.

21. See Archives d'Association: UNEF, AN-19870110, Article 134: "Projet de status présenté par le B.E.[de l'UGET]," Archives Nationales, Fontainebleau. Participants such as Ahmed Smaoui, Aïssa Baccouche, and Khaled Guezmir recalled the general assembly and its preceding events at Korba at the academic conference "Le Congrès de extraordinaire de l'UGET de février 1972, quarante années après," Tunis, 6–7 February 2012.

22. "Motion: Pétition proposée par le CAL-UGET (Base Vincennes)," undated, listed as "Document no. 8" in a booklet of tracts, "UGET 1972–1973," in Fonds FTCR, G2/2 (1), Section provisoire de Paris, Génériques, Paris.

23. "Bilan du comité d'action et de lutte de l'UGET Paris," February 1973, in Fonds FTCR, G2/2 (1), Section provisoire de Paris, Génériques, Paris.

24. *L'Action*, 2 February 1972.

25. *L'Action*, 2 February 1972; and *L'Action*, 3 February 1972. The latter article also notes that Lellouche was convicted by the Special Court, was not enrolled in the university, and was a foreign resident. Incidentally, this was also the only time that Simone Lellouche Othmani was ever granted permission to visit her husband at the civil prison in Tunis. See Lellouche Othmani, interview.

26. *L'Action*, 3 February 1972; and *L'Action*, 9 February 1972.

27. Portions of Masmoudi's interview in *Al-Amal*, the Arabic-language journal of the PSD, regarding the February movement were translated and published in the French daily *La Presse*, 2 March 1972. The Latin Quarter here refers to the primary site of student resistance during the French May 1968.

28. *La Presse*, 3 March 1972.

29. See *L'Action*, 11 March 1972; and "Communiqué de l'UD CFDT," Lyon, 28 February 1972, in Fonds *Cahiers de mai*, côte F delta res 578/68, BDIC, Nanterre.

30. "Bilan présenté par la commission d'information," GILT, 8 August 1972, Paris, in Fonds Othmani, SOL 3, BDIC, Nanterre.

31. *La Presse*, 2 March 1972.

32. "Communiqué de Novembre 1973," undated, in Fonds Othmani, SOL 3, BDIC, Nanterre, and Report of 5 June 1973, in Direction des Libertés Publiques et des Affaires

Juridiques, sous-direction étrangers, AN-19990260, Article 23, Archives Nationales, Fontainebleau.

33. See "Mouvement de février 1972 en Tunisie."

34. "Mouvement de février 1972 en Tunisie," 13.

35. See *Tribune Progressiste*, no. 13 (February–March 1972), 10.

36. *Tribune Progressiste*, no. 13 (February–March 1972), 16–17.

37. See "Bulletin d'Information du 14 mars 1972" and "Bulletin d'Information du 27 mars," GILT, in Fonds Othmani, SOL 3, BDIC, Nanterre.

38. "Perspectives: Nouvelles arrestations en Tunisie," Correspondance APL, 2 August 1972, in "Bulletin d'Information du 27 mars."

39. "Tentative de Bilan sur les problèmes de la défense," undated, CTIDVR, in Fonds Othmani, SOL 29, BDIC, Nanterre.

40. Lellouche Othmani provided her address and opened a bank account in her name for early iterations of *El Amel Tounsi*. See Lellouche Othmani, interview. Rights of association were not granted in full to foreigners until the arrival of Mitterrand's Socialist government and the law of 10 October 1981. See Rémy Leveau and Catherine Wihtol de Wenden, "Évolution des attitudes politiques des immigrés Maghrébins," *Vingtième Siècle. Revue d'histoire*, no. 7, numéro special: Étrangers, immigrés, Français (1985): 79.

41. "Bilan Novembre 73-Juin 74," undated, in Fonds Othmani, SOL 29, BDIC, Nanterre.

42. "Communiqué de Novembre 1973," undated, in "Bilan Novembre 73-Juin 74."

43. For more on the MTA, see Rabah Aissaoui, *Immigration and National Identity: North African Political Movements in Colonial and Postcolonial France* (New York: Palgrave Macmillan, 2009), 153–217; and "Le Discours du Mouvement des travailleurs arabes (MTA) aux années 1970 en France: Mobilisation et mémoire du combat anticolonial," *Hommes et Migration* 1263 (2006): 105–119.

44. Lellouche Othmani, interview. Unlike her husband, Lellouche Othmani was never an official member of Perspectives, though she maintained regular contact with many of its members.

45. "CISDHT - La lutte contre la répression: Information, assistance juridique, soutien des prisonniers," undated, in Fonds Othmani, SOL 28, BDIC, Nanterre.

46. Lellouche Othmani, interview.

47. "Rapport auto-critique," undated, CISDHT, in Fonds Othmani, SOL 28, BDIC, Nanterre.

48. The attempt on Hamchari's life was made on 8 December 1972, and he eventually died due to related complications on 9 January 1973 in Paris. See footnote in Abdellali Hajjat, "Les comités Palestine (1970–1972): Aux origines du soutien de la cause palestinienne en France," *Revue d'études palestiniennes* 98 (2006): 26. Hamchari is buried in the Père Lachaise cemetery in Paris. In 2011, Chammari was named Tunisian ambassador to UNESCO following the January revolution.

49. Numerous police reports from the prefecture on student activities and various organizations from June 1968 to February 1969 can be found, through *dérogation* in Direction Générale de la Police Nationale, AN-19910194, Article 09, Liasse 06: "tracts juin 1968 - février 1969," Archives Nationales, Fontainebleau. It should be noted that l'Office de Coopération et d'Accueil Universitaire also kept records of the activity of

African foreign students as early as the 1960s. See Office de Coopération et d'Accueil Universitaire, AN-20010120, Article 48, Archives Nationales, Fontainebleau.

50. See the "Liste des Arabes de Diverses Nationalités Susceptibles d'apporter leur soutien aux terroristes Palestiniens," created in September 1972 by the Direction de la Surveillance du Territoire, in Direction des Libertés Publiques et des Affaires Juridiques, sous-direction étrangers, AN-19990260, Article 23, Archives Nationales, Fontainebleau. Figures such as Michel Foucault, Alain Geismar, and Alain Krivine, leader of the Communist Revolutionary League, also appeared on surveillance lists.

51. On collaboration and French colonial surveillance techniques, see Kathleen A. Keller, "Political Surveillance and Colonial Urban Rule: 'Suspicious' Politics and Urban Space in Dakar, Senegal, 1918–1939," *French Historical Studies* 35, no. 4 (2012): 727–749; Robert Aldrich, "Conclusion: The Colonial Past and Postcolonial Present," in *The French Colonial Mind*, ed. Martin Thomas, vol. 2, *Violence, Military Encounters, and Colonialism*(Lincoln: University of Nebraska Press, 2011), 334–356.

52. These were the same oppositional groups cited by Mohamed Sayah, secretary-general of the Destourian Youth and deputy director of the PSD, in Parti socialiste destourien, *La Vérité sur la subversion à l'Université de Tunis* ([Tunis]: Parti socialiste destourien, 1968). See "La police coopère," *L'Express* (10–16 April 1972); "'Coopération franco-tunisienne' à la Cité Universitaire," *Politique-Hebdo* 18 (2 March 1972); and "La traite des tunisiens," GEAST-Paris, 13 June 1972, in Fonds Othmani, SOL 2, BDIC Nanterre.

53. The Neo-Destour, created in 1934 and led by Bourguiba, was renamed the Parti Socialiste Destourien in 1964 following Tunisian independence.

54. I treat the relationship between Tunisian student and worker movements in greater detail in Burleigh Hendrickson, "Student Activism and the Birth of the Tunisian Human Rights Movement, 1968–1978," in *Étudiants africains en mouvement: Contribution à une histoire des années 1968*, ed. Françoise Blum, Pierre Guidi, and Ophélie Rillon (Paris: Publications de la Sorbonne, 2016), 233–247.

55. *L'Action*, 11 February 1972.

56. Mahmoud Ben Romdhane, "Mutations économiques et sociales et mouvement ouvrier en Tunisie de 1956 à 1980," in *Le mouvement ouvrier maghrébin*, ed. Noureddine Sraïeb and the Centre de recherches et d'études sur les sociétés méditerranéennes (Paris: Éditions du Centre national de la recherche scientifique, 1985), 279.

57. Romdhane, "Mutations économiques et sociales," 280.

58. See Newsletter no. 02381 of the Collectif Tunisien 26 janvier, undated, in Fonds Othmani, SOL 34, BDIC, Nanterre.

59. Quoted in Marguerite Rollinde, "Les émeutes en Tunisie: Un défi à l'état?," in *Émeutes et mouvements sociaux au Maghreb: Perspective comparée*, ed. Didier Le Saout and Margureite Rollinde (Paris: Karthala, 1999), 113.

60. See Solène Leroux, "Ce jour-là: Le 26 janvier 1978, le 'jeudi noir' paralyse la Tunisie de Bourguiba," *Jeune Afrique* (26 January 1978), http://www.jeuneafrique.com/520107/culture/ce-jour-la-le-26-janvier-1978-le-jeudi-noir-paralyse-la-tunisie-de-bourguiba/.

61. Lellouche Othmani, interview; "Le rôle politique et culturel de Perspectives et des Perspectivistes dans la Tunisie indépendante," in *Mouvements nationaux tunisiens et maghrébins*, series 3, 17 (2008): 144; and "Interview - Dr. Saadedine Zmerli, ex-président de la Ligue Tunisienne des Droits de l'Homme," *Le Temps*, 16 February 2011.

62. See Nigel Disney, "The Working Revolt in Tunisia," *MERIP Reports*, no. 67 (May 1978), 12–14.

63. "Le massacre du 26 janvier," *Afrique-Asie* 154 (February 1978). After political claims against previous regimes were liberalized following the Tunisian revolution of January 2011, UGTT leaders called for an investigation into the Bourguiba regime's acts of torture associated with the events of Black Thursday.

64. "Procès des libertés démocratiques et syndicales en Tunisie," Bulletin spécial no. 27 (September 1978), CTIDVR, Paris, in Fonds Othmani, SOL 32, BDIC, Nanterre.

65. See the International Labor Organization, "Interim Report No. 197," Case No. 899 (Tunisia), November 1979, http://www.ilo.org/dyn/normlex/en/f?p =1000:50002:0::NO::P50002_COMPLAINT_TEXT_ID:2900103#1.

66. Othmani with Bessis, *Beyond Prison*, 21–22.

67. "Plateforme du Collectif," in Newsletter of Collectif Tunisien du 26 janvier, undated, in Fonds Othmani, SOL 34, BDIC, Nanterre.

68. "À Propos des évenements du 26-1-78 en Tunisie," letter from Simone Lellouche Othmani to the Collectif, 10 February 1978, in Fonds Othmani, SOL 34, BDIC, Nanterre.

69. See "L'Action d'Amnesty International," in Flash Info of the Collectif Tunisien du 26 Janvier, March 1979, in Fonds Othmani, SOL 34, BDIC, Nanterre; and *Amnesty International: Rapport 1979* (Paris: Éditions Mazarine, 1980), 210–214.

70. See Bulletin no. 4 of the Collectif Tunisien du 26 Janvier, undated, in Fonds Othmani, SOL 34, BDIC, Nanterre.

71. Flash d'information, "Témoignages de l'intérieur de la prison de Sousse sur la torture," undated, in Fonds Othmani, SOL 34, BDIC, Nanterre. BOP stands for Brigades de l'Ordre Public, similar to the French CRS.

72. See International Labor Organization, "Interim Report No. 197."

73. "Les structures syndicales provisoires de l'UGET soutiennent la classe ouvrière tunisienne dans sa lutte pour une UGTT autonome, démocratique, représentative et combattive," section provisoire de l'UGET, undated; and "À bas le congrès fantôche de l'UGTT!," le comité de section provisoire de Paris, UGET, 24 February 1978, in Fonds FTCR, G2/2 (2), Section provisoire de Paris, Génériques, Paris.

74. See "Les structures syndicales provisoires de l'UGET soutiennent la classe ouvrière"; "À bas le circulaire de Nouira," l'UGET, section provisoire de Paris, January 1978, in Fonds FTCR, G2/2 (2), Section provisoire de Paris, Génériques, Paris.

75. "Les structures syndicales provisoires de l'UGET soutiennent la classe ouvrière."

76. Sayah furnished me with a copy of the pamphlet and confirmed his authorship in 2010.

77. Parti socialiste destourien, *La politique contractuelle et les événements de janvier 1978* (Tunis: Éditions Dar el Amar, 1978), 29–30, 47.

78. Cited in "Le massacre du 26 janvier," *Afrique-Asie* 154 (February 1978), 25; and Disney, "The Working Revolt in Tunisia," 14.

79. Parti socialiste destourien, *La politique contractuelle*, 67, 82 (emphasis added).

80. Both MDS and MUP were illegal in 1978, though MDS was officially recognized in 1983. See Clement Henry Moore, "Tunisia and Bourguisme: Twenty Years of Crisis," *Third World Quarterly* 10, no. 1 (1988), 186; and interview with Mohamed Sayah, in Camau and Geisser, *Habib Bourguiba*, 633. Ben Salah's MUP had been involved in

the founding of the Tunisian Collective of 26 January, based in Paris, but severed ties at the behest of a political cartel within its ranks. See Flash Info of the Collectif Tunisien du 26 Janvier, January 1980, in Fonds Othmani, SOL 34, BDIC, Nanterre.

81. Parti socialiste destourien, *La politique contractuelle*, 66.

82. Parti socialiste destourien, *La politique contractuelle*, 66.

83. Rollinde, "Les émeutes en Tunisie," 126.

6. Immigrant Activism and Activism for Immigrants in France

1. Gordon lumped immigrants together, however. "An Andalucian in Barcelona, an emigrant from the *mezzogiorno* to northern Italy or a Portuguese worker in Paris, like a Breton or an Auvergnat in 19th-century Paris, was an immigrant and an excluded outsider in ways that differed only in degree from the classic (post-) colonial migrant from North Africa to France." Gordon, *Immigrants & Intellectuals*, 10.

2. Chérif Ferjani, interview by the author, Lyon, 10 February 2010.

3. *Le Monde*, 20–23 March and 19–20 April 1970.

4. See Amit Prakash, "Colonial Techniques in the Imperial Capital: The Prefecture of Police and the Surveillance of North Africans in Paris, 1925-circa 1970," *French Historical Studies* 36, no. 3 (2013): 479–510. Prakash also notes that a special French policing unit was created for the purpose of surveilling North Africans.

5. Pierre Milza, *Fascisme français: Passé et present* (Paris: Flammarion, 1987), 335.

6. On the shift from anti-Semitism to anti-Arabism, see Todd Shepard, "Algerian Reveries on the Far Right: Thinking about Algeria to Change France in 1968," in Jackson, Milne, and Williams, *May 68*, 77; and Pierre Milza, *L'Europe en chemise noire: Les extremes droits en Europe de 1945 à aujourd'hui* (Paris: Fayard, 2002), 202.

7. Shepard, "Algerian Reveries," 82.

8. See Patrick Seale and Maureen McConville, *Red Flag / Black Flag: French Revolution 1968* (New York: Putnam, 1968), 44–47. The Communist League was largely composed of the remaining members of the JCR, which was banned by the French government along with at least six other activist groups in 1968. Both the Communist League and the New Order were dissolved in the summer of 1973 after the two clashed at a New Order rally.

9. *Ce que veut la Ligue communiste, Section française de la 4e Internationale; manifeste du Comité central des 29 et 30 janvier 1972* (Paris: F. Maspero, 1972), 159.

10. *Ce que veut la Ligue communiste*, 89.

11. *Les Prisonniers politiques parlent: Le combat des détenus politiques: grève de la faim procès des diffuseurs de "La cause du peuple"* (Paris: François Maspero, 1970), 6.

12. *Les Prisonniers politiques*, 21.

13. *Le Monde*, 20 March 1970.

14. *Les Prisonniers politiques parlent*, 23. Canu was arrested in September 1970 for trying to reconstitute a dissolved illegal organization.

15. Alain Geismar, interview by Robert Gildea, Paris, 29 May 2007, quoted in Chris Reynolds, "From *mai-juin '68* to *Nuit Debout*: Shifting Perspectives on France's Antipolice," *Modern & Contemporary France* 26, no. 2 (2018): 153–154.

16. See interview with Hervé Bourges in *The French Student Revolt; the Leaders Speak*, trans. B. R. Brewster (New York: Hill and Wang, 1968), 46–47. Fausto Giudice cites

Geismar for having confused the events of 17 October 1961 and February 1962 into one "Charonne" in *Arabicides: Une chronique française, 1970–1991* (Paris: La Découverte, 1992).

17. Robert Linhart, *The Assembly Line*, trans. Margaret Crosland (Amherst: University of Massachusetts Press, 1981), 18–19.

18. Linhart, *The Assembly Line*, 85–106. Before organizing at the Citroën factory, Linhart and other UJC(ml) members were invited to the People's Republic of China in 1967 to witness the Great Proletarian Cultural Revolution. Reid, "*Établissment*," 85.

19. Linhart, *The Assembly Line*.

20. See, generally, Simont, Martin, and Le Dantec, *Ouvriers volontaires*.

21. *Le Monde*, 21 September 1973. See also Silverman, *Deconstructing the Nation*, 52.

22. Quoted in House and MacMaster, *Paris 1961*, 257.

23. "On assassine à Paris," tract signed by the Comités Palestines and Groupes Antiracistes, undated, in Fonds de la Gauche Prolétarienne, F delta res 576 5/9/2, BDIC, Nanterre.

24. See Thomas R. Flynn, *Sartre, Foucault, and Historical Reason*, vol. 1, *Toward an Existentialist Theory of History* (Chicago: University of Chicago Press, 2005), 239–243; and Mark Poster, *Foucault, Marxism, and History: Mode of Production versus Mode of Information* (Cambridge: Polity Press, 1984), chapter 1.

25. Mark G. E. Kelly, *The Political Philosophy of Michel Foucault* (New York: Routledge, 2009), 17.

26. Gordon, *Immigrants & Intellectuals*, 124–126. Djellali Ben Ali's sister wondered why it took the death of her brother to draw attention to the miserable living and working conditions of her neighborhood. See also David Macey, *The Lives of Michel Foucault: A Biography* (New York: Pantheon Books, 1993), 307–309.

27. See "On réprime ici [Paris], on réprime là-bas [Tunis]," undated tract, in Fonds Othmani, SOL 28 bis, BDIC, Nanterre.

28. Abdellali Hajjat, "Des Comités Palestine au Mouvement des Travailleurs Arabes (1970–1976)," in Boubeker and Hajjat, *Histoire politique des immigrations (post)coloniales*, 145–156.

29. Rabah Aissaoui, "Political Mobilization of North African Migrants in 1970s France: The Case of the Mouvement des Travailleurs Arabes (MTA)," *Journal of Muslim Minority Affairs* 26, no. 2 (August 2006): 172.

30. "Grève victorieuse à Penarroya Lyon," tract of SGEN-CFDT Bellevue, March 1972, in Fonds Cahiers de mai, cote F delta res 578/69, BDIC, Nanterre.

31. See "Penarroya: Les immigrés ont beaucoup à dire, et ils le disent," in *Politique-Hebdo* 17 (24 February 1972); and the documentary film by Daniel Anselme and Dominique Dubosc (dirs.), *Dossier Penarroya: Les deux visages du trust*, 1972.

32. After changing names several times through various acquisitions, remnants of the Penarroya Trust are currently grouped under the French multinational corporation Imerys, which specializes in mining and industrial mineral processing. On early signs of hazardous conditions, see "Correspondances et conventions collectives relatives aux salaires et conditions générales des employés de la société minière et metallurgique de Penarroya fonderie de Mégrine" (1936–1948), in Série SG/SG 2, carton 358, Archives Nationales de Tunisie, Tunis; and Gilbert Troly, "La Société minière et métallurgique de Penarroya," *Annales des Mines—Réalités Industrielles* 2008, no. 3 (2008): 31–32.

33. Certain factories employed primarily North African immigrants while others employed Portuguese, Italian, Spanish, and sub-Saharan African immigrants. The recruitment process is noted by Portuguese, Moroccan, and Tunisian workers who claimed that French companies targeted foreigners with little education and limited French fluency. See poster, "Pour vous faire savoir . . . qu'avec un contrat de travail on est un esclave," undated, publié avec le soutien de L'Union Nationale des Comités de Lutte d'Ateliers et le Comité de Défense de la vie et des droits des immigrés, in Fonds Cahiers de mai, côte F delta res 576/5/9/2, BDIC, Nanterre.

34. See "Convention Collective," signed in Tunis, 8 August 1936, in Série SG/SG 2, carton 358, Archives Nationales de Tunisie, Tunis.

35. Though there is little documentation of the Megrine strike outside of a reference in the 16 March 1972 issue of *Politique-Hebdo*, a Tunisian student activist stated that he had collected funds in support of the workers and confirmed Kharchi's leadership role. "Abdel," interview by the author, Tunis, 14 April 2011. The International Labor Organization also released a report listing UGTT members, including Belgacem Kharchi, who had been released by 1979. See International Labor Organization, "Interim Report No. 197."

36. Ross, *May '68 and Its Afterlives*, 95–96.

37. "Lettre collective des ouvriers de l'usine Pennaroya de Lyon aux ouvriers des usines Pennaroya de Saint-Denis et d'Escaudoeuvres," cote F delta res 578/68, Bibliothèque de Documentation Internationale Contemporaine, Nanterre.

38. "Bilan Financier au 1er mars 1972 du soutien aux travailleurs de Penarroya," signed by René Gauthier, Treasurer of the Committee of Support, in Fonds Cahiers de mai, côte F delta res 578/69, BDIC, Nanterre.

39. The Oued el Heimer Penarroya factory was located near Oujda in northeastern Morocco, close to the Algerian border. Michel Leclercq traveled to the factory in 1981 after the Association of Moroccans in France alleged the cause of the children's deaths. See Michel Leclercq, interview by the author, Lyon, 16 May 2011; and pamphlet of the Association des Marocains en France, "Pourquoi 31 enfants morts en un an et demi," in private archive of Michel Leclercq.

40. Ross, *May '68 and Its Afterlives*, 112.

41. Ross, *May '68 and Its Afterlives*, 112.

42. "Edmond Maire à Penarroya," *Politique-Hebdo* 19 (9 March 1972). It should be noted that although the Saint-Denis site halted its February 1972 strike after only one day once the CGT stepped in, it had already achieved significant gains during a previous January-February 1971 strike.

43. Tract "Mise au point des forgerons sur le tract 'gauchiste' du 16 juin 1971," 21 June 1971, in Fonds Cahiers de mai, côte F delta res 578/56, BDIC, Nanterre.

44. Official census data list increases in North African populations from approximately 40,000 in 1946 to over 1.1 million in 1975. In all likelihood these numbers were much larger since undocumented immigrants were not measured. I thank Jean-Philippe Dedieu and Aïssatou Mbodj-Pouye for pointing me to these statistics: "Étrangers selon la nationalité de 1946 à 1999," Institut national de la statistique et des études économiques, accessed 28 October 2017. https://www.insee.fr/fr/statistiques/fichier/2118512/rp99pipe_r6.xls

45. "Procès Verbal de la conférence nationale des travailleurs arabes," 17–18 June 1972, Paris, in Fonds de la Gauche Prolétarienne, côte F delta res 576 5/9/2, BDIC, Nanterre.

46. "Procès Verbal de la conférence nationale des travailleurs arabes."

47. The Amicales had been set up in France following independence in the Maghreb ostensibly to serve immigrant populations. Each nation had its own office and reported to the home government such that the Amicales had the dual function of assisting and surveilling immigrant populations. See Hajjat, "Les comités Palestine," 12–13; and Elise Franklin, "A Slow End to Empire: Social Aid Associations, Family Migration, and Decolonization in France and Algeria, 1954–1981" (PhD diss., Boston College, 2017).

48. Mahfoud Bennoune, "Maghribin Workers in France," *MERIP Reports*, no. 34 (1975), 12. See also Yvan Gastaut, "La flambée raciste de 1973," *Revue européenne de migrations internationales* 9, no. 2 (1993): 61–75. Violent attacks were particularly prevalent in the south of France, especially Marseille.

49. See Silverman, *Deconstructing the Nation*, 49–51; and Catherine Wihtol de Wenden, *Les Immigrés et la politique* (Paris: Presses de la Fondation Nationale des Sciences Politiques, 1988), 165–169.

50. Gordon, *Immigrants & Intellectuals*, 128. For the MTA's continued activities in the 1970s, see Abdellali Hajjat, "Le MTA et la 'grève générale' contre le racisme de 1973," *Plein droit* 67 (2005): 36–40; and Aissaoui, "Political Mobilization of North African Migrants," 171–186.

51. Aissaioui, "Political Mobilization of North African Migrants," 173.

52. Fonds Duyrat (1 1/4), côte F delta rés 708, BDIC, Nanterre.

53. See, generally, Fonds Duyrat (1 1/4), côte F delta rés 708, BDIC, Nanterre.

54. "Quel masque va mettre Bourguiba pour les prochaines élections," in Fonds Duyrat (1 1/4), côte F delta rés 708, BDIC, Nanterre.

55. Fonds Duyrat (1 1/4), côte F delta rés 708/2, BDIC, Nanterre.

56. From an unidentified and undated newspaper clipping of an article titled "Valence: Grève de la faim contre l'expulsion de 19 Tunisiens: Nous, ce qu'on demande, c'est d'avoir les papiers en règle," in Fonds Duyrat (1 1/4), côte F delta rés 708/2, BDIC, Nanterre.

57. *Le Monde*, 26 December 1972.

58. Coryell Schofield, "Europe's Immigrant Workers: New Grapes of Wrath," *Ramparts* 12, no. 8 (March 1974): 18–19.

59. Bennoune, "Maghribin Workers in France," 11–12.

60. Abdoulaye Gueye, "The Colony Strikes Back: African Protest Movements in Postcolonial France," *Comparative Studies of South Asia, Africa and the Middle East* 26, no. 2 (2006): 225–242. Jean-Philippe Dedieu has also addressed this imbalance in *La parole immigrée: Les migrants africains dans l'espace public en France (1960–1995)* (Paris: Klincksiek, 2012).

61. See figure 1, "Immigrant Population in France by Region of Origin," in David Lessaut and Cris Beauchemin, "Migration from Sub-Saharan Africa to Europe: Still a Limited Trend," *Population and Societies* 452, Institut national d'études démographiques (January 2009): 1. The figure for sub-Saharan immigrants may have jumped significantly by the mid-1960s, when Jean-Pierre N'Diaye estimates that between fifty thousand and sixty thousand Black African laborers made their way to France in 1962, and that figure continued to climb through 1969. See N'Diaye, *Négriers modernes; les travailleurs noirs en France* (Paris: Présence africaine, 1970): 21.

62. N'Diaye, *Négriers modernes*, 36–39.

63. *Le Monde*, 8 August 1973.

64. See N'Diaye, *Négriers modernes*, 12–13; and Yvan Gastaut, "Les bidonvilles, lieux d'exclusion et de marginalité en France durant les trente glorieuses," *Cahiers de la Méditerranée* 69 (2004): 6.

65. Quoted in Gastaut, "Les bidonvilles, lieux d'exclusion," 6. See also "Région Parisienne: Une éruption de microbidonvilles," *Politique-Hebdo* 15 (10 February 1972).

66. N'Diaye, *Négriers modernes*, 13.

67. Gordon, *Immigrants & Intellectuals*, 101–102.

68. Gueye, "The Colony Strikes Back," 228.

69. See Choukri Hmed, "Contester une institution dans le cas d'une mobilisation improbable: La 'grève des loyers' dans les foyers Sonacotra dans les années 1970," *Sociétés Contemporaines* 65, no. 1 (2007): 10.

70. N'Diaye, *Négriers modernes*, 113–114. The figures represented the equivalent of approximately 1,400 and 400 French francs, respectively, in 1963. These are most assuredly wild overvaluations of average immigrant monthly salaries. According to a study on private enterprises, the average salary of a French male employee in a non-managerial position in 1963 was 9,747 French francs per year (or around 810 French francs per month). See table 1, "Salaire net annuels moyens par sexe et catégorie socioprofessionnelle du 1950à 1975," in Christian Baudelot and Anne Lebeaupin, "Les salaires de 1950 à 1975," *Économie et statistique* 113, no. 1 (1979): 15.

71. N'Diaye, *Négriers modernes*, 116.

72. See Gillian Glaes, "Marginalised, yet Mobilised: The UGTSF, African Immigration, and Racial Advocacy in Postcolonial France," *French Cultural Studies* 24, no. 2 (2013): 178.

73. Gillian Glaes, "Sally N'Dongo, immigration africaine et aspects politiques du néocolonialisme en Afrique de L'Ouest et en France," *Migrance* 39 (December 2012), 99. See also Sally N'Dongo, *La "Coopération" franco-africaine* (Paris: François Maspero, 1972).

74. Despite comparatively weak coordination between sub-Saharan African students and workers, Jean-Philippe Dedieu and Aïssatou Mbodj-Pouye uncovered transnational efforts of journals like *Révolution Afrique* to support oppressed Africans in Europe and back home. See Dedieu and Mbodj-Pouye, "The First Collective Protest of Black African Migrants in Postcolonial France (1960–1975): A Struggle for Housing and Rights," *Ethnic and Racial Studies* 39, no. 6 (2016): 966–967.

75. "Abdou," interview by the author, Dakar, 1 December 2011.

7. The Birth of Political Pluralism in Senegal

1. Bathily, *Mai 1968 à Dakar*, 100–101.

2. Bianchini, *École et politique en Afrique noire*, 76.

3. Mamadou Diop Decroix, interview by the author, Dakar, 22 November 2011.

4. François Zuccarelli, *La vie politique sénégalaise*, vol. 2, *1940–1988* (Paris: CHEAM, 1988), 127–139.

5. Dispatch titled "Incidents à l'Université" of Hubert Argod (French ambassador to Senegal, who replaced Jean de Lagarde) to the Ministry of Foreign Affairs, 18 February 1970, ADMAE, Afrique: Sénégal (1959–1972), carton 51, Politique Intérieure:

situation politique, élections, agitation étudiante et syndicale (janvier 1970-décembre 1972), La Courneuve.

6. "Incidents à l'Université."

7. Dispatch of Hubert Argod to the Ministry of Foreign Affairs, 15 January 1971, ADMAE, Afrique: Sénégal (1959–1972), carton 36, Synthèses de l'ambassade de France au Sénégal, La Courneuve.

8. Bianchini, *École et politique en Afrique noire*, 76.

9. Dispatch of Hubert Argod to the Ministry of Foreign Affairs, 29 January 1971, ADMAE, Afrique: Sénégal (1959–1972), carton 36, Synthèses de l'ambassade de France au Sénégal, La Courneuve.

10. Dispatch of Hubert Argod to the Ministry of Foreign Affairs, 29 January 1971, ADMAE, Afrique: Sénégal (1959–1972), carton 36, Synthèses de l'ambassade de France au Sénégal, La Courneuve. One can only guess that the "hypocritical spectacle" was Pompidou's scheduled parade through the center of Dakar, where he eventually faced a foiled attack on 5 February.

11. See Annexe document no. 7, letter from Dr. Blondin Diop to President Senghor, 18 April 1970, in Sénégal, Ministère de l'information et des relations avec les assemblées, *Livre blanc sur le suicide d'Oumar Blondin Diop* (Dakar: Grande Imprimerie Africaine, 1973), 31; and "Mariane," interview by the author, Dakar, November 2011.

12. Dispatch of Hubert Argod to the Ministry of Foreign Affairs, 29 January 1971, ADMAE, Afrique: Sénégal (1959–1972), carton 36, Synthèses de l'ambassade de France au Sénégal, La Courneuve. See also Bianchini, *École et politique en Afrique noire*, 133.

13. See Bathily, *Mai 1968 à Dakar*, 136.

14. Dispatch of Hubert Argod to the Ministry of Foreign Affairs, 12 February 1971, ADMAE, Afrique: Sénégal (1959–1972), carton 36, Synthèses de l'ambassade de France au Sénégal, La Courneuve. On the Pompidou visit more generally, see Bianchini, *École et politique en Afrique noire*, 76–77.

15. Dispatch of Hubert Argod to the Ministry of Foreign Affairs, 12 February 1971, ADMAE, Afrique: Sénégal (1959–1972), carton 36, Synthèses de l'ambassade de France au Sénégal, La Courneuve.

16. Dispatch of Hubert Argod to the Direction des Affaires Africaines et Malgaches, "Procès des incendiaires," 28 July 1971, ADMAE, Afrique: Sénégal (1959–1972), carton 51, Politique Intérieure, La Courneuve.

17. "Procès des incendiaires."

18. Note of 29 November 1971, ADMAE, Afrique: Sénégal (1959–1972), carton 77, Politique Extérieure: Relation avec divers pays d'Afrique noire, La Courneuve.

19. Letter of P. Zundel to the Secretary of State of Foreign Affairs, "Affaire Ravel," 4 March 1971, ADMAE, Afrique: Sénégal (1959–1972), carton 57, Politique Extérieure, La Courneuve. Ravel directed his comments in part to cooperation advocate Yvon Bourges, who was secretary of state at the time of Ravel's arrest and later took on the role of minister of commerce in 1972.

20. Dispatch of Hubert Argod to the Ministry of Foreign Affairs, 11 March 1971, ADMAE, Afrique: Sénégal (1959–1972), carton 36, Synthèses de l'ambassade de France au Sénégal, La Courneuve.

21. "Mariane," interview.

22. See Jean-Paul Chabert, interview by Michel Béchir Ayari, in Ayari and Bargaoui, *Parcours et discours après l'indépendance.*

23. "Mariane," interview.

24. I explore this in greater detail in Burleigh Hendrickson, "From the Archives to the Streets: Listening to the Global 1960s in the Former French Empire," *French Historical Studies* 40, no. 2 (2017): 319–342.

25. "Abdou," interview by the author, Dakar, 1 December 2011.

26. Vincent Meessen also references this important phenomenon in Senegal through Omar Blondin Diop's role in the Jean-Luc Godard film *La chinoise* (1967) in *The Other Country / l'autre pays* (Brussels: WIELS, 2018), 34–35.

27. See Hendrickson, "From the Archives to the Streets," 332–336.

28. *Livre blanc,* 6–7.

29. *Livre blanc,* 8; and Bianchini, *École et politique en Afrique noire,* 76. Fougeyrollas occupied a tenuous position in which he damaged his close relationship with Senghor by supporting the student movement in 1968 and again in 1971, when he was expelled from Senegal in July for supporting the Dakar students.

30. *Livre blanc,* 8.

31. See *Lettre de Dakar* (Paris: Champ Libre, 1978), 44; and *Le Monde,* 9 April 1971.

32. *Le Monde,* 28 April 1971.

33. "Sénégal - Halte à la répression," signed FEANF and AESF, 2 May 1971, in Fédération des étudiants d'Afrique Noire en France, Collection: Documents d'information (1967–198?), Bibliothèque nationale de France, Paris.

34. See *Action,* 16 March 1968; and "Tunisie: Le divorce étudiant," *Jeune Afrique* 377 (25–31 March 1968).

35. For more on this strategy of limitation, see "Construction et equipement des Universités des états africains et malgache d'expression française," Committee Director of the Aid and Cooperation Funding, 1 July 1970, in Education Nationale: Organisation de l'Enseignement Supérieur en Afrique, AN-19770475, Article 1, Archives Nationales, Fontainebleau. Senegalese students were also upset about expedited programs like DUEST (dîplome universitaire d'études spéciales de technologie) and DUEG (dîplome universitaire d'études générales). "Abdou," interview.

36. *Livre blanc,* 9. Blondin Diop's coconspirators included Ibrahima Kanté, Alioune Sall (also known as "Paloma"), Moussa Kaba (Guinean), Dialo Blondin Diop (also known as "Papa Diop"), Nouhoum Camara (Guinean), Simon Artg (a British filmmaker), Mrs. Soukeyna M'Bodj (also known as "Lydia"), and Mrs. Anta Diouf.

37. Georges Kleiman, "Mort d'un militant africain," *Nouvel Observateur,* 21 May 1973.

38. Quoted in *Livre blanc,* 12.

39. *Lettre de Dakar.* Though the text was written anonymously, some believe it was penned by Omar's brother Ousmane. Journalist Samboudian Kamara makes this claim in "Anniversaire du décès d'Omar Blondin Diop," *Le Soleil,* 10 May 2013.

40. Champ Libre was founded in 1969 by publisher Gérard Lebovici, who was radicalized by the events of May 1968 in France. Lebovici was mysteriously shot and assassinated in his car on 7 March 1984. No one was ever arrested for his murder. See Gérard Lebovici, *Tout sur le personnage: Gérard Lebovici* (Paris: Éditions G. Lebovici, 1984).

41. *Livre blanc,* 6.

42. *Livre blanc*, 9.

43. *Livre blanc*, 12.

44. *Lettre de Dakar*, 11.

45. *Lettre de Dakar*, 11–12.

46. Parti socialiste destourien, *La Vérité sur la subversion*; and Comité international pour la sauvegarde des droits de l'homme en Tunisie, *Liberté pour les condamnés de Tunis: La vérité sur la répression en Tunisie* (Paris: F. Maspero, 1969).

47. *Lettre de Dakar*, 15.

48. *Lettre de Dakar*, 20–21.

49. *Lettre de Dakar*, 15–17.

50. "Mémorandum: Cahier de revendications," National Committee of the Rassemblement Démocratique des Élèves Sénégalais, 1 July 1968, reprinted as Annex III in Bathily, *Mai 1968 à Dakar*, 181–186.

51. Bathily, *Mai 1968 à Dakar*, 133. Here Bathily cites a proposal from the Democratic Movement of Senegalese Youth (Mouvement Démocratique de la Jeunesse Sénégalaise).

52. Bianchini, *École et politique en Afrique noire*, 97.

53. Bathily, *Mai 1968 à Dakar*, 44–45.

54. See Momar-Coumba Diop and Mamadou Diouf, *Le Sénégal sous Abdou Diouf: État et société* (Paris: Karthala, 1990), 39–40.

55. Léopold Sédar Senghor, "L'Université d'Abidjan: Pourquoi une idéologie Négro-Africaine?," speech, December 1971, in Dossier: Léopold Sédar Senghor, 1971, Archives Nationales du Sénégal, Dakar.

56. Zuccarelli, *La vie politique sénégalaise*, 133–134.

57. "La lettre du PAI au Ministre de l'Intérieur," 1 September 1976, in Dossier Partis politiques (O-U), ANS, Dakar.

58. Mamadou Diouf, "Beyond Patronage and 'Technocracy,'" in *Senegal: Essays in Statecraft*, ed. Momar-Coumba Diop (Dakar: Codesria, 1993), 248.

59. Diouf, "Beyond Patronage and 'Technocracy,'" 248.

Conclusion

1. "On the Poverty of Student Life," in Knabb, *Situationist International Anthology*, 409.

Bibliography

Archives

Archives de l'École de Police, Dakar, Senegal
Archives Diplomatiques du Ministère des Affaires Étrangères, La Courneuve, France
Archives Nationales de France, Fontainebleau, France
Archives Nationales de Sénégal, Dakar, Senegal
Archives Nationales de Tunisie, Tunis, Tunisia
Bibliothèque Centrale de l'Université Cheikh Anta Diop de Dakar, Dakar, Senegal
Bibliothèque de Documentation de Internationale Contemporaine, Nanterre,
    France (renamed as La Contemporaine)
Bibiliothèque Municipale de Lyon-Part Dieu, Lyon, France
Bibiliothèque Nationale de France, Paris, France
Bibiliothèque Nationale de Tunisie, Tunis, Tunisia
Centre des Archives Diplomatiques de Nantes, France
Centre d'Histoire Sociale du XXe Siècle, Paris, France
Fondation Temimi Pour la Recherche Scientifique et d'Information, Tunis, Tunisia
Génériques, Paris, France
Goerthe-Insitut Sénégal, Dakar, Senegal
Institut de recherche sur le Maghreb contemporain, Tunis, Tunisia

Newspapers and Periodicals

Actu Toulouse
Combat
Dakar-matin
Jeune Afrique
La Presse de Tunisie
L'Action
Le Monde
Le Soleil
L'Express
L'Humanité
L'Obs Politique
Perspectives Tunisiennes
Politique Hebdo
VOA News
Xarébi

Films

Dubosc, Dominique, and Daniel Anselme. *Dossier Penarroya: Les deux visages du trust.* Directed by Dominique Dubosc and Daniel Anselme. 1972.

Godard, Jean-Luc, Anne Wiazemsky, Jean-Pierre Léaud, Michel Semeniako, Juliet Berto, et al. *La Chinoise.* DVD. Directed by Jean-Luc Godard. Port Washington, NY: Distributed by Koch Entertainment, 2008 [1967].

Published Sources

Abbassi, Driss. *Entre Bourguiba et Hannibal: Identité tunisienne et histoire depuis l'indépendance.* Paris: Karthala, 2005.

——. *Quand la Tunisie s'invente: Entre Orient et Occident, des imaginaires politiques.* Paris: Éditions Autrement, 2009.

Adotevi, Stanislas Spero K. *Négritude et négrologues.* Paris: Union générale d'éditions, 1972.

Aijaz Ahmad. *In Theory: Classes, Nations, Literatures.* London: Verso, 1992.

Aissaoui, Rabah. *Immigration and National Identity: North African Political Movements in Colonial and Postcolonial France.* London: Tauris Academic Studies, 2009.

——. "Political Mobilization of North African Migrants in 1970s France: The Case of the Mouvement des Travailleurs Arabes (MTA)." *Journal of Muslim Minority Affairs* 26, no. 2 (2006): 171–186.

Aldrich, Robert, and John Connell. *France's Overseas Frontier: Départements et Territoires D'outre-mer.* Cambridge: Cambridge University Press, 1992.

Alexander, Christopher. *Tunisia: Stability and Reform in the Modern Maghreb.* Milton Park, Abingdon, Oxon, England: Routledge, 2010.

Ali Mhoumadi, Nassurdine. *Un métis nommé Senghor.* Paris: Harmattan, 2010.

Almeida-Topor, Hélène d', Chantal Chanson-Jabeur, and Monique Lakroum, eds. *Les Transports en Afrique: XIXe et XXe siècles.* Paris: Harmattan, 1992.

Almeida-Topor, Hélène d', Catherine Coquery-Vidrovitch, Odile Goerg, and Françoise Guitart, eds. *Les Jeunes en Afrique: La Politique et la ville.* Tome 1. Paris: L'Harmattan, 1992.

Althusser, Louis. *Lenin and Philosophy, and Other Essays.* London: New Left Books, 1971.

Amnesty International: Rapport 1979. Paris: Éditions Mazarine, 1980.

Andereggen, Anton. *France's Relationship with Subsaharan Africa.* Westport, CT: Praeger, 1994.

Anderson, Samuel D. "Domesticating the Médersa: Franco-Muslim Education and Colonial Rule in Northwest Africa, 1850–1960." PhD diss., University of California Los Angeles, 2019.

Appadurai, Arjun. "Putting Hierarchy in Its Place." *Cultural Anthropology* 3, no. 1 (1988): 36–49.

Arsan, Andrew Kerim. "Failing to Stem the Tide: Lebanese Migration to French West Africa and the Competing Prerogatives of the Imperial State." *Comparative Studies in Society and History* 53, no. 3 (2011): 450–478.

Artières, Philippe, and Michelle Zancarini-Fournel, eds. *68: Une histoire collective, 1962–1981.* Paris: La Découverte, 2008.

Ayari, Michaël Béchir. "S'engager en régime autoritaire." PhD diss., Université Paul Cézanne (Aix-Marseille), 2009.

Ayari, Michaël Béchir, and Sami Bargaoui, eds. *Parcours et discours après l'indépendance.* Tunis: Éditions DIRASET, 2011.

Azaiez, Boubaker Letaief. *Tels syndicalistes, tels syndicats ou Les péripéties du mouvement syndical tunisien.* Tunis; Carthage: Éditions Imprimerie S.T.E.A.G., 1980.

Badiou, Alain. *The Rebirth of History: Times of Riots and Uprisings.* Translated by Gregory Elliott. New York: Verso, 2012.

Bailleul, André. "L'Université de Dakar, institution et fonctionnement (1950–1984)." PhD diss., Université de Dakar, 1984.

Balandier, Georges. "La Situation Coloniale: Approche Theorique." *Cahiers internationaux de sociologie* 11 (1951): 44–79.

Balans, Jean Louis, Christian Coulon, and Alain Ricard, eds. *Problèmes et perspectives de l'éducation dans un État du Tiers monde: Le cas du Sénégal.* Bourdeaux: Centre d'étude d'Afrique noire, 1972.

Ball, Olivia. *"Every Morning, Just Like Coffee." Torture in Cameroon.* London: Medical Foundation for the Care of Victims of Torture, 2002.

Ballantyne, Tony. *Orientalism and Race: Aryanism in the British Empire.* Houndmills, Basingstoke, Hampshire: Palgrave, 2002.

Bathily, Abdoulaye. *Mai 1968 à Dakar: Ou, La révolte universitaire et le démocratie.* Paris: Éditions Chaka, 1992.

Baudelot, Christian and Anne Lebeaupin. "Le salaires de 1950 à 1975 dans l'industrie, le commerce et les services." *Économie et statistique* 113, no. 1 (1979): 15–22.

Beauvoir, Simone de, and Gisèle Halimi. *Djamila Boupacha.* Paris: Gallimard, 1962.

Ben Rouina, Afef. "Islamisme et démocratie: Le cas de la Tunisie, 1970–1990." Master's thesis, Université de Tunis, 2000.

Ben Slimane, Fatma. "Entre deux empires: L'élaboration de la nationalité tunisienne." In *De la colonie à l'État-nation: Constructions identitaires au Maghreb,* edited by François Pouillon, Jean-Claude Vatin, M'hamed Oualdi, and Pierre-Noël Denieuilal., 107–117. Paris: L'Harmattan, 2013.

Benjamin, Walter. *The Arcades Project.* Translated by Howard Eiland and Kevin McLaughlin. Cambridge, MA: Belknap Press of Harvard University Press, 1999.

Bennoune, Mahfoud. "Maghribin Workers in France." *MERIP Reports,* no. 34 (1975): 1–12.

Bertaux, Sandrine. "The Return of the Native: Postcolonial Smoke Screen and the French Postcolonial Politics of Identity." *Public Culture* 23, no. 1 (2011): 201–215.

Bhabha, Homi K. *The Location of Culture.* London: Routledge, 1994.

Bianchini, Pascal. *École et politique en Afrique noire: Sociologie des crises et des réformes du système d'enseignement au Sénégal et au Burkina Faso (1960–2000).* Paris: Karthala, 2004.

Blanchard, Pascal, Nicolas Bancel, and Sandrine Lemaire. *La fracture coloniale: La société française au prisme de l'héritage colonial.* Paris: La Découverte, 2005.

Blum, Françoise. "Années 68 postcoloniales? 'Mai' de France et d'Afrique." *French Historical Studies* 41, no. 2 (2018): 193–218.

——. "Sénégal 1968: Révolte étudiante et grève générale." *Revue d'Histoire Moderne et Contemporaine* 59, no. 2 (2012): 144–177.

Boahen, A. Adu. *The Role of African Student Movements in the Political and Social Evolution of Africa from 1900 to 1975*. Paris: UNESCO, 1994.

Boittin, Jennifer Anne. *Colonial Metropolis: The Urban Grounds of Anti-imperialism and Feminism in Interwar Paris*. Lincoln: University of Nebraska Press, 2010.

Boubeker, Ahmed, and Abdellali Hajjat, eds. *Histoire politique des immigrations (post) coloniales: France, 1920–2008*. Paris: Éditions Amsterdam, 2008.

Bougerra, Abdeljalil. *De l'histoire de la gauche tunisienne: Le mouvement Perspectives, 1963–1975*. Tunis: Cérès, 1993.

Bourg, Julian. "The Red Guards of Paris: French Student Maoism of the 1960s." *History of European Ideas* 31, no. 4 (2005): 472–490.

Bourges, Hervé. *The French Student Revolt; the Leaders Speak*. Translated by B. R. Brewster. New York: Hill and Wang, 1968.

Breckenridge, Carol Appadurai, Peter van der Veer, and South Asia Seminar. *Orientalism and the Postcolonial Predicament: Perspectives on South Asia*. Philadelphia: University of Pennsylvania Press, 1993.

Brown, Timothy S. "'1968' East and West: Divided Germany as a Case Study in Transnational History." *American Historical Review* 114, no. 1 (2009): 69–96.

——. *West Germany and the Global Sixties: The Anti-authoritarian Revolt, 1962–1978*. New York: Cambridge University Press, 2013.

Bryant, Kelly M. Duke. *Education as Politics: Colonial Schooling and Political Debate in Senegal, 1850s-1914*. Madison: University of Wisconsin Press, 2015.

Bsais, Abdeljabbar, and Christian Morrisson. *Les coûts de l'éducation en Tunisie*. Tunis: Université de Tunis, Centre d'études et de recherches économiques et sociales, 1970.

Burton, Antoinette. *After the Imperial Turn: Thinking with and through the Nation*. Durham, NC: Duke University Press, 2003.

Byrne, Jeffrey James. *Mecca of Revolution: Algeria, Decolonization, and the Third World Order*. New York: Oxford University Press, 2016.

Camara, Ousmane. *Mémoires d'un juge africain: Itinéraire d'un homme libre*. Paris: Éditions Karthala, 2010.

Camau, Michel, and Vincent Geisser, eds. *Habib Bourguiba: La trace et l'héritage*. Paris: Karthala, 2004.

Castro, Roland. *1989*. Paris: Barrault, 1984.

Caute, David. *The Year of the Barricades: A Journey through 1968*. New York: Harper & Row, 1988.

Ce que veut la Ligue communiste, Section française de la 4e Internationale; manifeste du Comité central des 29 et 30 janvier 1972. Paris: F. Maspero, 1972.

Chakrabarty, Dipesh. *Provincializing Europe: Postcolonial Thought and Historical Difference*. Princeton, NJ: Princeton University Press, 2000.

Chaplin, Tamara, and Jadwiga E. Mooney-Pieper, eds. *The Global 1960s: Convention, Contest, and Counterculture*. London: Routledge, 2018.

Charfi, Mohamed. *Mon combat pour les Lumières*. Léchelle, France: Zellige, 2009.

Chatterjee, Partha. *The Nation and Its Fragments: Colonial and Postcolonial Histories*. Princeton, NJ: Princeton University Press, 1993.

Chenoufi, Kamel, and Gilles Gallo. *La Tunisie en décolonisation (1957–1972): Genèse des structures de développement et des structures de la République*. Le Pradet, France: LAU, 2003.

Christiansen, Samantha, and Zachary A. Scarlett. *The Third World in the Global 1960s*. New York: Berghahn Books, 2013.

Clancy-Smith, Julia Ann. *Mediterraneans: North Africa and Europe in an Age of Migration, c. 1800–1900*. Berkeley: University of California Press, 2011.

——. *Rebel and Saint: Muslim Notables, Populist Protest, Colonial Encounters (Algeria and Tunisia, 1800–1904)*. Berkeley: University of California Press, 1994.

Cohn-Bendit, Daniel, and Gabriel Cohn-Bendit. *Obsolete Communism: The Left-Wing Alternative*. Translated by Arnold Pomerans. New York: McGraw-Hill, 1968.

Cole, Joshua. "Massacres and Their Historians: Recent Histories of State Violence in France and Algeria in the Twentieth Century." *French Politics, Culture & Society* 28, no. 1 (2010): 106–126.

——. "Remembering the Battle of Paris: 17 October 1961 in French and Algerian Memory." *French Politics, Culture & Society* 21, no. 3 (2003): 21–50.

Comeau, Robert, D. Cooper, and Pierre Vallières. *FLQ: Un Projet Révolutionnaire: Lettres et Écrits Felquistes (1963–1982)*. Outremont, Québec: VLB, 1990.

Comité international pour la sauvegarde des droits de l'homme en Tunisie. *Liberté pour les condamnés de Tunis: La vérité sur la répression*. Paris: F. Maspero, 1969.

Conklin, Alice L. *A Mission to Civilize: The Republican Idea of Empire in France and West Africa, 1895–1930*. Stanford, CA: Stanford University Press, 1997.

Cooper, Frederick. *Citizenship between Empire and Nation: Remaking France and French Africa, 1945–1960*. Princeton, NJ: Princeton University Press, 2014.

——. *Colonialism in Question: Theory, Knowledge, History*. Berkeley: University of California Press, 2005.

Cooper, Frederick, and Ann Laura Stoler. *Tensions of Empire: Colonial Cultures in a Bourgeois World*. Berkeley: University of California Press, 1997.

Cornevin, Robert. "La France et l'Afrique noire." *Études internationales* 1, no. 4 (1970): 88–101.

Daily, Andrew. "Race, Citizenship, and Antillean Student Activism in Postwar France, 1946–1968." *French Historical Studies* 37, no. 2 (2014): 331–357.

Damamme, Dominique, Boris Gobille, Frédérique Matoni, and Bernard Pudal, eds. *Mai-Juin 68*. Ivry-sur-Seine, Paris: Éditions de l'Atelier, 2008.

Debord, Guy. *La société du spectacle*. Paris: Gallimard, 1992.

Dedieu, Jean-Philippe. *La parole immigrée: Les migrants africains dans l'espace public en France (1960–1995)*. Paris: Klincksiek, 2012.

Dedieu, Jean-Philippe, and Aïssatou Mbodj-Pouye. "The First Collective Protest of Black African Migrants in Postcolonial France (1960–1975): A Struggle for Housing and Rights." *Ethnic and Racial Studies* 39, no. 6 (2016): 958–975.

Deleuze, Gilles, Felix Guattari, and Michel Foucault. *Anti-Oedipus: Capitalism and Schizophrenia*. Minneapolis: University of Minnesota Press, 1983.

Dewerpe, Alain. *Charonne 8 février 1962: Anthropologie historique d'un massacre d'État*. Paris: Éditions Gallimard, 2006.

Dewitte, Philippe. *Les mouvements nègres en France, 1919–1939*. Paris: L'Harmattan, 1985.

Diané, Charles. *Les grandes heures de la F.E.A.N.F.* Paris: Chaka, 1990.

Dieng, Amady Aly. *Les grands combats de la Fédération des étudiants d'Afrique noire: De Bandung aux indépendances, 1955–1960.* Paris: L'Harmattan, 2009.

——. *Mémoires d'un étudiant africain: De l'Université de Paris à mon retour au Sénégal.* Vol. 2. Dakar: Codesria, 2011.

Diop, Momar-Coumba. *Gouverner le Sénégal: entre ajustement structurel et développement durable.* Paris: Karthala, 2004.

——. *La société sénégalaise entre le local et le global.* Paris: Karthala, 2002.

——, ed. *Senegal: Essays in Statecraft.* Dakar: Codesria, 1993.

——. *Sénégal: Trajectoires d'un État.* Dakar: Codesria, 1992.

Diop, Momar-Coumba, and Mamadou Diouf. *Le Sénégal sous Abdou Diouf: Etat et société.* Paris: Karthala, 1990.

Diop Decroix, Mamadou. *La Cause du Peuple: Entretien avec El Hadj Kassé.* Dakar: Panafrika, 2007.

Dirlik, Arif. "Chinese History and the Question of Orientalism." *History and Theory* 35, no. 4 (1996): 96–118.

——. "The End of Colonialism? The Colonial Modern in the Making of Global Modernity." *Boundary 2* 32, no. 1 (2005): 1–31.

Dramé, Patrick, and Jean Lamarre. *1968, des sociétés en crise une perspective globale.* Quebec: Presses de l'Université Laval, 2009.

Dressen, Marnix. *De l'amphi à l'établi: Les étudiants maoïstes à l'usine (1967–1989).* Paris: Berlin, 2000.

Dreyfus-Armand, Geneviève, Robert Frank, Marie Françoise Lévy, and Michelle Zancararini-Fournel. *Les années 68: Le temps de la contestation.* Paris: Éditions complexe, 2008 [2000].

Dreyfus-Armand, Geneviève, and Laurent Gervereau, eds. *Mai 68: Les mouvements étudiants en France et dans le monde.* Paris: Éditions La Découverte, 1988.

Einaudi, Jean-Luc. *La bataille de Paris: 17 octobre 1961.* Paris: Seuil, 1991.

——. *Octobre 1961: Un massacre à Paris.* [Paris]: Fayard, 2001.

Eley, Geoff. *Nazism as Fascism: Violence, Ideology, and the Ground of Consent in Germany, 1930–1945.* London: Routledge, 2013.

Entelis, John P. "Ideological Change and an Emerging Counter-culture in Tunisian Politics." *Journal of Modern African Studies* 12, no. 4 (1974): 543–568.

Eribon, Didier. *Michel Foucault.* Cambridge, MA: Harvard University Press, 1991.

Fanon, Frantz. *The Wretched of the Earth.* Translated by Constance Farrington. New York: Grove Press, 1982 [1963].

Filiu, Jean-Pierre. *Mai 68 à l'ORTF: Une radio-télévision en resistance.* Paris: Nouveau Monde, 2008.

Fink, Carole, Philipp Gassert, and Detlef Junker, eds. *1968, the World Transformed.* Washington DC: German Historical Institute, 1998.

Flynn, Thomas R. *Sartre, Foucault, and Historical Reason.* Vol. 1, *Toward an Existentialist Theory of History.* Chicago: University of Chicago Press, 1997.

——. *Sartre, Foucault, and Historical Reason.* Vol. 2, *A Postructuralist Mapping of History.* Chicago: University of Chicago Press, 2005.

Fogarty, Richard Standish. *Race and War in France: Colonial Subjects in the French Army, 1914–1918.* Baltimore: Johns Hopkins University Press, 2008.

Foucault, Michel. *Discipline and Punish: The Birth of the Prison*. New York: Pantheon Books, 1977.

Franklin, Elise. "A Slow End to Empire: Social Aid Associations, Family Migration, and Decolonization in France and Algeria, 1954–1981." PhD diss., Boston College, 2017.

Gamble, Harry. *Contesting French West Africa: Battles over Schools and the Colonial Order, 1900–1950*. Lincoln: University of Nebraska Press, 2017.

Gani, Léon. *Syndicats et travailleurs immigrés*. Paris: Éditions Sociales, 1972.

Gassert, Philipp, and Martin Klimke. *1968: Memories and Legacies of a Global Revolt*. Washington, DC: German Historical Institute, 2009.

Gastaut, Yvan. "La flambée raciste de 1973." *Revue européenne de migrations internationales* 9, no. 2 (1993): 61–75.

——. "Le rôle des immigrés pendant les journées de mai-juin 1968." *International Migration* 23, no. 4 (1993): 9–29.

——. "Les bidonvilles, lieux d'exclusion et de marginalité en France durant les trente glorieuses." *Cahiers de la Méditerranée* 69 (2004): 233–250.

Geismar, Alain, Serge July, and Erlyne Morane. *Vers la guerre civile*. Paris: Éditions et publications premières, 1969.

Gildea, Robert. *The Past in French History*. New Haven, CT: Yale University Press, 1994.

Gildea, Robert, James Mark, and Anette Warring. *Europe's 1968: Voices of Revolt*. Oxford: Oxford University Press, 2013.

Gilroy, Paul. *Against Race: Imagining Political Culture beyond the Color Line*. Cambridge, MA: Harvard University Press, 2000.

——. *The Black Atlantic: Modernity and Double Consciousness*. Cambridge, MA: Harvard University Press, 1993.

Giudice, Fausto. *Arabicides: Une chronique française, 1970–1991*. Paris: La Découverte, 1992.

Glaes, Gillian Beth. "Marginalised, yet Mobilised: The UGTSF, African Immigration, and Racial Advocacy in Postcolonial France." *French Cultural Studies* 24, no. 2 (2013): 174–183.

——. "The Mirage of Fortune: West African Immigration to Paris and the Development of a Post-colonial Immigrant Community, 1960–1981." PhD diss., University of Wisconsin–Madison, 2007.

——. "Sally N'Dongo, immigration africaine et aspects politiques du néocolonialisme en Afrique de L'Ouest et en France." *Migrance* 39 (December 2012): 95–108.

Gobille, Boris. *Mai 68*. Paris: La Découverte, 2008.

Goebel, Michael. *Anti-imperial Metropolis: Interwar Paris and the Seeds of Third World Nationalism*. Cambridge: Cambridge University Press, 2015.

Gonidec, P. F. *Les systèmes politiques africains*. Paris: Librarie générale de droit et de jurisprudence, 1978.

Gordon, Daniel A. "'À Nanterre, ça bouge': Immigrés et gauchistes en banlieue, 1968 à 1971." *Historiens et Géographes* 385 (2004): 75–86.

——. *Immigrants & Intellectuals: May '68 & the Rise of Anti-racism in France*. Pontypool, Wales: Merlin Press, 2012.

Groupe D'Études Et D'Action Socialiste Tunisien. *Procès de Tunis [1968]: Mémoires de militants*. Paris: G.E.A.S.T., 1968.

Gueye, Abdoulaye. "The Colony Strikes Back: African Protest Movements in Postcolonial France." *Comparative Studies of South Asia, Africa and the Middle East* 26, no. 2 (2006): 225–242.

——. "Sacre ou sacrifice: La condition des chercheurs africains dans la mondialisation universitaire." *Cahiers du Brésil Contemporain* 57/58–59/60 (2004–2005): 305–318.

Guèye, Omar. *Mai 68 au Sénégal: Senghor face aux étudiants et au mouvement syndical.* Paris: Karthala, 2017.

Guimont, Fabienne. *Les étudiants africains en France, 1950–1965.* Paris: Harmattan, 1997.

Gupta, Akhil, and James Ferguson. "Beyond 'Culture': Space, Identity, and the Politics of Difference." *Cultural Anthropology* 7, no. 1 (1992): 6–23.

Hajjat, Abdellali. *Immigration postcoloniale et mémoire.* Paris: L'Harmattan, 2005.

——. "Les comités Palestine (1970–1972): Aux origines du soutien de la cause palestinienne en France." *Revue d'études palestiniennes* 98 (2006): 1–27.

Hardt, Michael, and Antonio Negri. *Empire.* Cambridge, MA: Harvard University Press, 2001.

Haroun, M-Ali. *La 7e Wilaya: La guerre du FLN en France, 1954–1962.* Paris: Seuil, 1986.

Hendrickson, Burleigh. "Student Activism and the Birth of the Tunisian Human Rights Movement, 1968–1978." In *Étudiants africains en mouvement: Contribution à une histoire des années 1968*, edited by Françoise Blum, Pierre Guidi and Ophélie Rillon, 233–247. Paris: Publications de la Sorbonne, 2016.

——. "Finding Tunisia in the Global 1960s." *Monde(s): Histoire, espaces, relations* 11 (2017): 61–78.

——. "From the Archives to the Streets: Listening to the Global 1960s in the Former French Empire." *French Historical Studies* 40, no. 2 (2017): 319–342.

——. "March 1968: Practicing Transnational Activism from Tunis to Paris." *International Journal of Middle East Studies* 44, no. 4 (2012): 755–774.

——. "Migrations intellectuelles, *Indépendance Inachevée* et 1968 à Dakar et à Tunis," *Migrance* 39 (September 2012): 111–122.

——. "Periphery and Intimacy in Anti-imperial Culture and Politics: From French Others to Othering Frenchness." *French Politics, Culture & Society* 38, no. 2 (2020): 105–125.

Hmed, Choukri. "Contester une institution dans le cas d'une mobilisation improbable: La 'grève des loyers' dans les foyers Sonacotra dans les années 1970." *Sociétés Contemporaines* 65, no. 1 (2007): 55–81.

Horn, Gerd-Rainer. *The Spirit of '68: Rebellion in Western Europe and North America, 1956–1976.* Oxford: Oxford University Press, 2007.

Horne, Janet. "'To Spread the French Language Is to Extend the Patrie': The Colonial Mission of the Alliance Française." *French Historical Studies* 40, no. 1 (2017): 95–127.

House, Jim, and Neil MacMaster. *Paris 1961: Algerians, State Terror, and Memory.* Oxford: Oxford University Press, 2006.

Hymans, Jacques Louis. *Léopold Sédar Senghor: An Intellectual Biography.* Edinburgh: Edinburgh University Press, 1971.

Jackson, Julian. "The Mystery of May 1968." *French Historical Studies* 33, no. 4 (Fall 2010): 625–653.

Jackson, Julian, Anna-Louise Milne, and James S. Williams, eds. *May 68: Rethinking France's Last Revolution*. Houndmills, Basingstoke, Hampshire: Palgrave Macmillan, 2011.

Jebari, Idriss. "'Illegitimate Children': The Tunisian New Left and the Student Question, 1963–1975." *International Journal of Middle East Studies* (2022): 1–24.

Jennings, Eric Thomas. *Vichy in the Tropics: Pétain's National Revolution in Madagascar, Guadeloupe, and Indochina, 1940–1944*. Stanford, CA: Stanford University Press, 2001.

Jobs, Richard Ivan. "Youth Movements, Travel, Protest, and Europe in 1968." *American Historical Review* 114, no. 2 (2009): 376–404.

Kalter, Christoph. *The Discovery of the Third World: Decolonization and the Rise of the New Left in France, c. 1950–1976*. Cambridge: Cambridge University Press, 2016.

——. "Tiers-monde et gauche radicale." In *Histoire des mouvements sociaux en France de 1814 à nos jours*, edited by Michel Pigenet and Danielle Tartakowsky, 378–389. Paris: La Découverte, 2012.

Kantrowitz, Rachel. "Triangulating between Church, State, and Postcolony: *Coopérants* in Independent West Africa." *Cahiers d'Études africaines* 1/2, no. 221 (2016): 219–242.

Kastner, Jens, and David Mayer. *Weltwende 1968? Ein Jahr aus globalgeschichtlicher Perspektive*. Wien: Mandelbaum, 2008.

Katsiaficas, George N. *The Imagination of the New Left: A Global Analysis of 1968*. Boston: South End Press, 1987.

Katz, Ethan. *The Burdens of Brotherhood: Jews and Muslims from North Africa to France*. Cambridge, MA: Harvard University Press, 2015.

Keenan, Bethany S. "Vietnam Is Fighting for Us: French Identities and the U.S.-Vietnam War, 1965–1973." PhD diss., University of North Carolina, 2009.

Keller, Kathleen A. "Political Surveillance and Colonial Urban Rule: 'Suspicious' Politics and Urban Space in Dakar, Senegal, 1918–1939." *French Historical Studies* 35, no. 4 (September 21, 2012): 727–749.

Kelly, Mark G. E. *The Political Philosophy of Michel Foucault*. New York: Routledge, 2009.

Khuri-Makdisi, Ilham. *Contextualizing Radicalism in the Eastern Mediterranean: Globalization and Change, 1860–1914*. Berkeley: University of California Press, 2010.

Klimke, Martin. *The Other Alliance: Student Protest in West Germany and the United States in the Global Sixties*. Princeton, NJ: Princeton University Press, 2010.

Knabb, Ken, ed. and trans. *Situationist International Anthology*. Berkeley, CA: Bureau of Public Secrets, 2006 [1981].

Kraïem, Mustapha. *Le parti communiste tunisien pendant la période coloniale*. Tunis: Institut supérieur d'histoire du mouvement national, Université de Tunis I, 1997.

Kraïem, Mustapha. *Nationalisme et syndicalisme en Tunisie, 1918–1929*. Tunis: Union Générale Tunisienne du Travail, 1976.

Kraushaar, Wolfgang. *Frankfurter Schule und Studentenbewegung: Von der Flaschenpost zum Molotowcocktail, 1946–1995*. Frankfurt am Main: Rogner & Bernhard bei Zweitausendeins, 1998.

Kurlansky, Mark. *1968: The Year That Rocked the World*. New York: Ballantine, 2004.

Le Combat des détenus politiques: Grève de la faim, procès des diffuseurs de "la Cause du peuple." Paris: François Maspero, 1970.

Le Mouvement étudiant tunisien, 1950–1972: Itinéraire idéologique et politique. Tunis: Publication An-Nidhal, Organe Tunisien de la Révolution Arabe, 1972.

Le Saout, Didier, and Marguerite Rollinde, eds. *Émeutes et mouvements sociaux au Maghreb: Perspective comparée.* Paris: Karthala, 1999.

Lebovici, Gérard. *Tout sur le personnage: Gérard Lebovici.* Paris: Éditions G. Lebovici, 1984.

Lefebvre, Henri. *The Explosion; Marxism and the French Revolution.* Translated by Alfred Ehrenfeld. New York: Monthly Review Press, 1969.

Lessaut, David, and Cris Beauchemin. "Migration from Sub-Saharan Africa to Europe: Still a Limited Trend." *Population and Societies* 452, Institut national d'études démographiques (January 2009): 1–4.

Lettre de Dakar. Paris: Champ libre, 1978.

Lewis, Mary Dewhurst. *Divided Rule: Sovereignty and Empire in French Tunisia, 1881–1938.* Berkeley: University of California Press, 2014.

Linhart, Robert. *The Assembly Line.* Translated by Margaret Crosland Amherst: University of Massachusetts Press, 1981.

Lô, Magatte. *Sénégal: Syndicalisme et participation reponsable.* Paris: L'Harmattan, 1987.

Ludden, David. "Orientalist Empiricism: Transformations of Colonial Knowledge." In *Orientalism and the Postcolonial Predicament: Perspectives on South Asia*, edited by Carol Appaduria Breckenridge and Peter van der Veer, 250–278. Philadelphia: University of Pennsylvania Press, 1993.

Macey, David. *The Lives of Michel Foucault: A Biography.* New York: Pantheon Books, 1993.

Mamdani, Mahmood, E. Wamba-dia-Wamba, and Codesria. *African Studies in Social Movements and Democracy.* Dakar: Codesria, 1995.

Manning, Patrick. *Francophone Sub-Saharan Africa, 1880–1995.* Cambridge: Cambridge University Press, 1998.

Marker, Emily. "France between Europe and Africa: Youth, Race, and Envisioning the Postwar World, 1940–1960." PhD diss., University of Chicago, 2016.

Marwick, Arthur. *The Sixties: The Cultural Revolution in Britain, Italy, France, and the United States, c. 1958–1974.* Oxford: Oxford University Press, 1998.

Maussen, Marcel, Veit Bader, and Annelies Moors, eds. *Colonial and Post-colonial Governance of Islam: Continuities and Ruptures.* Amsterdam: Amsterdam University Press, 2011.

Mbembe, Achille. "Provincializing France?" *Public Culture* 23, no.1 (2011): 85–119.

McClintock, Anne. "The Angel of Progress: Pitfalls of the Term 'Post-colonialism.'" *Social Text* 31/32 (1992): 84–98.

McDonnell, Hugh. "Water, North African Immigrants, and the Parisian Bidonvilles, 1950s–1960s." *Radical History Review* 2013, no. 116 (2013): 31–58.

McDougall, James. "Dream of Exile, Promise of Home: Language, Education, and Arabism in Algeria." *International Journal of Middle East Studies* 43, no. 2 (2011): 251–270.

Meessen, Vincent. *The Other Country / l'autre pays.* Brussels: WIELS, 2018.

Mehta, Gita. *Karma Cola: Marketing the Mystic East*. New York: Fawcett Columbine, 1991.

Metzger, Jean-Luc. "Dressen M., De l'amphi à l'établi. Les Étudiants Maoïstes à l'usine (1967–1989)." *Politix* 15, no. 57 (2002): 224–229.

Mills, Sean. *The Empire within Postcolonial Thought and Political Activism in Sixties Montreal*. Montreal: McGill-Queen's University Press, 2010.

Milza, Pierre. *Fascisme français: Passé et present*. Paris: Flammarion, 1987.

——. *L'Europe en chemise noire: Les extremes droits en Europe de 1945 à aujourd'hui*. Paris: Fayard, 2002.

Mohandesi, Salar. "Bringing Vietnam Home: The Vietnam War, Internationalism, and May '68." *French Historical Studies* 41, no. 2 (2018): 219–251.

Moore, Clement Henry. *Politics in North Africa: Algeria, Morocco, and Tunisia*. Boston: Little, Brown, 1970.

——. "Tunisia and Bourguisme: Twenty Years of Crisis." *Third World Quarterly* 10, no. 1 (1988):176–190.

Moore, Clement Henry, and Arlie Russell Hochschild. "Student Unions in North African Politics." Daedalus 97, no. 1 (1968): 21–50.

Morgenthau, Ruth Schachter. "Old Cleavages among New West African States: The Heritage of French Rule." *Africa Today* 18, no. 2 (1971): 6–16.

Moyn, Samuel. *The Last Utopia: Human Rights in History*. Cambridge, MA: Belknap Press of Harvard University Press, 2010.

Naccache, Gilbert. *Qu'as-tu fait de ta jeunesse? Itinéraire d'un opposant au régime de Bourguiba, 1954–1979: Suivi de récits de prison*. Paris: Cerf, 2009.

N'Diaye, Jean-Pierre. *Négriers modernes; les travailleurs noirs en France*. Paris: Presence africaine, 1970.

N'Dongo, Sally. *Coopération et Néocolonialisme*. Paris: François Maspero, 1976.

——. *La "Coopération" franco-africaine*. Paris: Maspero, 1972.

Othmani, Ahmed with Sophie Bessis. *Beyond Prison: The Fight to Reform Prison Systems around the World*. Translated by Marguerite Garling. New York: Berghahn Books, 2008.

Pallier, Denis. "Les bibliothèques universitaires de 1945 à 1975." *Bulletin des bibliothèques de France* 3 (1992): 58–73.

Pandey, Gyanendra. *Routine Violence: Nations, Fragments, Histories*. Stanford, CA: Stanford University Press, 2006.

Parti socialiste destourien (Tunisie). Parti socialiste destourien. *La Politique contractuelle et les événements de janvier 1978*. Tunis: Dar El Amal, 1978.

——. *La Vérité sur la subversion à l'Université de Tunis*. [Tunis]: Parti socialiste destourien, 1968.

Pensado, Jaime M. *Student Unrest and Authoritarian Political Culture during the Long Sixties*. Stanford, CA: Stanford University Press, 2013.

Perkins, Kenneth J. *A History of Modern Tunisia*. New York: Cambridge University Press, 2004.

Perks, Robert, and Alistair Thomson. *The Oral History Reader*. London: Routledge, 2006.

Pitti, Laure. "La lutte des Penarroya contre le plomb." *Santé et Travail* 62 (2008): 48–50.

——. "Ouvriers algériens à Renault-Billancourt, de la guerre d'Algérie aux grèves d'OS des années 1970." PhD diss., Université de Paris 8, 2002.

Poster, Mark. *Foucault, Marxism, and History: Mode of Production versus Mode of Information*. Cambridge: Polity Press, 1984.

Prakash, Amit. "Colonial Techniques in the Imperial Capital: The Prefecture of Police and the Surveillance of North Africans in Paris, 1925-circa 1970." *French Historical Studies* 36, no. 3 (2013): 479–510.

Reid, Donald. "Daniel Anselme: On Leave with the Unknown Famous." *South Central Review* 32, no. 2 (2015): 109–130.

——. "*Établissement*: Working in the Factory to Make Revolution in France." *Radical History Review* 88 (2004): 83–111.

——. *Opening the Gates: The Lip Affair, 1968–1981*. London: Verso, 2018.

Reynolds, Chris. "From *mai-juin '68* to *Nuit Debout*: Shifting Perspectives on France's Anti-police." *Modern & Contemporary France* 26, no. 2 (2018): 145–163.

Riesz, János. "Senghor and the Germans." Translated by Aija Bjornson. *Research in African Literatures* 33, no. 4 (2002): 25–37.

Ross, Kristin. *May '68 and Its Afterlives*. Chicago: University of Chicago Press, 2002.

Rousseau, Jean-Jacques. *Discourse on the Origins of Inequality (second discourse)*. Edited by Roger D. Masters and Christopher Kelly. Translated by Judith R. Bush. Hanover, NH: Dartmouth College, 1992.

Sabatier, Peggy R. "Educating a Colonial Elite: The William Ponty School and Its Graduates." PhD diss., University of Chicago, 1977.

——. "'Elite' Education in French West Africa: The Era of Limits, 1903–1945." *International Journal of African Historical Studies* 11, no. 2 (1978): 247–266.

Safir, Gershon. *A Half Century of Occupation: Israel, Palestine, and the World's Most Intractable Conflict*. Berkeley: University of California Press, 2017.

Sarr, Amadou Lamine. "Mai 68 im Senegal. Fortsetzung des Unabhängigkeitsprozesses in Afrika?" In *Weltwende 1968? Ein Jahr uas globalgeschichtlicher Perspektive*, edited by Jena Kastner and David Mayer, 130–142. Vienna: Mandelbaum, 2008.

Schnapp, Alain, and Pierre Vidal-Naquet, eds. *The French Student Uprising, November 1967-June 1968; an Analytical Record*. Boston: Beacon Press, 1971.

Schofield, Coryell. "Europe's Immigrant Workers: New Grapes of Wrath." *Ramparts* 12, no. 8 (March 1974): 16–20.

Seale, Patrick, and Maureen McConville. *Red Flag / Black Flag; French Revolution, 1968*. New York: Putnam, 1968.

Secrétariat d'Etat à l'Education Nationale. *Une récente réalisation du gouvernement Bourguiba: Nouvelle conception de l'enseignement en Tunisie*. Tunis: La Presse, 1959.

Seidman, Michael. *The Imaginary Revolution: Parisian Students and Workers in 1968*. New York: Berghahn Books, 2004.

Sénégal, Ministère de l'information et des relations avec les assemblées. *Livre blanc sur le suicide d'Oumar Blondin Diop*. Dakar: Grande Imprimirie Africaine, 1973.

Senghor, Léopold Sédar. *Leopold Sedar Senghor: The Collected Poetry*. Charlottesville: University Press of Virginia, 1991.

——. *On African Socialism*. Translated by Mercer Cook. New York: Praeger, 1964.

Shepard, Todd. *The Invention of Decolonization: The Algerian War and the Remaking of France.* Ithaca, NY: Cornell University Press, 2006.

——. "'Of Sovereignty': Disputed Archives, 'Wholly Modern' Archives, and the Post-decolonization French and Algerian Republics, 1962–2012." *American Historical Review* 120, no. 3 (2015): 869–883.

——. *Sex, France & Arab Men, 1962–1979.* Chicago: University of Chicago Press, 2017.

——. "'Something Notably Erotic': Politics, 'Arab Men,' and Sexual Revolution in Post-decolonization France, 1962–1974." *Journal of Modern History* 84, no. 1 (2012): 80–115.

Siino, François. *Science et pouvoir dans la Tunisie contemporaine.* Paris: Karthala, 2005.

Silverman, Maxim. *Deconstructing the Nation: Immigration, Racism, and Citizenship in Modern France.* London: Routledge, 1992.

Simont, Juliette, Jean-Pierre Martin, and Jean-Pierre Le Dantec, eds. *Ouvriers volontaires: les années 68: l'"Établissement" en usine.* Paris: Les Temps Modernes, 2015.

Singer, Daniel. *Prelude to Revolution: France in May 1968.* Cambridge, MA: South End Press, 2002.

Slobodian, Quinn. *Foreign Front: Third World Politics in Sixties West Germany.* Durham, NC: Duke University Press, 2012.

Smouts, Marie-Claude, ed. *La situation postcoloniale: Les postcolonial studies dans le débat français.* Paris: Fondation nationale des sciences politiques, 2007.

Sot, Michel, ed. *Étudiants africains en France (1951–2001): Cinquante ans de relations France-Afrique, quel avenir? Études et témoignages.* Paris: Karthala, 2002.

Sraïeb, Noureddine, and Centre de recherches et d'études sur les sociétés méditer-ranéennes, eds. *Le Mouvement ouvrier maghrébin.* Paris: Éditions du Centre national de la recherche scientifique, 1985.

Stoler, Ann Laura, ed. *Imperial Debris: On Ruins and Ruination.* Durham, NC: Duke University Press, 2013.

——. "Imperial Debris: Reflections on Ruins and Ruination." *CUAN Cultural Anthropology* 23, no. 2 (2008): 191–219.

Stora, Benjamin. *Le transfert d'une mémoire: De l'Algérie française au racism anti-arabe.* Paris: La Découverte, 1999.

Sugiyama, Yoshiko. "Sur le même banc d'école: Louis Macheul et la rencontre franco-arabe en Tunisie lors du Protectorat français (1883–1908)." PhD diss., Université de Provence, 2007.

Temkin, Moshik. "Europe and Travel Control in an Era of Global Politics: The Case of France in the Long 1960s." In *Peoples and Borders: Seventy Years of Migration in Europe, from Europe, to Europe [1945–2015],* edited by Elena Calandri, Simone Paoli, and Antonio Varsori, 109–120. Baden-Baden, Germany: Nomos, 2017.

Thomas, Lynn M. "Modernity's Failings, Political Claims, and Intermediate Concepts." *American Historical Review* 116, no. 3 (June 2011): 727–740.

Thomas, Martin, ed. *The French Colonial Mind.* Vol. 2, *Violence Military Encounters, and Colonialism.* Lincoln: University of Nebraska Press, 2012.

Traore, Sekou. *La Fédération des étudiants d'Afrique noire en France: (F.E.A.N.F.).* Paris: L'Harmattan, 1985.

Troly, Gilbert. "La Societe minière et metallurgique de Penarroya." *Annales des Mines—Réalités Industrielles* 2008, no. 3 (2008): 27–34.

Tunisia and Kitābat al-Dawlah lil-Tarbiyah al-Qawmīyah. *Nouvelle conception de l'enseignement en Tunisie: Une récente réalisation du gouvernement Bourguiba, 1958–1959.* [Tunis]: Le Secrétariat, 1959.

UNESCO. *The Role of African Student Movements in the Political and Social Evolution of Africa from 1900 to 1975.* Paris: UNESCO, 1994.

Union générale des étudiants de Tunisie. *Étudiant tunisien: organe de l'Union générale des étudiants de Tunisie.* Tunis: [s.n.], 1968. (19).

Vaillant, Janet G. *Vie de Léopold Sédar Senghor: Noir, Français et Africain.* Translated by Roger Meunier. Paris: Karthala, 2006.

Vaïsse, Maurice, ed. *Mai 68 vu de l'étranger: Les événements dans les archives diplomatiques françaises.* Paris: CNRS Éditions, 2008.

Van Stralen, Hans. "Sartre and Foucault on Bataille and Blanchot." *Orbis Litterarum* 61, no. 6 (December 2006): 429–442.

Vigna, Xavier. *L'insubordination ouvrière dans les années 68: Essai d'histoire politique des usines.* Rennes: Presses universitaires de Rennes, 2009.

Vigna, Xavier and Michelle Zancarini-Fournel. "Les rencontres improbables dans 'les années 68.'" *Vingtième Siècle. Revue d'histoire* 101, no. 1 (2009): 163–177.

Vogel, Jakob. "Senghor et l'ouverture culturelle de la RFA en 68. Pour une histoire transnationale l'Allemagne—France—Afrique." *Vingtième Siècle* 94, no. 2 (2007): 135–148.

Von der Goltz, Anna. "Making Sense of East Germany's 1968: Multiple Trajectories and Contrasting Memories." *Memory Studies* 6, no. 1 (2013): 53–69.

Walsh, Catherine E., and Walter D. Mignolo. *On Decoloniality: Concepts, Analytics, Praxis.* Durham, NC: Duke University Press, 2018.

Weidhaas, Peter. *Life before Letters.* Translated by Lawrence Schofer. New York: Locus Publishing, 2010.

Wihtol de Wenden, Catherine. *Les Immigrés et la politique.* Paris: Presses de la Fondation Nationale des Sciences Politiques, 1988.

Wilder, Gary. *Freedom Time: Negritude, Decolonization, and the Future of the World.* Durham, NC: Duke University Press, 2015.

———. *The French Imperial Nation-State: Negritude & Colonial Humanism between the Two World Wars.* Chicago: University of Chicago Press, 2005.

Williams, R. J. Patrick, and Laura Chrisman. *Colonial Discourse and Post-colonial Theory: A Reader.* New York: Columbia University Press, 1994.

Wlassikoff, Michel, Marc Riboud, Jean-Claude Gautrand, and Philippe Vermès. *Mai 68, l'affiche en héritage.* Paris: Éditions Alternatives, 2008.

Wolin, Richard. *The Wind from the East: French Intellectuals, the Cultural Revolution, and the Legacy of the 1960s.* Princeton, NJ: Princeton University Press, 2010.

Zeilig, Leo. *Revolt and Protest: Student Politics and Activism in Sub-Saharan Africa.* London: Tauris Academic Studies, 2007.

Zuccarelli, François. *La vie politique sénégalaise.* Vol. 2, *1940–1988.* Paris: CHEAM, 1988.

INDEX

3 May Action Committee, 65–66
1968 protests: Arab Spring as continuum of,
  1–5; in Dakar, 86–105; in France, 4, 61–70;
  as postcolonial moment, 6–10; transnational networks of, 50–58, 66–67, 115–16;
  in Tunis, 6, 30–31, 45–49; universities and
  global collaboration of, 12–13, 14–17,
  33–37. *See also* activism; student activism;
  worker activism
1972 protests, 116–27. *See also* activism
1978 protests, 127–35. *See also* activism

Abya Yala, as term, 180n15
Achour, Habib, 128, 133, 135
L'Action (publication), 55, 56, 57, 121, 122,
  131, 133
activism: global decolonization movements,
  6–14, 85–86, 111, 173–76; by Group of
  Incendiaries *(blondinistes)*, 159–64; by
  immigrant laborers, 69–83, 136–56;
  transnational networks of, 50–58, 66–67,
  115–16, 123–27, 174; by university students,
  12–17, 24–37, 100–101, 175–77; by workers,
  16, 61–62, 91–94, 127–34, 152-155. *See also*
  1968 protests; 1972 protests; 1978 protests;
  names of specific groups
AEMNA(F) (Association des Étudiants
  Musulmans Nord-Africains en France):
  activist network and, 28, 67; Bourguiba's
  speech to, 22; establishment of, 185n44;
  Paris activist meetings with, 50–51,
  120–21, 123, 124
AESF (Association des Étudiants Sénégalais
  en France), 99, 101, 112, 165
African House, 152, 153
African Independence Party. *See* PAI
African Institute of Economic Planning and
  Development, 102
Africanization of education system, 24, 32,
  36, 48, 84, 90, 93, 107–8, 169–71. *See also*
  education system

African Socialism, 8, 108, 170
Afrique-Asie (publication), 125, 129
Algeria: French citizenship for, 70; as French
  colonial territory, 20, 62, 63; French
  military base in, 29; French student
  activism on, 66, 67; resistance movement
  in, 63–65, 137–38; student activism in, 50,
  51, 124, 141
Algerian immigrants in France, 69
Algerian War (1954–1962), 15, 19, 27, 66,
  177
Alliance Française, 22
alphabétisation project, 142
Althusser, Louis, 71, 73, 74, 82, 137
Al-Amal (publication), 203n27
Amel Tounsi (populist group), 130, 202n5
El Amel Tounsi (publication), 118, 125,
  188n26, 202n5
Amicale organizations, 149, 154, 210n47
Amnesty International, 125, 131
Anselme, Daniel, 74
anti-Americanism, 158–59
anti-Arabism, 60, 137, 138, 149, 185n46.
  See also racism
antiracist movements, 16, 28, 101–2, 136.
  See also immigrant laborers and activism
anti-Semitism, 27, 42, 60, 67, 137, 187n3,
  192n17. *See also* racism
anti-Vietnam War movement: in Dakar, 96,
  198n52; in France, 7, 13, 61, 68–69, 82; in
  U.S., 7. *See also* Vietnam War
AOF (Afrique-Occidentale Française), 18–20,
  22–23, 25, 182n2
Arabic studies, 22
Arabization of education system, 36, 115,
  188n23. *See also* education system
Arab League, 67–68
Arab Spring, 1–5
Arab Workers' Movement. *See* MTA
Association of Muslim North African
  Students. *See* AEMNA(F)